CLIMBING THROUGH

CLIMBING THROUGH
A Courageous Story of Grit, Healing, and Second Chances

MELISSA STRONG

FALCON

ESSEX, CONNECTICUT

FALCONGUIDES®

FalconGuides, an imprint of The Globe Pequot Publishing Group, Inc.
64 South Main Street
Essex, CT 06426
www.globepequot.com

Falcon and FalconGuides are registered trademarks and Make Adventure Your Story is a trademark of Globe Pequot Publishing Group, Inc.

Copyright © 2026 by Melissa Strong

All rights reserved. No part of this book may be reproduced in any form or by any electronic or mechanical means, including information storage and retrieval systems, without written permission from the publisher, except by a reviewer who may quote passages in a review.

British Library Cataloguing in Publication Information available

Library of Congress Cataloging-in-Publication Data available
ISBN 9781493086689 (paperback) | ISBN 9781493086696 (epub)

Limit of Liability / Disclaimer of Warranty: The author and The Globe Pequot Publishing Group, Inc. (GPPG) expressly disclaim any and all liability for the use of any materials, information, or methods described in this book, including, without limitation, for accidents, injuries, illnesses, damages, or death sustained by readers who engage in the activities described or promoted herein. No representations or warranties are made as to the accuracy or completeness of the contents of this work, and all warranties, express or implied—including, without limitation, warranties of fitness for a particular purpose—are expressly disclaimed. The opinions presented are solely those of the author and are provided for informational purposes only.

Endorsement Disclaimer: Reference to any individual, organization, website, or other resource in this book does not constitute an endorsement by the author or GPPG of such party or the information, products, or services they may provide, now or in the future.

This book is dedicated to

Adam, my champion, for standing by my side.
Mom and Dad, who believed in me and helped make
their little girl's dream come true.
My sister, Alison, and her wonderful children, Andrew, Emelia, and Mary.
My friends and the Estes Park community.
The team at Bird & Jim and Bird's Nest.
and
Ashley Ignatiuk, MD, Seth TeBockhorst, MD,
and the doctors, nurses, and staff at UCHealth.

Some names have been changed to protect
the privacy of the individuals involved.

Follow the story with pictures on melissaistrong.com/prior-during-post
—warning, graphic content.

Contents

Preface xi

Chapter 1: As I Stand Dying 1
Chapter 2: A Foggy Fortune 5
Chapter 3: What Does that Palm Reader Know? 7
Chapter 4: No Pain, No Gain .11
Chapter 5: The Road Taken 15
Chapter 6: Between a Rock and My Happy Place 23
Chapter 7: Pebble Wrestling 29
Chapter 8: A Real Job 37
Chapter 9: Adam 43
Chapter 10: How Many Children Do You Have? 51
Chapter 11: The Road Not Taken 57
Chapter 12: When One Door Closes, Don't Yank 61
Chapter 13: Dollar, Dollar Bills 69
Chapter 14: Lichtenberg 77
Chapter 15: Amped Up 81
Chapter 16: The Forest 85
Chapter 17: The Scream 87
Chapter 18: Helicopter, Please 93
Chapter 19: No Light at the End of the Tunnel 97
Chapter 20: Forgiveness 103
Chapter 21: Four Fingers 107
Chapter 22: Net Worth 111
Chapter 23: Tiny Pools of Hope 115
Chapter 24: New Home 121
Chapter 25: The Way 127

Chapter 26: *I Dream of Jeannie* 131
Chapter 27: Grapefruit Pellegrino? 139
Chapter 28: Beyond a Ten 143
Chapter 29: Surf's Up 149
Chapter 30: Snap On 155
Chapter 31: Spinning My Wheels 163
Chapter 32: Straitjacket 169
Chapter 33: Paws Before Hands 175
Chapter 34: The Big Reveal 183
Chapter 35: Home 191
Chapter 36: The Slow Race 195
Chapter 37: Out with the Old, In with the New 201
Chapter 38: Narwhal 209
Chapter 39: The Final Countdown 215
Chapter 40: Bird & Jim 221
Chapter 41: Opening the Climbing Trunk 229
Chapter 42: Every Girl's Dream 233
Chapter 43: Hello, Old Friend 239

Epilogue 245
Appendix: Surgery Notes 249
About the Author 265

Some people think it's an insult to the glory of their sickness to get well. But the time poultice is no respecter of glories.
—JOHN STEINBECK, *EAST OF EDEN*

Preface

Looking back, it all seems completely unreal. But my hands are right there, a constant reminder: Yes, this happened. It's always there, whether I'm trying to climb a boulder or type these words. People say my life sometimes sounds like a horror story or a gruesome movie. But that poor girl wasn't a made-up character.

She was me.

"I am one of the luckiest unlucky people I know," I tell people.

After it happened, my life was put on hold for a year. My very identity—Melissa Strong, independent woman, strong rock climber, businesswoman—was threatened as a new life morphed around me. This would change me for both the good and the bad. Time stood still, yet flew by.

I lived Robert Frost's advice: "The best way out is always through." I was eager to get through and see what was on the other side. I had a restaurant to create, a huge loan, and a contractor hired. I had business partners who had quit their jobs to work with me, and there were people who believed in me and my vision for my town of Estes Park, Colorado.

So I couldn't quit, slow down, or skip a beat. I could not accept statements like *You will not have thumbs or fingers*, or *You won't be able to run a restaurant*, and *You will never rock-climb again*. I heard these messages from others and in my own head.

But I did not give in to despair. For that, I thank my doctor, husband, family, friends, partners, and community, all of whom fueled my will and resolve. Instead, I dived deep within and surfaced to find a safety net woven from past experiences, gratitude, family, community, love, self-acceptance, forgiveness, inner strength, and fortitude. All of this kept me on the right side of hopelessness.

My career dream was my distraction and salvation: I would open my restaurant, Bird & Jim, my first in Estes Park. That vision helped save me. It provided something else to focus on besides my recovery, self-pity, and the looming unknown future of my hands. Of course, there were moments of grieving, there were times of despair, and there still are. But I stared down the fears and doubts and would not allow them to defeat or define me. My perseverance was a gift that grew out of gratefulness that I'd survived, and from my hopes and dreams.

Thank you for taking the time to read my story. I hope it will inspire you, and encourage you to find your strength within—you have what it takes to overcome, whatever the nature of your challenges.

—Melissa Strong
Estes Park, Colorado
October 2025

Chapter One

As I Stand Dying
Estes Park, Colorado, April 2, 2017

It wasn't much of a debate. I could head into the mountains to do some climbing, knowing that springtime in the Rockies means post-holing through snow, wet climbing shoes, and crash pads sliding down snowbanks instead of staying put to cushion my fall.

Or I could stay home and climb on our home wall.

I had too much on my mind, too many things to accomplish as I worked to open my first restaurant. It was a dream I'd nurtured for years. I couldn't take the time to drive to the trailhead and hike to dry rock in the Front Range. Years earlier, I had turned our two-car garage into a climbing gym with an overhanging 60-degree wall.

Not a hard call: I opted for an at-home session.

I'd recently returned from Hueco Tanks State Park & Historic Site in east El Paso, our home away from home, where we operate a concession, guiding climbers to restricted bouldering areas. I'd cut the trip short because I was consumed with securing finances for the soon-to-be restaurant back in Estes Park. I'd put the cart before the horse—I'd bought an old restaurant, which a crew was currently tearing down to the studs before the loan came through. So a gym session made sense. No matter how much work there is, I told myself, you've got to stay fit.

Climbing was my life. I'd been a climber for seventeen years; I met my husband Adam while climbing; we were both sponsored by climbing-gear companies. We split our time between Hueco Tanks and the Rocky

Mountains, bouldering and helping with climbing access. When we could afford to, we traveled to Switzerland, France, Spain, South Africa, and Australia, just to climb.

Besides, if I stayed at home, I could work on the tables for the restaurant. I'd decided to keep the pine tables from the old restaurant, especially with no money in the tight budget for new ones. But I wanted to make them look like they fit into the renovations.

Adam had come across an intriguing idea online: the Lichtenberg technique, which uses electricity to burn designs into a wood surface. You take a microwave transformer, wire it to mini jumper cables, paint some baking soda and water on the wood, attach the cables to the wood, and activate the machine. The electricity takes over and creates amazing designs that look like rivers on a map.

I went ahead with my workout, working my way up and across our wall repeatedly for two and a half hours, followed by a finger-strengthening routine on our hangboard. It was a series of repeaters, hanging on 12 mm edges from my fingertips, 7 seconds on, 3 seconds off. Do that six times, rest a minute, repeat until failure.

After the training session, I moved some of the old tables outside onto the driveway. Adam had made the machine and tested it, and we had done a burn together. I'd already branded a few table legs on my own.

I placed the machine in my work area, plugged the long orange extension cord into the wall, and then into the machine, which had no on–off switch; it was on when you plugged it in.

Oops—forgot the baking soda and water.

I dropped the cords, went inside to mix the solution, and came back out. I bent down to pick up the two mini jumper cables and instantly realized my mistake. I hadn't unplugged the machine. I felt a prickling sensation in both of my hands.

What's happening? Electricity pulsated through my body. *Shit! This is exactly what Adam told me not to do.* The tingling intensified in my hands. My mind raced.

Let go! As much as I tried, the electricity seemed to force my hands to tighten their death grip. *Scream for help!* I tried, but couldn't. It was one of those nightmares where you try to call out but you can't. My brain could not command my vocal cords to produce a sound. *Shake your hands!* The current froze my arms.

The humming of the transformer grew louder and the tingling amplified and traveled up my arms. *Fall over—dislodge a clamp!* Again, no connection between brain and body. I could not even fall over. My body and my will betrayed me. I was a statue, rigid, ensnared by electricity, frozen in my last motion.

The current grew stronger and my grip only tightened. Everything was involuntary, the opposite of what I desperately wanted to do. I was seized by the pulsing current.

Well, shit. I guess this is it.

I am dying.

My last thought was almost a whine: *I don't want to die. How can I die before I finally get to open my restaurant?*

Then everything went dark.

CHAPTER TWO

A Foggy Fortune

Cayman Islands, December 1995

We rolled into the small sandy parking lot of the local dive bar and the five of us spilled out of the car into a warm, humid evening. Waves sonorously met the reef not far from the shore. A warm breeze carried a relaxed, melodious reggae beat as we approached the door. Smiling faces of old regulars greeted us. *Do they ever leave this bar?* I thought. Pool balls clacked and couples swayed to the music in the smoky room. A local dive never gets old, especially in your early twenties on an island paradise with your family.

My father, Paul, and his namesake, my brother Paul, placed quarters on the edge of the pool table to claim the next game. My mom, Sheila, and sister Alison found friends at a table, and I caught up with folks we hadn't seen since our last visit to the island. One drink followed another.

"Missy, get yuh brothah," my dad called across the room in his Massachusetts accent. "We're up."

I slid off the stool, wondering where Paul had gone off to. I poked my head out the back door and found him at a bright aqua-blue wooden picnic table in need of a new coat of paint. Not surprisingly, he was with some ladies. "Hey, Dad says you're up next," I announced.

"Okay, just a minute. Jada is reading my palm." He grinned at me and then back at the beautiful young woman holding his hand.

Curiosity drew me closer. I'd never had my palm, cards, fortune, or anything read.

Jada traced a line on my brother's palm and giggled as she stared into his light blue eyes, the color of the Cayman waters. *They always fall for the baby blues.* She said he'd have many romances in his future, but maybe not marriage.

Paul smiled and stood up, lingering at the table. A family friend traveling with us slid into his place. Jada talked of finding love after a broken heart and living a long life.

Then Jada looked at me and read my eager expression. She gestured for me to sit down and gently cradled my hand. She narrowed her eyes and furrowed her brow. Remaining quiet, she looked up and shook her head from side to side.

"No," she said.

"Oh, come on," I pleaded. "What do you see?" Again she shook her head. "I cannot," she said. I stared back quizzically.

"Are you in a relationship?" she asked.

"I'm getting married in June," I replied.

Jada shook her head. "This spring?" she said.

"Yes, June sixth, 1996," I replied.

Jada turned and looked at Paul and our friend. "Do not let her get married, and just love her as much as you can." She would say nothing more.

"Paul, come on," my father yelled from the window.

Weird, I thought.

I went back inside, trying to shake off Jada and her messages. But what she'd said would linger.

CHAPTER THREE

What Does that Palm Reader Know?
New Orleans and Massachusetts, 1990–1996

THE FORTUNETELLER'S MARITAL ADVICE EERILY MATCHED MY GUT feeling.

I only shared it with my mother. "I think I'm having doubts about marrying Trey," I confided one afternoon in the kitchen.

"Melissa," she said, "we already mailed the invitations."

I was seventeen when I graduated from an all-girls Catholic high school. Our senior class consisted of twenty-six girls, small enough that we all fit on the stage for the graduation ceremony.

"I'm going to apply to the University of Hawaii," I announced to my mother one day.

"Too far" was the response. "There are so many good schools in New England, Melissa. And if you are going to go away for school, it has to be a Jesuit college." Her requirements were meant to reinforce my religious rearing, limit my scheming, and provide structure for her rebellious youngest child. Who was I to argue? I was fortunate that my parents were paying for school.

I found a couple of Jesuit colleges outside of New England I thought I might like: Loyola University in New Orleans, and Regis University in Denver. The quaint New Orleans campus won me over, with its old redbrick buildings, gigantic live oaks dripping with Spanish moss, the fragrance of magnolias and gardenias, sunny days, clanking streetcars, ornate architecture. Not to mention the music, culture, and the outstanding cuisine of that great city. And the drinking age of eighteen was an added incentive for a willful teen like me.

I met Trey during my first semester and eventually was swayed into a date when he got onstage at a bar and sang the Allman Brothers' "(Sweet) Melissa." After one year of reveling in the party scene, I got my act together and graduated in four years with a good GPA. I had no intention of sticking around, though I'd enjoyed my time in Louisiana and our trips to nearby states, exploring their unique cultures.

In that good-ol'-boy world, I stuck out like a sore thumb, a Yankee in the Southland. My future husband and in-laws taught me their ways: fishing for catfish in the bayou, hunting white-tailed deer in Covington (I shot the deer with my camera), cooling off in a pool in Mandeville fed by artesian well water. I learned how to pinch the tails and suck the heads at crawfish boils and caught blue crabs in drainage ditches. I loved it all, but was ready to move on. And I wasn't in a hurry to return to Massachusetts.

My graduation party was a crawfish boil and a kegger in Trey's parents' backyard. When Trey got down on one knee and took out a diamond ring at the celebration, I was surprised but not shocked. We'd started getting wedding pressure from our Catholic families when we'd announced our plan of living together first. I was twenty-two and he was twenty-three.

I said yes.

Our youthful grand plan was to live in the mountains for one year prior to starting "real life." Eventually I would become a professor of literature and he'd become a lawyer, working at my father's law firm. We'd driven back and forth from New Orleans to Massachusetts several times over the years, stopping in Asheville, North Carolina, and the Smoky Mountains. "If we are going to live in the mountains," I declared, "let's go to the real mountains, out west." No argument—he was game.

Despite Jada's (and my) misgivings, we went ahead with our plans.

The wedding was a grand event, held on the manicured lawn of my family's home on Cape Cod with the Atlantic Ocean as our backdrop. I was the youngest of three siblings, but the first to wed. My mom and I nailed every detail, from the handmade paper invitations to the entree—filet mignon and lobster—to the extravagant flower arrangements centered on king protea blooms. I looked like a princess, and felt like one, too.

One problem: My husband-to-be was not speaking to me. I'm sure we're not the only couple to quarrel on their wedding day, but we barely exchanged words outside of our vows. I cried in our quaint B&B on our wedding night as he yelled at me for something trivial concerning his friends.

After honeymooning in Alaska, we flew back to Massachusetts, packed up my gray Toyota 4Runner, and headed west in search of a place to live. Trey liked Whitefish, Montana; too remote, I said. We motored on. I voted for Bend, Oregon, and Trey said no. "Well, let's head to Colorado." We'd each visited the state separately, years ago.

We drove through Fort Collins, heading into the mountains. A ski resort could work for a year, we theorized. We headed up to Estes Park and over the Continental Divide on Trail Ridge Road, through the tundra. We got into yet another argument at a Super 8 in Dillon, Colorado, when we realized that the ski towns would be too expensive.

"Let's flip a coin," Trey said. "Heads, we go to Massachusetts, tails, we go to New Orleans." That was his solution.

"I'm not ready to move home," I retorted, "and obviously you have never listened to me, because I said I would never live in New Orleans." I caught my breath and said, "How about Estes Park?" It was affordable and not too remote, I told him, and soon I was gripping the steering wheel and fighting tears as I drove back the way we'd come.

As we neared Estes Park, driving through green meadows on either side of Highway 36, cresting the final hill, something felt right for the first time since leaving Massachusetts. The Rocky Mountains were dazzling in late September, framed by a cloudless, crisp blue sky. A dusting of early snow frosted the peaks, showing off their ridges, bluffs, and escarpments. The Estes Valley was sprawled out below, welcoming us.

I rolled down the window and the thin, clean, piney, invigorating mountain air rushed over my face. I breathed deeply. This was where I was supposed to be.

Ten months later, after I'd told my mom I was getting a divorce, my dad called and hollered into the phone. "Do you know how much that wedding cost me?"

"Well, Dad, at least it was the best party we've ever been to," I replied.

Trey drove back to New Orleans and enrolled in law school. He made one return trip to Colorado, attempting to retrieve his soon-to-be ex-wife. I happily declined the offer.

Dad called again and said he never liked Trey anyway. He told me to get on a plane home and he'd arrange to get my belongings and car back east.

I also declined that offer. It was time to start living for me.

CHAPTER FOUR

No Pain, No Gain
Belmont, Massachusetts, 1980s

GYM TEACHERS LOVE TO SHOUT "NO PAIN, NO GAIN!" Ms. TSHANG WAS one of them. Whether she was in the school gym (also its auditorium) or the grassy field out back, you could count on hearing it. My parents thought the strictness of an Opus Dei school was right for their rebellious son and outspoken daughter. I went to Montrose School for girls, grades six through twelve, and my brother Paul went to the all-boys brother school.

Although our family was Catholic, we never joined the ranks of Opus Dei, the strict sect of Catholicism that "accepts the teaching authority of the church without question."* Years later, I asked a numerary (a celibate lay member) what was meant by "mortification," the teaching that members should perform penance through "self-inflicted pain or discomfort." *Like what*, I wondered? The teacher explained that it could include anything from sitting next to a person you dislike to wearing itchy, uncomfortable undergarments, or tapping yourself on the wrist with a coarse rope when praying. We had Mass daily, religious instruction three times a week, and confession weekly.

I entered Montrose School at grade seven, with twenty-five other girls. My brother was "asked to leave" the boys' school the same year I started, prompting our peeved mother to question her support of the

---
* "Opus Dei," Britannica.com, https://www.britannica.com/topic/Opus-Dei.

organization. But I would stay. Paul slid down a slope of roguishness, escalating to malefaction. He was a troublemaker. My parents hoped the school would keep their second daughter and third child from going down the same road as the brother she idolized.

"Melissa, pull up your knee socks, or that will be another demerit for you." It was Ms. Stack, walking past me as I peered into my locker, hoping my gym bag would magically appear. I yanked my gray, cable-knit socks up and turned to my friend.

"Katy, do you have any extra gym clothes?" I asked desperately. "Ms. Tshang is going to kill me—I forgot my gym bag again." Katy shook her head and told me I'd better hustle and face the music. "You don't want to be late too!"

Ms. Tshang was different from the other teachers. She was one of the few not affiliated with Opus Dei. She was sinewy and fit, young and approachable, down-to-earth and on her own path. She also led two classes I loathed—math and gym. Math was not my subject, and I detested running laps. Later in life, learning I was dyslexic might have explained my difficulties with math a bit. Word problems made me sweat and algebra gave me a headache, though geometry was okay. (However, the only thing I remember from geometry—not taught by Ms. Tshang—was a cartoon of a squirrel and a tree in the textbook margin: "What did the tree say to the squirrel? Gee-amatree.")

Something besides that hokey joke must have stuck, as after placement tests, Loyola put me in advanced math. I still have a classic nightmare about being unprepared for a math test—hadn't studied, didn't have a pencil, panicking as I tried to find the classroom, declaring "I swore I'd dropped this class." In high school I'd lacked motivation, focusing on boys and gossiping more than grades and homework.

"Melissa, I cannot believe you forgot your gym clothes again!" Ms. Tshang said. "There is a bag of lost-and-found gym clothes. I'm not sure if they're clean, but it's what you get."

I picked out the least-offensive white polo and red shorts, quickly changed, and joined the rest of the class running laps around the basketball court because the field was covered with snow. I settled in next to my best friend and started chattering.

"Do you want to come skiing this weekend?" I asked.

After school on most winter Fridays, my parents drove the family up to Waterville Valley, New Hampshire, and we'd come home on Sunday. I started skiing at four—I remember the snowbanks towering over me. My dad nestled me between his skis as the basket lift towed us up the bunny slope and we snowplowed down.

I'd been active my whole life. After a day of skiing, I'd jump in the hotel's indoor/outdoor pool and stay in until my skin was pruned. "Mom, watch me!" I'd yell from the diving board. I never got tired. Eventually, they bought a condo, and Dad would drive through snowstorms to get us there.

In the summer, we went to Hull, Massachusetts, situated on a peninsula at the southern end of Boston Harbor, and lived across the street from the ocean on Nantasket Beach. At home in Belmont, on the outskirts of Boston, we played kickball in the yard and basketball in our driveway, fighting over who got to be Larry Bird or Spud Webb.

Our family had rollicking good times, constantly active. But team sports weren't for me; I felt intimidated and insecure. Our small school had just one sports team, softball, led by Ms. Tshang. I mustered my courage and tried out as a freshman but didn't make the team. I agreed to be the student manager for the season, but after that, I wrote off team sports.

I was the classic teenager cliché of the late 1980s: permed hair, lace bows, arms full of rubber and metal bracelets, Swatch watches. Swimming in the waves gave way to tanning, listening to the radio, and walking the beach to check out boys. Most of my exercise came from dancing and mimicking the moves of pop stars on VH1 and MTV, like Madonna, Cyndi Lauper, Michael Jackson, and George Michael, and dreaming of being a "Solid Gold" dancer. I put posters of Scott Baio and Rob Lowe on my bedroom walls.

"Come on, Melissa and Jeannine, pick it up! Let's go—stop your gibbering and finish your laps—no pain, no gain!" Ms Tshang bellowed.

I was hopeless, even in volleyball, which I wanted to like. I just had trouble with sports where balls rapidly approached my face. "Stop ducking, Melissa! Hit the ball!"

When I opened my report card, there was a big "C" for both math and gym.

"A 'C' in gym class, Missy—really?" my mother said.

"Mom, she *hates* me," I replied dramatically.

Years later, as a sponsored athlete, Ms. Tshang would come to mind. I'd wonder what she would think of me today.

CHAPTER FIVE

The Road Taken
Estes Park, 1996

IN THE LATE 1990S, ESTES PARK WAS NOT A HAPPENING WINTER DESTInation. It's the gateway to Rocky Mountain National Park, which is jammed in the summer with visitors but pretty empty in the winter. The sidewalks rolled up early. Most of the residents were retirees and second-home owners. It's not a ski town. If you wanted to ski, you'd "skin up" the closed slopes of the former Hidden Valley resort on backcountry skis and ski down. As locals would say, you had to "Earn your turns."

One of the established restaurants on the main drag, Elkhorn Avenue, was (and still is) Ed's Cantina, a Mexican place. When Trey and I first landed in Estes Park in 1996, I walked in, asked for the manager, and had a job fifteen minutes later. I figured restaurant work would do for our one-year stint. My coworkers were transplants like me, drawn to the mountains to avoid life—or maybe, to start living it.

After Trey and I split, I kept my job at Ed's. My coworkers and I worked hard, to a symphony of beeping microwaves, hustling burritos and burgers to tourists with screaming children. The kids poured milk into light fixtures, drew on the wood tables with crayons, and pierced the booth fabric with forks as their parents slurped margaritas, taking the sting out of their family vacation. After work, we spent our hard-earned tips at a local joint, usually the Wheel Bar down the street. We closed the bar down and hosted the crew at our rented house for dance parties until dawn. We would sleep and repeat. I lived the single life I had never really had, since I met my ex-husband after just turning eighteen.

One night at the Wheel, a climbing guide in town for the summer invited me to climb with him the next day. We'd go to Lumpy Ridge, he said, just outside of town. I'd had a few beers and said "Sure!"

Lumpy Ridge is a line of granite slabs that form a beautiful backdrop to our town. It's much older than the mountains towering over the valley—the Mummy Range to the north, and the Continental Divide wrapping around to the west. For 1.8 billion years they've been sculpted by nature, and now they are home to traditional, old-school crack climbs sprinkled with some vertical bolted routes.*

The following day, hungover and roasting on the sunbaked slabs, I questioned my decision-making. *How did I let myself get talked into this?* My weak legs shook (climbers call this "Elvis leg"). My barfly existence wasn't compatible with climbing. I went one more time and was relieved when the excursion ended and I was off the hook from my inebriated commitment and safely back on flat ground.

The work-drink-sleep cycle in this mountain paradise would eventually lose its luster, though it took a few years. I'd sleep through beautiful days and then hear coworkers gushing about the beautiful destinations they hiked to or the radical climbs they scaled. The nonstop party to celebrate my freedom did little but fill the till at the bar. Something was missing in me: joy, a spark, bliss.

One typical night I looked through the gloomy, smoke-filled saloon and wondered, *Were my fellow barflies indeed my friends?* I decided to call it a night and went home early.

The next day I woke up, resolved to go for a run. New day, new Melissa.

After a half-mile around Lake Estes, I was coughing, wheezing, and desperate. At twenty-six years old, how could I not even run half a mile? *What the heck, Melissa.* (Maybe it was the pack-a-day cigarette habit?)

---

* "Lumpy Ridge Loop," *Rocky Mountain Hiking Trails.com*, https://www.rockymountainhikingtrails.com/lumpy-ridge-loop.htm.

Frustration and disappointment welled up in me. Right then and there—bent over, gasping, hands on my knees—I looked up at the beautiful mountains around me and vowed to change. I needed something to do—a reason to wake up and not sleep until my shift started. Passionate climbers surrounded me at work. They were not closing the bar down nightly but instead poring over the latest *Climbing* magazine, planning what to climb on their days off. I decided I had to give climbing an honest try. I went back to my cabin and called Bronson.

Bronson was my friend and coworker, a vivacious, petite, cute blonde, and an incredibly enthusiastic climber. She'd always encouraged me to try the sport. Instead of taking her up on it, contrarily we endeavored to drag her to the bars. Despite our corrupt efforts, she mostly avoided our negative influence and stayed home. She'd tell us she was climbing the next day and wanted to feel fresh. "I don't want to waste my money at the bars," she'd say. "I've got to save up for winter climbing road trips." Or she'd tell my roommate and mutual bestie Karla, another beautiful blonde, and me about a place called Hueco Tanks down in Texas, and how great it was as a winter climbing destination. She kept bugging me to join her.

Over the phone I told her I was ready to take her up on her offer.

"Yes!" she exclaimed. "Perfect timing—a group of gals and I are going to the Monastery on Wednesday, a cluster of crags about twenty miles east of town."

I hung up feeling excited, and apprehensive. *Would climbing be for me?*

I'd already tried it a few times. This time would be different, though. *I won't be hungover, and it's a fun group of ladies*, I told myself. *I will be different.*

Just in case, I called the golf course and booked a lesson for the same day, hoping I'd like one of these options. I was determined to find something that would light the spark that cigarettes and alcohol had dimmed. *Life for me would change!* Oh, and since I was doing all of this, I might as well quit smoking a pack a day, throwing this into the life-overhaul mix.

I borrowed some gear—rope, harness, climbing shoes, and quickdraws—and carried my share of the weight on the hike to the crag. Some trepidation crept in about this first sport-climbing experience. I knew this area differed from the multi-pitch, traditional climbing and the slabs of Lumpy Ridge that I had scaled with a little desperation and a lot of coaxing. With Bronson leading the hike—*Man, her little legs move fast!*—I struggled to keep up. I asked her questions so she'd have to talk, and I could breathe. As I tried to maintain pace and keep my panic down about the climbing challenge ahead, I mentally committed to running, and unquestionably, to quitting smoking.

We got to our spot, a single-pitch sport-climbing crag. Bronson went over some basics. "I am going to lead the climb and run the rope through the anchors. Then I will rappel down, and you can climb with the rope already set up. It's called top-roping."

She was a reassuring teacher. "The lead climber ties one end of the rope to their harness," Bronson said, demonstrating the figure-eight knot. "The belayer, also in a harness, runs the rope through a GriGri. That's a belaying device attached to the harness with a locking carabiner." Bronson's friend Lizzy acted out her instructions, running the rope through the gear.

"The belayer, Lizzy, will feed the rope to the lead climber, me, as I climb. I will stop and clip one quickdraw carabiner into the bolt and the other to the rope," Bronson said, looking up at the first bolt. "If I fall, the rope pulls quickly, the GriGri locks, and Lizzy catches me. I will fall to the last quickdraw I placed, plus some rope stretch." It made sense as I looked on, and her confident explanations bolstered my conviction. *I can do this.*

Traditional and sport-climbing have the same climber setup—a lead and a belayer—but they differ. Trad climbing follows a seam or cracks in the rock. The lead climber places gear in the rock's natural features. The gear most often used is a spring-loaded camming device, but back then, wired hexes and nuts were still popular placement gear—metal on one end, which the climber inserts into the crevice, with wire on the other end. The wire connects to the rope with webbing and a carabiner. In sport-climbing, the lead climber clips "quickdraws"—two carabiners on each end of strong webbing. One carabiner clips into a bolt that is permanently secured on the rock face and the other clips to the rope that freely slides through the carabiner, feeding up to the climber.

Constant communication, Bronson emphasized, is crucial between the climber and the belayer. "It doesn't seem necessary when you are standing next to each other," she said, "but it's important when you are at the anchors, and during multi-pitch climbing, when you cannot see each other." She turned to Lizzy and they checked to ensure that each other's harnesses and ropes were properly secured. Then Bronson said "Climbing," and Lizzy responded "Climb on."

I felt a surge of excitement.

Bronson floated up the yellowish-brown granite face, cautious yet confident, pausing at each bolt, clipping the quickdraw to the bolt, and hauling the rope up to clip to the carabiner on the other side of the quickdraw. She reached the top of the single-pitch climb and secured the rope at the top of the route, clipping into the anchor chains. She and Lizzy yelled back and forth, "Off belay!" Bronson ran the rope through fixed anchor chains that hung from bolts and rappelled down, allowing the inexperienced climber—me—to top-rope the climb.

Top-roping is beginner-friendly, taking the plummet out of the fall and removing the fear—and consequences—that come with leading. On a top rope, if you fall, you're quickly stopped, suspended by the secured rope. If you're leading, you plunge to the last bolt clipped, plus you have the stretching of the dynamic rope.

I stepped forward. I tied into one end of the rope and Bronson checked my figure-eight knot and harness. She then checked her own harness and ran the rope through a belaying device, and then it was time. I approached the granite face, dipped my hands into a chalk bag around my waist, and laid my hands on the rock. Wondering just how I was going to mount this rock face, I skeptically placed my right foot on a protruding crystal.

And I started to climb. Bronson reminded me that I forgot to say "Climbing." I was so focused on transferring my weight off the ground and balancing on the wall, I had forgotten.

"Climbing," I muttered, almost not believing it.

My mind went blank as the impossible happened, and before I knew it, I was 5 feet off the ground.

In my nominal trad-climbing experience, I'd learned that natural features on the routes provide obvious hand- and footholds—there's a straightforward sequence following crack systems. On a face like this, handholds were less obvious.

As I moved—slowly, carefully—from the low-angled slabby beginning to the vertical face, I wondered where, or what, to grab onto. The granite wall was striped with fluorescent green and yellow lichen, but not fissures. I felt a tingle of panic take hold and my legs began shaking. It was obvious to me (and the others) that I didn't have the muscles required for the task, but you have to start somewhere.

I pushed through a few more moves, groping for a hold. I looked down at my feet, balanced on crystal granite swells. *Would my foot stay on? Where should I move it? How could I continue?* The more I thought about falling, the tighter I gripped the small crystals, causing blood to pump into my forearms, rendering my grip—and the muscles I did have—useless.

"I think I'm going to fall!" I called out. My knuckles were white, and I was sweating profusely.

"It's okay. You're not going anywhere—I've got you," Bronson said. "If you need a break, just sit back on the rope and rest." *Was she crazy—rest up here? Sit on the rope?* I had no choice but to trust her, since I couldn't hold onto the rock any longer. My damp, clenched fingers relaxed, and my weight shifted off my feet. I felt the rope tighten, and I dropped a foot or two as the rope stretched with my weight. It worked.

I hung in the air partway up the rock face. I stared at the stone in front of me and then up to the top. The sunlight beamed over the rock precipice against a brilliant blue sky. I took a breath and shook out my forearms. They were taut with lactic acid, making it difficult to open or close my hands. I looked down at Bronson.

"Do you want to come down?" she asked.

A desire to reach the top flooded over me. "No, I want to keep trying." I dipped my hands into my chalk bag. Breathing deeply, I reached out, pulled myself back onto the rock, and resumed climbing. I trusted the sticky rubber on my borrowed climbing shoes. I stepped on crystals I did not have faith in. I grabbed onto holds I couldn't quite see, and kept going. Soon I was at the top.

Pure satisfaction overwhelmed me. What an odd sensation! I wasn't sure I'd ever felt anything like it.

After some glorious moments, Bronson told me to sit back on the rope—I was fully trusting now—and she would lower me. As I dangled on the rope and slowly descended, I was able to enjoy the view. I looked out over the tops of the pine trees and between the corridors of granite framing the Rockies in the distance. Filled with joy, I knew I would be a rock climber from this moment on.

With solid ground under my feet, I was still floating with elation. I was ready for my next climb, but told my friends I had to leave. I had a golf lesson. They laughed, and when I asked when we could do this again, they knew I was hooked.

I hiked out by myself with a spring in my step. The fire was lit. I couldn't wait to climb again.

I have been climbing, and golfing, ever since. I excel at one more than the other, dedicating more time, focus, and training to climbing, but they're both part of my life.

And back then I was enjoying life.

Chapter Six

Between a Rock and My Happy Place
Estes Park, 1999

I CAN FATHOM HOW NONSENSICAL ROCK CLIMBING MUST APPEAR TO someone who does not climb. Why would you want to launch yourself up a steep rock face almost impossible looking to scale when there is an easier way to the top? Or why cling on to the underside of a roof, the steep overhanging rock face that can sometimes be horizontal? I totally get it.

Then again, what's the point of hitting a tiny white ball across miles of green fairways and tapping it into a little cup? Or smacking a yellow ball across a net? Why do massive men slam into each other to move a pigskin from one end of a field to another?

The simple answer: Enjoyment. We can discuss how each sport offers different rewards and triggers different emotions, but it all comes down to enjoyment. Surely feel-good dopamine plays a role. Indeed, in some endeavors we approach a kind of addiction, depending on an individual's circumstances or quest.

It's not just about standing on top of a cliff or a boulder. It's the process. It's how you get there that captivates me. For us climbers, much of the appeal is the puzzle of it all—putting together the pieces of a route. Figuring out what to hold onto, how to hold onto it, where to place your foot, when to shift your weight. Move dynamically or lock off and reach up statically? We face all of these challenges, every second, on the rock. The satisfaction of bringing the sequences together was a pure rush!

But before I could ever dance up a rock with finesse and aptitude, I needed to tackle the challenge of the sheer physical demand of climbing. For this unathletic barfly, hanging onto small undulations of a rock face activated muscles I never knew were in my body. After that first serious outing, my shoulders, back, biceps—hell, every part of my body—ached with soreness.

And yet, the soreness felt great. I was excited to tear down these newly discovered muscles, build them up again, and strengthen them for our next excursion. Getting to the top of my first rock just meant I wanted more. I was weak as a kitten, yet I distinctly saw a route to learning. It was a glimmer of newfound power, an avenue toward improvement (in a sport where balls don't come at your head!).

My climbing friends made it look effortless, simply floating up the rock. Then there was me: I over-gripped each hold and didn't trust my aptitude. I was convinced my grasp would fail or that my shaking leg would pick off a foothold. I had a long way to go, starting at zero fitness at twenty-six years old.

First, I needed to start running to build cardio fitness and endurance. Carrying ropes and gear at 8,000 feet had exhausted me before I'd even reached the cliffs to start climbing. If I was going to make it up the rock "clean" (that means, no falling) and with any style, I had to improve my fitness.

When the climbing bug bit me, I lived less than a block from Lake Estes. The nearly 4-mile path around the lake became my regular training run. It took months of pushing through cold-weather jogs and downhill sprints, battling fierce winds on many days, before I could run the trail without stopping. Ms. Tshang's "No pain, no gain" echoed through my head. With time, I could keep up with my climbing partners as we hiked to the base of climbs at Lumpy Ridge and the Monastery.

Some of my colleagues at Ed's Cantina were keen on climbing. If they were desperate for a climbing partner, I could talk them into taking out the gumby. Following people up easier climbs, I became proficient at jamming my feet and fists into cracks (ouch) and "cleaning" (removing) the gear they had placed as I followed them on a multi-pitch route up the rock.

In multi-pitch trad climbing, your partner climbs away from the belayer, placing gear into cracks in the rock and connecting the cam (a spring-loaded camming device), hex, or nut to the rope with webbing and a carabiner. The lead climber ascends to a ledge or stopping point, creating anchors out of their gear and slings, then belays the second climber up to them. The placed gear will ideally catch the lead, along with their belayer, if they fall. The second climber "cleans" the gear as they climb, taking it out of the rock seams and clipping it to their harness or sling. As the season progressed, I seconded up more challenging classic cracks like J-tree to Fat City to Lay Back and Like It.

Then there was the gear. I was excited to see my tip money adding up so I could drive down to Neptune Mountaineering in Boulder and buy my own 5.10 climbing shoes and chalk bag (after borrowing Bronson's) and started to assemble my first "rack," purchasing a gear sling, nuts, hexes, and cams. I even toyed with the idea of leading, but was reluctant. If I led a climb, my life, and my partner's, would depend on my skill and gear placement. I wasn't there yet.

One sunny morning I ventured out with someone similarly skilled but with more experience, Karla. My roommate and coworker, Karla was a corn-fed Kansas blonde beauty whose kindness and personality were as stunning as her looks.

As we planned the day, Karla said she was up for the challenge. "I'm going to do this, and I'm going to lead," she said. "Are you in?"

"Yeah, I'm psyched," I said, happy to have a partner to get out with. Plus, it was just the two of us, and someone had to lead.

We packed up. "I'll carry the gear," she said. "You've got the rope?"

"Yup. I'm even going to remember my harness," I joked. Last time out, we'd hiked to the base of a cliff before I realized I'd forgotten my harness. *Rookie!*

We chatted our way to the bottom of the Book, a feature in the Lumpy Ridge.

"I decided on White Whale," Karla said, referring to the route, "because on the first pitch, you can sling a tree as an anchor."

"Sounds good to me," I said.

Easing into the thought of lead climbing, I had happily followed climbers who led the route, watching and learning, intrigued by the notion and progression. I practiced anchors with friends; getting up to their anchors, they would explain their systems, created with nuts and cams placed into cracks, usually on ledges, connected by slings equalizing two to three points in the rock. After building these anchors, the leader would clip into them and belay the second climber up to them. The second climber would clip into the anchors and belay the lead climber as they climbed the next pitch.

Being the second climber provided me with time to spend next to the anchors, examining them; then, I would disassemble them before moving up. I practiced creating anchor points, equalizing them, and having an experienced friend review my work. I knew that I also needed to be mentally ready and confident before I started leading. Lives depended on these anchors, and my life depended on the gear I placed going up to the anchor point. It's serious business. The gravity of it all is a huge mental challenge, and you need the requisite skill and confidence before you can lead.

We got to the base of the climb and took out Bernard Gillett's guidebook to Lumpy Ridge. Karla had done this climb before, so she knew where it started. I liked checking out route descriptions—for instance, what the second pitch was like if we decided to continue, and what were the climbs next to it. With shoes and harnesses on, double-backed and checked by each other, we also checked each other's figure-eight knots connecting the rope to our harnesses.

"All good, all good," we declared.

Karla put the gear sling over her shoulder, approached the granite wall, and paused for a minute. She turned back and looked at me. "I'm not ready," she said. "Can you do it?"

Shit, I thought. I got her reluctance. This was terrifying. I had only followed up to this point.

I paused. I really wanted to climb; I was super stoked; it was a beautiful day; and here we were. Climbers have a saying: If you hike and don't climb, it's called "taking your gear for a walk." I didn't want to retreat.

"Let me reread the description," I said, wanting to make sure I could sling a tree as an anchor. I finally came up with "Well, I think I can."

The climb difficulty was beginner level, graded 5.7. After a bit of mental vacillating, I told myself that I'd followed much harder climbs than this, and knew I could climb 5.7 without falling. (*Though I could always slip.*)

"I got it," I spat out. "But let's do the first pitch only, and rappel down—I don't trust my anchors yet, and like your tree idea."

I pulled onto the rock. The gear felt heavy. I paused after a few moves, questioning my decision. *Just keep climbing*, I told myself.

I placed my first cam about 10 feet up and clipped it to the rope. *Okay, that's a start, but if you fall, you will hit the ground.*

Keep climbing, I told myself again. Get the next piece in, and you'll be fine.

Moving up another 10 feet, I sank the next piece of protection into the rock.

Oh my God, I am high up here. Also true: *Too committed to reverse and downclimb.*

Just keep climbing, I commanded myself.

My legs started shaking; *Elvis had entered the building.* I told myself they'd shake less if I climbed, and so I did. My inner voices were having quite the debate.

I got to the ledge and wrapped the tree with webbing and clipped the ends together with a locking carabiner. I shook with excitement. "I did it!" I yelled down to Karla, "On belay." "Climbing," she yelled back.

I did it! I couldn't believe it. The terror drained away and I was overwhelmed with achievement. *My first lead.*

I looked out at the vista of MacGregor Ranch, the crowns of pine trees dotting the landscape. Just past the cliff's edge of the Bookmark, I could see the peaks of Hallett, Otis, and Taylor in the heart of Rocky Mountain National Park. Vibrating with accomplishment, I breathed in deeply and absorbed the panorama.

From then on, when encouraged by a patient friend, I would swing leads. I led easy trad pitches, constantly questioning my skills and gear placement. I got more comfortable creating anchors, but never absolute. I always took it very seriously—life was on the line. I stepped up only if I felt I could safely lead and create an anchor.

I was learning and loving it.

CHAPTER SEVEN

Pebble Wrestling
Rocky Mountain National Park, September 1999

I WAS NOW A COMMITTED CLIMBER, EAGER TO LEARN AND GET OUT. BUT finding rope-climbing partners whose days off lined up with mine was not always easy. My coworkers were looking to push their limits, and a newbie was not the best partner. My days off were Tuesday and Wednesday, so I couldn't tag along with the weekend warriors.

One day at work, Stephen Greenway, a climbing fanatic, invited me to join him and some friends who were going bouldering at Emerald Lake in Rocky—our moniker for Rocky Mountain National Park (RMNP), along with ROMO (the abbreviation used by the National Park Service). I knew one thing for sure about bouldering, and shared it with Stephen: "Bouldering is hard." I'd never tried it, but knew it required power and strength—two things that were developing slowly for me.

Something I was learning about was the grading systems used for climbing routes, including the fact that rope climbing and bouldering have different scales. A rope climb starts with the numeral 5, and after a decimal point is a second number, from 2 to 15d. The bouldering system went from V0 to V16. As I understood it, the easiest bouldering climb was the equivalent of a 5.10 rope climb.

"That would be similar to the hardest climb I've followed," I told Stephen. "I don't think I could even get my ass off the ground."

Stephen wasn't going to lie. "There are not a lot of easy boulder problems in the area."

He was using "problem" as the term for a particular route, so called because you had to figure out how to solve it.

"We are going to go work this V5 called Lobster Claw," he said, "but I am sure there are a few warm-up problems you can try."

"I don't have a crash pad," I said lamely, when in truth I was wary about falling even if I had one. Stephen shrugged that off, saying he had an extra pad I could carry.

I had no more excuses, and since I desperately wanted to climb on my days off, I decided to get out of my comfort zone.

"Sure," I said. "I guess I'll try it."

The climbing scene in Estes Park in the early 2000s was dominated by trad climbers who dismissed bouldering as "pebble wrestling." In rope climbing, the hardest, trickiest section of a climb is called the "crux." In bouldering, the crux is right there in front of you, on a boulder. From the ground to the top, you are pulling on and executing a demanding sequence of moves. There are no ropes, harnesses, quickdraws, or gear slings, just thick foam mats that you hope to land on when you fall. The whole effort might get you 20 feet off the ground; if you are doing an overhanging "roof," sometimes no more than 5 feet. But there are fellow climbers spotting on the ground below, directing a climber to the crash pads when he or she falls.

The most popular trailhead in Rocky Mountain National Park is at Bear Lake, a beautiful spot below Hallett Peak. Amid the crowds of tourists in the vast parking lot, we looked a bit odd. I laid my borrowed crash pad on the asphalt and looked to Stephen and his wife to figure out how to pack and carry this large, awkward foam square. I put my climbing shoes, chalk, water, food, sweatshirt, coat, and rain jacket on the open crash pad, folded it, and cinched tight the buckles on the edge and bottom. I wondered if all my stuff would fall out as I hiked. Backpack carrying straps were attached to the pad, and I heaved the cumbersome mass onto my back.

The picturesque hike to Emerald Lake was beautiful, even under the bulky pad. We cut up a fire trail to Nymph Lake, delightfully adorned with lily pads. The open water reflected Longs Peak—the national park's only "14'er," at 14,259 feet. Nymph looked vastly different from the past winter when Karla and I had whiled away an afternoon building a snowman on the frozen lake. Next came Dream Lake, with water so clear you could see trout cruising below the surface. Above Dream Lake, we headed up a steep section.

I sweated profusely as the straps dug into my shoulders. *Are we there yet?*

We veered from the trail up a gneiss slab next to a small cataract. Across the stream, I could see towering boulders rising out of the pine forest. *Shit, those are tall.* The creek was gushing with snowmelt, and after a hop over the rushing water, we ascended a gray rock slab and dropped our pads. We had arrived.

Boulders surrounded us. To my relief, some were not as towering as others. Some were as high as a van, maybe 7 feet. Some were more like RVs, up to 20 feet high. Others were as big as houses, 40 feet high. On the rock I could see smudges of chalk, showing where others had climbed. This area was recently discovered, Stephen told me, and that chalk had been left by some elite climbers, like Tommy Caldwell, Dave Graham, Dean Potter, and Jim Belcer—climbers I would get to know well in the coming years.

We rested briefly, cooling down from the hike and fueling up with a snack. We placed pads under an overhanging lichen-covered wall of gneiss and pulled on our sticky rubber climbing shoes. I stood and watched as Stephen dipped his hands into a chalk bucket and reached out to the lowest chalked "feature" (a term for any useful protrusion or depression in a rock face). He carefully placed his feet on tiny edges at the bottom of the rock and pulled his weight off the crash pad.

I watched intently. He quickly latched the next hold with his right hand, moved his left foot up, shifted his weight over his bent knee, and grabbed a flat edge with the fingers of his left hand. He then used a "back step"—moving his right foot, turning his hip to the wall, and putting the outside edge of his shoe on the rock—extending his arm to the next hold.

After a few more moves he was grasping the lip of the boulder with both hands. He looked down, then put his left foot on a hold he had just been crimping with his fingertips, and swung his right leg up to the lip of the boulder, hooking it with his heel. This allowed him to shift slightly over the edge as he reached up and back to a large hold called a "jug." With his left hand on the jug, he hauled his weight off the face and over the lip of the rock; in a smooth "mantling" movement, he turned his right hand backward and flat on the lip and pushed himself up onto the top of the boulder. *Voila!*

He looked down at us.

"That's a nice little warm-up. Maybe V0 or V1," he said as he turned to find a path off the boulder.

Warm-up? For him, maybe. He made it look effortless, fluidly reaching for holds. I longed to match this level of expertise, but knew I'd look more like a toddler trying to climb up on a couch.

Stephen's partner, Sonya, tried next. She and Stephen and their friend who had joined us were far better climbers than I was, and stronger than anyone I'd rope-climbed with. Sonya pulled on, executed a few moves, then reached up, missed a hold, and fell. She landed harmlessly on the crash pad, her friend's hand on her back.

"See, the fall is not bad," she told me. "You go, I'll take a minute."

I looked up at the boulder. The top was only 8 feet above the crash pad, not much higher than the top bunk of a bunkbed, but the steepness of the boulder angling over me made me wonder if I could even hold on, let alone climb. Until then, I'd primarily climbed slabs or vertical cracks and faces. I'd managed one "crack roof move" (hands in a crack in an overhang) on a route called Fat City, at Lumpy Ridge. But that wasn't clean—I'd hung on the rope and tried the sequence repeatedly.

Despite my concerns, I grabbed the starting holds and pressed the edges of my climbing shoes onto small protrusions on the rock, wondering if my feet would stay on. Summoning a lot of *grrr*, I pulled myself off the ground. *Miracle!* I looked up at the next chalked right-hand hold and flung my arm at it. I felt my fingers skin scrape off of the edges and my ass hit the pad.

"I touched it!" I said, surprised, and immediately resituated and pulled back on. This time I managed to grab the hold, then tried to "lock it off"—that is, to reel the hold in creating a bent arm position and hold it while moving your feet or your other arm—but I fell again, falling

Pebble Wrestling

short of the next crimp. I wasn't bummed; I was excited about putting this puzzle together. I pulled back on again, and fell again.

Sonya chuckled. "You have to remember to rest a bit between tries," she said, advising that my "rapid-fire burns" (repeated tries) would tire me out fast.

I stepped aside.

She pulled back on and did the problem, topping out as we spotted. She came back around and explained the "beta"—the info on handholds, foot placement, and other tips for a problem—to me before I tried and fell again.

Since where I was falling was only 4 feet off the ground, she walked over to the holds and explained, "You can pull on here," touching the last holds I could get to from the bottom, "and try to figure out the next move. Once you have all of the moves, try from the bottom. You will figure out the beta and save strength."

I laughed, as this obvious tip had not occurred to me at all. "Great point," I said, pulling on the middle of the problem, attempting to rock my weight over my foot and lock off to the hold I kept missing, Sonya spotting and encouraging me along the way.

Hours of climbing, resting, climbing, watching, and absorbing beta and climbing lingo flew by. I tried other problems and the guys threw themselves at Lobster Claw after The Kind, which looked impossible to me. My body was completely destroyed and my mood was utterly elated.

"This was so much fun!" I exclaimed as we packed up. "Way better than I thought it would be." I jabbered away, saying things they'd realized moons ago: It was fun trying moves and working out the beta with other people instead of being isolated on a rope. The skin on my fingers was scuffed and I could barely lift my arms. I hadn't even "topped out" a boulder problem, but I was totally psyched. As we hiked back down to the Bear Lake lot, I invited myself back, saying "I'd be super psyched to come back and try it again next time you come up."

In the shower that evening, my arms felt like heavy blobs of Jell-O. I was barely able to wash my hair.

When I woke the next day I felt like I'd lost a wrestling match with a giant. *Pebble wrestling? I was more sore than I had ever been.* I could tell this form of climbing would make me stronger. Lying in bed, I played the moves in my head, thinking about the holds and positions. It was all so different from crack climbing. I pictured myself climbing through the bottom, reaching up and catching the hold that I couldn't hit, and executing the problem. My heart sped up and my hands began to sweat.

I was addicted. Bouldering was it.

That fall, whenever I could find a crew, I would hike back to Emerald Lake, throwing myself at boulders that strong climbers just warmed up on. I was happily surprised that advanced boulderers invited me along. I practically jogged behind Dean Potter and Jim Belcer to keep up with their next-level fitness and Dean's long stride—and they were wearing flip-flops! They were establishing new climbs across the canyon from Emerald Lake's main boulders.

"This shit is going to be too hard for me," I lamented to these superheroes.

"Just try," they said. "We got you."

I pushed past my comfort zone, falling a lot but feeling completely safe with the long arms of Dean reaching 7 feet in the air to catch me and guide me to the pad.

I found blocks that were close enough to visit before work. Sometimes I'd go alone if I couldn't summon a posse. I finished the season with a new crash pad, some new muscles, and a new attitude. Also a new project: a V2 traverse at Boxcar Boulder. A "traverse" means working your way horizontally across a rock face. Boxcar was perfect: Located just off a road near the Wild Basin entrance of Rocky, twenty minutes south of town, it was a seam traverse, with tiny feet and some slopey, crimpy holds. It wasn't too far off the ground and it did not top out, making it easy to try it alone.

I could shuttle a few pads up there in no time. It was a perfect place to spend beautiful fall days staring at foot jibs, trying different grips and sequences—working the problem. The low-angled sunlight shimmered through yellow aspen leaves that flickered a winsome song in the light breeze. I found pure happiness outdoors in the resplendent scenery, trying moves repeatedly until I "sent" (cleanly finishing a boulder problem), then proceeding on to the next problem. I went back to these rocks every chance I could.

I didn't entirely abandon rope climbing. After the snow arrived, the sunny slabs of Lumpy Ridge were still accessible. I found myself back there often, cruising up a climb and pulling the Fat City roof clean. My partner, who hadn't climbed with me for months, wondered where I'd gotten this new strength.

"Doing that pebble wrestling," I said, laughing. "It works. You should come out someday." I looked down at the crack we had climbed to get to the roof. "You don't have to go through all of this rigmarole to get to the crux of the climb," I added. "And you don't have to jam your hands and fists into these painful cracks." I shook my hands, which were purple and mashed up from the granite crystals.

"What are you talking about?" he said, flexing his hands. "I love this! Plus, look at the views." He gestured toward the peaks of Meeker, Longs, and Mount Lady Washington across from us. He was right. We all had our own path, and passions.

Here I was, proselytizing to a rope climber about bouldering. I was a fan, a groupie, obsessed. I couldn't get enough of the fun and freedom of bouldering—hanging out with friends in stunning settings, figuring out sequences, falling, topping out, and laughing.

I built a climbing wall in my garage with the help of some enthused friends. My climbing rope and harness hung there, collecting chalk dust.

Looking back, I realize I would have become a better overall climber if I'd kept up *all* aspects of the sport. But I always do what I love in life, and at this point, it was bouldering.

Chapter Eight

A Real Job

Estes Park, Spring 2004

"So, how'd you end up bartending?"

There it was. The inevitable question, one in which I always sensed a subtext. Customers weren't being rude, but they probably assumed something must have gone awry in my life. My automatic punch line, delivered with a smile: "My degree in literature from Loyola New Orleans qualifies me to bartend." And then we'd have a nice chat.

I am a restaurant worker with a degree, like many of my coworkers. We chose this job; we didn't settle for it after some sad travails. In Estes Park—or any mountain town, really—you'll find people who work nights in hospitality so their days are free to live a wonderfully active life in a gorgeous setting. Others are moms taking care of young children during the day, then picking up cash working nights. I often thought the subtext for some customers was quiet envy, or complete bafflement at our unconventional lives. Another question I'd get: "What will you do next? You know, for a *real* job?"

They didn't get it. I would explain that the hospitality industry is a real job for around 17 million people in the United States. I was happy and fulfilled with serving, bartending, and managing the popular Dunraven Inn on the outskirts of Estes Park, and had done so for almost five years (and would stay for thirteen more). Sure, it was far from the career path I'd imagined when sitting in Dr. Wasserman's Medieval Literature class in 1993. My passionate, enthusiastic professors had made teaching literature at a university seem like the perfect job.

I even dipped my toe back into that idealistic dream at age twenty-six when I began working toward a master's degree at the University of Colorado in Boulder, an hour's drive from Estes Park.

It didn't last. Writing a paper on the fourteenth-century poem, "Piers Plowman," I wondered, *What's the point?* Even if I came up with some groundbreaking insights about this medieval narrative poem, who would care? Do I want to put two years into a master's and six for a PhD, with no guarantees on a job, or good pay, or choosing where I'd live? Within a specialty like medieval lit, I'd have to take any opening, wherever it appeared. What if there was no climbing there? Plus, I loved my little mountain town of Estes Park—not just the climbing, but the community, the magnificence, and, of course, my friends.

I finished the semester and then dropped the idea.

One year of hospitality work turned into two; two years turned into four, and four, eventually, to twenty-one (Ed's Cantina, plus a three-month stint at The Other Side restaurant, and then the Dunraven before Bird & Jim). I'd try to explain the appeal and satisfaction of restaurant work to curious customers: the physicality and the constant motion, making moving pieces come together. Every night we'd skirt disasters, tame the chaos, and orchestrate the flow, from the front door to the kitchen. I wanted to give customers more than a great meal—an experience that would be felt, and remembered. "Plus time off in the winter to travel!" I'd say, and the customer would usually nod with understanding, or feigning so.

Another question: "Why are your arms so big?" I'd usually bartend in a tank-top dress on warm summer nights (the Dunraven was an old restaurant with no air-conditioning). "I like to rock-climb," I'd explain. As I zoomed from one end of the bar to the other, they'd ask more questions—"You sleep on ledges?"—and I'd explain the differences between traditional climbing and bouldering.

"And you fall—on mats?"

"Repeatedly!" I'd say. "But you have spotters who try to direct you to the mats. You've probably walked by a few people carrying them in the park."

A Real Job

In the early 2000s, bouldering was still new to many people. When they'd ask "Are you good?" eventually I could reply modestly, "Well, a few companies sponsor me. I get free crash pads, shoes, chalk, clothing, and even some traveling money." Which meant, "Yeah, I'm decent."

I was happy to be excelling in my passion, growing muscles and technique, becoming more confident, honing my skills and progressing up the grade scale. However hard I worked, whatever trials life presented, I had my escape: getting outside in beautiful settings to figure out sequences on the rocks. Restaurant work was the perfect complement; plus, I excelled at that, too. I'm a multitasker by nature, always aiming to please, wanting to delight and grow smiles, and I never liked to sit still (something to which my mom can attest).

My life evolved into a pattern: working and climbing in the busy summer season, saving up for winter road trips to sunny, warm boulders in California. Climbing trumped any career that might dictate where I could live. It gave me the kick in the ass to get out of the bar scene, to become healthy and embrace nature. Standing under rocks that radiated energy ignited something inside me. This fit my personality: climbing, extrapolating sequences, trying and failing repeatedly, and then succeeding.

I quickly became aware that the world was full of distinct rocks that presented unique challenges and various styles, which made me want to travel more. Restaurant work was perfect; I could climb all day and work at night. My boss didn't care if I traveled in the winter, as long as I worked hard from May through October. My constant improvement made it even more addictive—not that I needed much encouragement.

In 2001, I did my first V4, a lower level on the overall grade scale but a new plateau at the time. My ambitions were high and each grade was a celebration.

"That's it," I announced to my girlfriends. "Let's go to France. I want to climb in Fontainebleau." I had a VHS tape of *The Real Thing*, a 1996 bouldering movie about Ben Moon and Jerry Moffatt, two celebrated British climbers, as they road-tripped to the bouldering mecca near Paris. The film played a big part in the popularization of bouldering.[*]

---

[*] "*The Real Thing*—The Original Bouldering Movie," *Moonclimbing.com*, https://moonclimbing.com/News/post/the-real-thing-climbing-film.

My friends were up for it, so Bronson, Karla, and Lisa Foster (a climbing friend and Dunraven colleague) came, along with non-climbing besties Jen and Marsha.

The forests of Fontainebleau, France, are magically littered with sandstone boulders. We rented a car and a *gîte* (vacation house) and packed an English-to-French dictionary, a *Let's Go France* guidebook, and a hot-off-the-press *Fontainebleau Climbs* bouldering guide. We drove in circles, got lost, found boulders, made new friends, drank lots of wine, and got our asses handed to us at the boulders. The infamous sandstone slopers of Font were entirely different from the gneiss edges of Rocky, and entirely challenging. We were humbled every day, but adored every second.

At first I focused on a few classic climbs, thinking I could match my hardest grade from back home. Not so much. After a few days of sliding down sandstone and creating glistening pink centers in my fingertips, I turned to easier climbs. There were entire circuits of them, comprised of hundreds of problems or more, and we could top out as many boulders in a day as our bodies allowed. I returned home after two weeks, rededicated to working, saving, climbing, training—and returning.

Restaurant work made it all possible.

As a child, restaurants were magical to me. I was the kid all servers wanted at their table, the six-year-old ordering lobster and scallops. Walking into a red-carpeted restaurant felt like a movie: happy people, smiling faces, kind greetings. "The Garganos! Welcome back!" The maître d' would usher us to a large round booth, hand us gigantic leather menus, and glide away.

In the 1980s, my family would go to Fantasia in Cambridge, Massachusetts. Everything enthralled me, including the red velvet wallpaper in the bathroom, where I'd narrate my bowel movements to my embarrassed sister Alison, assigned to monitor me. Oh, the excitement of the soap, which magically changed from dry powder to bubbles! "Come on, Missy," Alison would say. "Hold on, I have to wipe the counter" I'd tell her. Back at the table, my mother laughed: "I can't get her to do that at home." I'd order a frozen virgin grasshopper to go with chocolate cake for my dessert.

A Real Job

My first job was at Jake's, a fried-seafood joint in the beach town of Hull, Massachusetts, where we spent summers. Hull was close enough that my dad could still commute to his law office. Working in a fish fry joint was vastly different from the glamorous excursion to Fantasia as a six-year-old. After one month of picking up tartar-sauce-smeared, greasy red plastic baskets and plates, I swore I'd never again work in a restaurant. But the subsequent six years of working summers in my father's law firm also convinced me I'd never again work in an office, or be a lawyer.

My restaurant work in Estes Park won me over. "This is a real job for me," I'd assure any skeptical customer. "And I like it."

I figured out what I would be by identifying what I did not want to be.

Chapter Nine

Adam
Estes Park, 2004–2016

Another sunny day, climbing with friends Heather and Glen, who were spending their second summer working and climbing in Estes Park after a winter in Hueco Tanks. They and their Akita, Sugar, rented my spare room. Being a single young female with a mortgage, I rented out not only the apartment above the garage but also the small spare room off my kitchen. We met at the Suzuki boulders, a roadside cluster in Rocky Mountain National Park named for Hidetaka Suzuki, an old-school climber who would dash there on his lunch break from Komito Boots to get in a quick workout. We were trying an unnamed boulder problem—a dumpy, lowball (topping out at 4 or 5 feet), sharp, V8 (estimated grade level at the time) roof that was not a high quality line, but challenging for me and easily accessible.

A friend of Heather and Glen's also showed up—Adam Strong, a new guy in town. He strolled up from the nearby parking area with a crash pad slung over one shoulder. He wore green army fatigue pants cut off to shorts, and an orange polyester short-sleeved, button-front, vintage collared shirt. A fluorescent orange trucker's hat bearing the Tide detergent logo covered unruly light brown hair wadded into dreadlocks. His loose, open shirt revealed a sinewy physique. He was an arborist, my friends informed me, and a formidable climber of rocks and trees.

He had recently moved to Estes Park for the summer climbing season, migrating north with the climbing weather from Hueco Tanks.

With abundant tree-climbing experience and little fear, he quickly landed a job at Mike's Tree Service. He lived in his 1996 white Subaru and soon discovered how difficult it is to be a dirtbag climber trying to camp around Estes Park with few free camping options or forest service roads accessible to a Subaru.

Adam was on his own unstructured path, the only requirements being climbing and minimal responsibility. After declining academic and track scholarships at Stanford, Adam headed to Alaska for college. The outdoors, rock climbing, and ice climbing called him to the remote wilderness state. Removed from his family's nest for the first time and exposed to an uncloistered life, Adam diverged from his sheltered Southern Baptist upbringing. He dived into this world unencumbered. Eventually he ventured back to warmer states, leaving ice climbing and academia behind. Adam found warm dry rocks, like-minded climber friends, and tree work to pay the bills. Alternately climbing rocks and trees, he roamed the continent in sync with the weather.

"Melissa, this is Adam," Heather said.

"Hey," I said.

Adam tilted his head and said "Hi," revealing a pleasantly handsome, ruddy face and a sweet smile. A chipped front tooth lent a touch of goofiness to his grin, which was fringed by a red goatee. At first glance, he seemed simultaneously pleasant and intense, and I was unsure which would dictate his personality.

I had dated here and there since my divorce and had had a few relationships that went nowhere. At the time, I was single and happy. My passion was climbing, which grew more robust each year. My limited glimpse into dating in the climbing world didn't make me eager to rush into the scene. At that time there was not a plethora of women climbing, which led to significant drama, leaving me a reluctant participant. I had a small circle of climbing friends, and we ventured to California, Utah, and France (where I had returned in 2003). I was content with a life that revolved around climbing and traveling. I'd lost contact with my barfly friends; I had rocks to focus on.

With a small inheritance from my grandfather and some help from my parents, I was able to make a minimal down payment on a house that had a rental apartment over the garage, to help pay the mortgage. Over the winter, John Willson, climbing enthusiast and my roommate, helped me build a 60-degree overhanging climbing wall in the two-car garage. (I kicked my 4Runner outside.)

The ceilings were only 10 feet high, so we had no other choice regarding the angle. It was steep. Once we'd framed the footprint, we drilled holes in the plywood face and lined them with t-nuts. After affixing the plywood to the frame, we put some holds on the wall. "I'm not sure I can even climb on this!" I said, laughing as I screwed them in. Fortunately, I had a lot of large holds ("jugs," in climbing jargon) to start with. I barely managed my way up the jug haul lines at first, but within a few months I'd progressed to pulling through sequences on smaller plastic holds.

This was exciting—my training-wall investment was proving to be effective. I had a space of my own and work that supported my lifestyle. I was happy being single.

Of course, that's precisely when you meet someone.

Adam tossed his pad down. He put his climbing shoes on and did a few warm-up problems. He came over to check out what we were climbing on. With a smoldering hand-rolled cigarette between his lips, he pulled onto the start to feel it out, and with little effort, did the V8 roof I was trying. *He's strong if this is a warm-up.*

I was aware of his presence throughout the day, but tried to dismiss him. That night was going to be the soft opening for a remodeled Ed's Cantina, which Karla had recently bought from her brother-in-law. I asked if we could add one more to the list, and Adam joined the group.

Bouldering in Rocky was becoming better known, and seasonal climbers moved through the area with the summer. I put Adam in that category: another transient climber who lives in his car and would leave with the first snowfall. *Not interested.*

At dinner, I learned how he'd bounced around from Texas to Tennessee to Arizona, always ending up in Hueco Tanks for the winter. I'd heard of Hueco, but chose to make the longer drive to Bishop, California, to avoid the notorious restrictions at Hueco Tanks State Park & Historic Site.

A few days later, a bouldering friend named Paul Otis called to tell me his buddy Adam Strong was in Estes Park. "You two would be perfect for each other," he said. I laughed and told him we'd already met, and changed the subject.

I ran into Adam a few more times with mutual friends; he got my phone number and asked me to go climbing. "Sure," I said. I was always happy to have psyched people to climb with.

We met at the Lumpy Ridge parking lot. "Is anyone else coming?" I asked.

"No, just us."

I was surprised, since I had only seen him with groups of people.

"Sounds good. These boulders aren't too high, so we should be okay with these pads."

I told him my friend Ashley might come by to take photos; I'd sometimes test gear and write reviews (hence, the lightweight techy top I was wearing). Ashley met us, took some pictures, hung out briefly, and left.

Adam and I climbed on some of Lumpy Ridge's classic sharp, challenging boulders and then we went out to eat. We had fun; the climbing was good and the conversations easy, and I saw a pleasant, sincere guy behind his powerful, confident presence.

The next day, snippets of our time together popped into my head, and I caught myself wondering if he would call again. And he did. I was a little annoyed at myself for my swooning thoughts. *Come on, Melissa—he'll be gone with the season.*

The following day, he came to my work to say hi and asked me on a proper date. It was a rom-com suffer-fest for him—he'd scratched his cornea at work and showed up with an eye patch of wadded-up tissue paper. Clearly in pain the entire day, he still managed to keep his spirits up.

After a few weeks of climbing together, going out to eat, hanging out with friends, and cooking for him (cooking and enjoying good food was one of my hobbies), Adam announced, "I'm not going anywhere."

I looked at him. "What are you talking about?"

"I just wanted to let you know I'm not leaving—I like it here. And you."

On our next date, I cooked stuffed eggplant for dinner, a little healthier than the sausage calzones I first made for him. He ate everything, including the skin. *Wow, this guy really likes eggplant.* (I found out later that he hated it, but wanted our time together to be great, so choked it down with a smile—the courting games.)

Later that evening, he told me about every untoward thing he had done in his life, saying "If you're going to hear anything about me, I want it to come from me." *An interesting approach to relationship building, but I get it,* I thought, as I listened to stories of his younger, wilder days. I didn't quite realize what was happening, but he was falling in love and forming the foundation for what was coming next.

Three months of spending most of our time together passed quickly. Adam moved in after his basement apartment flooded. By then, I had fallen in love. Before leaving for my restaurant shift, I would leave notes for him to find when he came home from tree work, along with a pre-cooked dinner for him to reheat. I talked about him incessantly to my girlfriends and wrote some sappy stanzas, another sure sign.

One evening in September, I was at my desk, writing a climbing story I hoped to get published in a magazine. Adam was preparing to head out the next day with some friends for a weekend speed-climbing competition. He came over and knelt by my chair.

"Will you marry me?" he said.

Stunned, I said, "What?"

He repeated himself.

"Are you serious, or just feeling bad that you're leaving town?" I was bewildered. "Have you thought about this?"

"Yes," he said. "I've been thinking about it for a while."

I heard myself say "Where is the engagement ring?"

"Let's pick one out together," he said, in response to my conventional request, meant as a curveball.

My head was spinning.

"This is kind of crazy, but yes," I said, quickly adding, "Let's wait a year, though—we really just met." Adam leaned in and kissed me passionately.

Well, let's hope the second time's the charm.

How committed was he? Instead of making his annual pilgrimage to Hueco Tanks, we worked through that winter to save for a springtime climbing trip to a newly discovered bouldering area, the Rocklands in South Africa. When we returned, we planned our small wedding in a meadow in Estes Park with a view of the Continental Divide, surrounded by family and friends. My parents were supportive, my mother's only wish being no dreadlocks for the wedding. Adam's father, Charlie Strong, married us on his birthday, September 17, 2005.

Life progressed quickly and unexpectedly. In our first year of marriage, we agreed to buy Mike's Tree Service, which became Adam's Tree Service. Adam would officially take over in April 2006, allowing us to spend that winter at Hueco Tanks State Park & Historic Site.

For years, I had snubbed this popular bouldering destination because of the restricted access put in place in the late 1990s to protect its historic and cultural resources, like ancient pictographs, dwellings, and burial sites. It's considered one of the top three bouldering destinations in the world. Depending on your strengths and preferred style, you can choose between Fontainebleau, Rocklands in South Africa, or Hueco Tanks.

Hueco is a fascinating place. The park consists of four significant rock formations: three "mountains" in the Texas Chihuahuan Desert, and a rock spur. *Hueco* (pronounced "Way-co") is Spanish for "hollow," referring to geological depressions that hold water. Magma pushed up into an older limestone formation millions of years ago, and weathering has eroded the limestone and sculpted the now-exposed igneous rock.[*]

Ten thousand to twenty thousand years ago, Hueco's water, shelter, and game drew migrating Indigenous people to the area to hunt giant long-horned bison. Later, Hueco became home to tribes who built huts and dams and grew crops, including the Jornada Mogollon, Apache,

---

[*] "Interpretive Guide: Hueco Tanks State Park and Historic Site," Texas Parks & Wildlife Department, https://tpwd.texas.gov/publications/pwdpubs/media/pwd_br_p4501_0095.pdf.

Kiowa, and Tigua. The park contains a multitude of rock art sites, mortar holes, pottery shards, former dwellings and hearths, arrowheads and tools, and burial sites. It's a sacred, spiritual environment. Some Westerners migrating to California found shelter and water here when the Butterfield Overland Mail stage line briefly used Hueco as a stop in 1858–1859. The travelers etched their names into the rock during their respite. Decades later, it became a ranch before becoming a state park and historic site in 1970.[*]

By the late 1980s and early 1990s, the sacred land had been scarred by social trails, graffiti, vandalism, and litter, and artifacts were stolen. A new public use plan was created to protect Hueco Tanks by restricting day-use capacity. Some sections allowed self-guiding after an education session while others required a certified guide.

My first trip to this area captivated me—860 acres of some of the world's best bouldering in a beautiful high desert surrounded by intriguing history. The climbing was as unique as the setting. Boulders are scattered on and around rock cliffs. Conjoining rock piles produce overhanging roofs, steep faces, slabs, corridors, tunnels, and arches. The boulders and rock cliffs are marked with seams and pocked with *huecos*. It's a beautiful landscape infused with tribal culture that you can see and feel. I found my own deep nexus with Hueco and became ardently dedicated to the area. I learned to appreciate the restrictions that protect Hueco Tanks while keeping it accessible to all users.

My first season there was intimidating and a bit overwhelming. People would stop by to visit their old pal Adam Strong, who was deeply ensconced in the climbing scene. "I wanted to come meet the girl Adam Strong would marry," I heard from his friends. Everyone was sociable, and most had a "remember that one time" Adam story to tell.

We agreed to do what we could to devote ourselves, at least part-time, to this precious place. We financed 5 acres of land using a credit card check, splitting the land with Heather and Glen, who eventually sold it to us when they invested in more acreage across the valley for a campground. In February 2006, we hacked a driveway into the plot with

---

[*] "Hueco Tanks," *Texas Beyond History*, https://www.texasbeyondhistory.net/hueco/story.html.

pickaxes, shovels, and the help of friends, and parked our 13-foot camper on the land. We milked that season as long as possible, driving back to Colorado on April 2 to be ready for Adam to take over the tree service. He was committed to a lifestyle plan of working minimally and climbing more. I was game, but was firmly pushing Adam toward a "Let's create a lasting life plan" mentality. Our courtship and first dreamy season in Hueco was over, and we had challenges ahead.

That June, we drove back to Texas to attend a training program to become Hueco Tanks State Park–certified guides to restricted areas. We applied to the state park system for a guiding concession. Wagon Wheel Co-opt became the second business we'd acquired in one year, which also happened to be our first year of marriage and second year of knowing each other. People say the first year of marriage is the hardest, and we proved them right. We endured challenges and growing pains, but I broke my previous record of being married for ten months. We evolved as people together and grew closer with each year, weathering what came our way and strengthening our bond and our love.

We moved with the seasons, from Estes Park and Rocky Mountain National Park (RMNP) to El Paso and Hueco Tanks State Park & Historic Site. Adam and I became volunteers at RMNP, working with the climbing rangers to help protect access. Through Wagon Wheel and my participation in local climbing organizations, I applied for grants to create special projects to help educate users of Hueco Tanks. The restrictions that I once resented I now appreciated. The growth of climbing gyms and the increased popularity of rock climbing can lead to excessive use, causing damage and access issues. Hueco's restrictions protect the sacred rocks and cultural resources while allowing people to respectfully climb.

Over the years, Adam and I occasionally broke out of our Colorado–Texas cycle and traveled wherever the rocks were calling: Yosemite, Utah, back east to Tennessee and New England, plus Squamish in British Columbia, Fontainebleau in France, South Africa (again), Switzerland, Italy, and even Australia. It's a big world, and we were enjoying every bit of it, finding rocks to climb and wines to taste.

Chapter Ten

How Many Children Do You Have?
Estes Park, 2006–2016

We were young(ish), in love, and utterly headstrong. We were in our early thirties when we met and married fifteen months later. By this age, many couples are already settled down with a toddler and maybe another baby on the way. For us, it was different. Adam was a transient climber when he rolled into Estes Park. Starting a family was not a priority, and we'd discussed this before marrying.

"I want to have a child someday," I said. He wasn't eager, but said "Down the road." We focused on climbing and working enough to fund the next excursion or winter in Hueco. Despite our somewhat nomadic life, I did cling to some stability—I wasn't moving into a Subaru or a van. A home base was essential for me, as was the idea of children in our future. For now, though, I was all in for a convivial climbing life.

We threw ourselves at rocks, spending long days in the mountains and continuing the fun into the evening, cooking and drinking with friends while reveling in the day's challenges and triumphs. We also nursed our injuries. Climbing pushed our bodies to the limit, or beyond. On occasion, the tendons in our fingers and knees popped loudly, and elbow pain (epicondylitis, or climber's elbow) was endemic in our circle. Rotator cuffs were strained and torn. Still, we scarcely slowed down. Climbing trips, winters in Hueco, home in Estes Park—it was a nice life. Owning the tree service meant stress and responsibility, but Adam was his own boss, and always found help to let us get away for a few months each year.

As time passed, though, I yearned for something more. I got off birth control at age thirty-eight—not too late, I convinced myself. Six years of marriage, of growing into our relationship, learning, maturing, mellowing—*You are ready*, I told myself.

But I was also terrified. I dreamed of the joys of motherhood, longed to feel a baby shift and kick in my womb—to hold our baby close to my chest and breathe in that baby smell, sharing an intense connection with our child. But I was less sure about the challenges of carrying and birthing a child, let alone raising one.

I was an athlete, hesitant to sacrifice my body—selfish and short-sighted view I see in hindsight, but I had other reasons. I'd heard stories about abdominal muscles ripping apart and sometimes never mending. Some women had no issues, of course, but others struggled with the physical and mental challenges of pregnancy, childbirth, and motherhood. I looked at my sister and her husband, happy with their three beautiful, healthy children. I wanted to add cousins to the family, and looked forward to holidays together and family gatherings.

A child would change so much, I knew. For instance, winters in Texas fell in the middle of the school year—no more Hueco? Homeschooling was always an option, but was that selfish? Unfair to our little one? I nudged these future worries aside for now.

I also thought often of my brother. Intelligent, hilarious, and capable of so much love, but a problem child from birth. He was a person with an addiction, skillful in figuring out ways to continue and cover his dependence. Would our child be a victim of some merciless random strand in our family DNA? My parents endured years of anxiety because of my brother. I fielded calls or messages from him that were full of twisted pain, confusion, and rants. "Mom and Dad never loved me" he would say. "Of course they love you, Paul—they support you, they take care of you. They have always loved you unconditionally. How could you even say that?" There was no way to understand his brain process.

Seeing my parents' pain and countless quarrels about their son added to my misgivings about becoming a mother. Could I endure that kind of anguish? I lived in uncertainty and apprehension.

These selfish deliberations were among my excuses as the years passed. But in 2014, I told myself that it was now or never. After a year off the pill, nothing. I purchased ovulation tests and tracked my cycles. After another eighteen months of planned sex and lunch-break quickies, I broached the idea of getting doctors involved. Adam unreservedly supported this.

The doctors told me gently that I had old eggs, but said women younger than me face the same issues. There was no telling if it was because I'd waited too long. We decided to give in vitro fertilization a try, but it took years just to reach our first IVF trial. There were tests, medication, hope—and delays. The timing of egg-retrieval surgery was difficult due to labs and ultrasounds and doctors' schedules and holidays. My body did not react well to some medications, which resulted in temporary cysts that caused further delay.

The IVF schedule allowed us to squeeze in a short trip to sunny Hueco in the snowy winter of 2016. While we waited for a friend of Adam's to arrive to run the tree crew, we got a nice 10-inch dump of snow. I had recently embraced backcountry skiing. Skinning up was a great workout, and I could get in a few runs without driving to a resort and buying a lift ticket.

I told Adam we should head up to Hidden Valley, which features vestiges of old ski runs. Adam was not a winter sports enthusiast but had been playing along, and he'd recently bought a split board—a snowboard that splits apart so you can tour uphill. We tossed our gear in the car and drove into the park.

Hidden Valley is nestled into a hillside off the windy Trail Ridge Road. At the foot of the basin there is a long creek with a parking lot that once provided access to a ski resort, with T-bars and chairlifts operating from 1955 to 1991. Above that entrance, Trail Ridge Road is closed, though it switches back and crosses the run far above the lot. The upper section is mostly a treeless bowl.

After an intensely aerobic uphill slog, we reached the top of the upper section of Hidden Valley. We removed the skins from our skis, clipped back into our bindings, and started down. Just a few moments into the run, I felt my skis sink deep into the layer underneath the fresh snow. I tried to force a turn and heard three loud pops in my left knee. I went down, instantly knowing it was bad. I called out to Adam, who made his way over.

"My knee—I heard it. It was loud. I think I'm screwed."

We were still in the upper bowl, the section above Trail Ridge Road. I slid down to the flat but snow-covered road. I tried to see if I could put any weight on my leg, using my poles to inch myself upright. My knee slogged off to the side, dislocating (visible through the baggy ski pants), and as I collapsed back into the powder, I heard Adam scream at the sight.

Good god. This was grim.

I told Adam I thought I could slide down the rest of the slope to the parking lot, but that was quite a way down the mountain. The chairlift that once served this area had been removed in the early 1990s. A few skiers stopped to offer help and convinced me that sliding down was not a good idea. There was a ski litter (a stretcher-sled) stashed nearby by park rangers. We formed a plan. The Good Samaritans would skin down Trail Ridge Road, pulling me along on the litter for the 5 winding miles down to the entrance to the parking area. Adam would snowboard down the run, get the car, and meet us at the road.

My mind was in turmoil on the slow, cold ride down. I was enormously thankful to these kind strangers, upset that I'd ruined their day, and wracked with regret and disappointment about my leg. It only got worse at the orthopedics office a few days later. The diagnosis: torn ligaments, both the anterior cruciate and medial collateral, a torn meniscus, and a fractured tibia. The surgery and recovery were tough enough, but it also meant pausing fertility treatments for several months before starting the entire process over again.

Finally, our time had come. I had trouble accepting a nurse's admirable attempt to describe the process as a natural path to fertility. When the FedEx man arrived with a large box of medication that cost about

$7,500, I tried not to fall apart. I had to inject the entire contents of that box into myself over a ten- to thirteen-day period. I called it Hell Week. Talk about traumatic. I blundered the first injection badly, using the wrong needle (the mixing needle versus the injection one), resulting in a burning lump of fluid between my skin and muscle. I screamed and tears welled up. When I realized my mistake, I was slightly relieved. The injections got easier.

Each morning, I woke early, injected hormones, got in the car, and drove to the doctor's office, ninety minutes to two hours, depending on the day and which office was open. I did this for ten days, listening to Loggins and Messina's "Danny's Song" ("People smile and tell me I'm the lucky one / . . . Think I'm gonna have a son / He will be like she and me, as free as a dove / conceived in love"), usually crying a bit, with hope and hormones off the charts. Blood tests, ultrasounds, then finally the "trigger shot" and egg-extraction surgery. With seven or eight mature follicles, I was hopeful.

When I awoke, they told me they only got two eggs. *Better than none*, I thought. Then came the wait to see if they could be fertilized.

I wanted to feel hopeful but was numb. My life, our future, and our potential child all hung in an eerie world of vagueness utterly beyond my control. To distract myself as I waited, I chose a Sisyphean home project that was necessary for fire safety: move a wood pile that was too close to our house 25 feet farther away, log by log. The mundane task perfectly fit my mood. I picked up as many logs as my fragile post-surgery body would allow and walked them over to a new stack. Hour after hour, methodically. My knee, still swollen from surgery, slowed me down, but there was no hurry. All I was doing was waiting for a call that might change our lives.

The phone rang. Only one egg fertilized; again, better than none. Now, we had five or six days to wait to see if the fertilized egg would reach the blastocyst stage. Each day, I tried not to focus on our lonely little zygote. Parents are warned about all possible failures: The transfer to my uterus might be unsuccessful, and there were no guarantees I could successfully carry this child to term.

If it's healthy, please let the egg make it, I thought. *If not, let it end now.* I couldn't take much more of this.

I got updates that the egg was still growing, cultivating hope in my heart. On day six, the phone rang. Adam was home for lunch, and I was finishing some knee therapy and rolling out a mat for an ab workout. I could hear it in her voice before she said anything—her empathy was audible. The fertilized egg had not matured.

I tried to choke the tears back when I ended the call. Adam hugged me and told me he would see me through another round if I wanted. He assured me that he loved me and that our lives would be good with or without a baby. I accepted his love and told him I'd better get back to my ab workout. It felt like an ending that I needed to learn how to accept. *It wasn't meant to be,* I told myself.

I told Adam to please get online and buy us tickets to Australia.

If we weren't going to have a child, I wanted to continue living like a childless couple, and that meant jetting off on adventures whenever we pleased. The best consolation would be meeting our good friend Mike on a climbing trip in the Grampians, a range of sandstone mountains in southeast Australia. My family offered to help financially with another round of IVF if I changed my mind, but they understood our decision, even though they had varying opinions of their own. My dad wanted to meet a grandchild from his baby girl. My mom said no children was the way to go. My sister reminded me I was godmother to Andrew, her oldest child, and I would always have my nieces.

Chapter Eleven

The Road Not Taken

Estes Park, Early 2016

"Andy, I am ready," I said one day at work.

Andy had been the owner of the Dunraven for six years, and I had worked for the previous owner for twelve years before that. I was always full of ideas and freely shared suggestions, so Andy wasn't surprised. At one point we'd even discussed bringing me in as a partner, but that plan hadn't come together.

"Ready?"

"For something new," I said. "To make a different restaurant in Estes Park."

Andy nodded, understanding. The bigger question was whether Estes Park was ready. This was a tried-and-true tourist town, a classic gateway for a national park that had four million visitors every year. But much of it was stuck in the 1970s. Restaurants operated with the "If it's not broke, don't fix it" mentality, and kept the same menu offerings for years.

This included the Dunraven, whose hearty Italian fare had refueled hikers and visitors for decades. Its interior was warm and homey, beloved by countless repeat customers, both locals and tourists. Also, basically unchanged for ages. I couldn't blame the restaurant owners—with a captive clientele, there was no pressing need to invest in change or rock the boat.

But I saw what was happening around us. There was a fantastic food scene growing all across the Front Range. It was easy for food suppliers to focus on Denver, Boulder, and the ski resorts, overlooking our little mountain town. Plus, Estes had its heels firmly dug into the past, with a few exceptions. I loved what my friend Karla had done with Ed's Cantina. She saw her way through a complete remodel and matched the new look with fresh, seasonally inspired new menus. Of course, local resistance was quite vocal. People loved the old No. 8, a loaded burrito, as well as the broasted chicken. But they adapted to the change because they were forced to. Gone was the microwaved fare and precooked burgers.

Deep down, I was thinking, *If I'm not going to have a baby, I can give birth to something else.* I looked at Andy and asked, "Are you interested in another restaurant, creating something different, together?"

He paused, then said, "Yeah, yeah, for sure, I would consider it."

I had hustled for others for years, working in restaurants since I landed in Estes. Everywhere I worked—or ate, for that matter—I would look around, scheming and redesigning, thinking of how I'd change things, or what my own restaurant would look like if I ever got the chance. Instead of putting my work efforts into the Dunraven, why not open new doors and create the restaurant I'd always dreamed of? If children were not part of our future, this would give me something to pour myself into.

I realized dreaming could go on indefinitely. I had to act—but how? What would be my *kairos*—my moment of opportunity?

A few nights later I tended bar at the Dunraven, keeping an eye on diners, mixing drinks, pouring beers, and slicing up peaches and oranges for our signature sangria. Always listening while working (a key to the hospitality industry), I overheard some customers at the bar and realized they were talking about a struggling restaurant in town. I slid into the conversation.

"Are you talking about The Other Side?" I asked. "I worked there briefly before I came here." I had heard the current owners were finding operations to be challenging.

"We're new to town," one of the men said, "and we just bought the Country Supermarket complex." Everyone knew the place—a low-slung group of buildings a couple of miles back toward town that included a small grocery store, a souvenir shop, and a tired restaurant. Out back was a pond and RV park. "I'm not sure they'll make it," the gentleman said, referring to The Other Side.

I wondered if my excitement showed.

How horrible that another's misfortune could be my chance. Should I say anything?

I paused before blurting out, "Andy and I are looking to start a different restaurant together." It's one of my secret powers—proclaiming what was on my mind (even if in this case, I was stretching the truth a bit, since Andy was not committed yet, only interested). Over the years, I'd learned to use it for good; sometimes, it works, and sometimes people don't want to hear it.

"I'm Dave," the man said, offering his hand.

"Hi, Dave, I'm Melissa," I said with gusto.

He nodded. "I've seen you working here—bartending, waiting tables, managing the place. You're a hard worker."

"Thanks—I try hard. I love this place," I said, trying to contain myself. "But I'm ready to start something new and different. And Andy is game to partner with me," I said, smiling at Andy in an attempt to sway his enthusiasm for another venture.

Dave smiled and said, "Well, let's see what happens. I sense we will have an open space. I'd like to talk with you and Andy when that happens."

Bam! Yes!

I was bubbling over with joy but managed to maintain a collected exterior. There was interest, there was a space, and there was the potential for a conversation. This might be the opportunity I'd been waiting for.

The parking lot of the Country Supermarket is as utilitarian and uninspiring as you might imagine, with a Conoco gas station right there for added charm. But to the west is a spectacular view: the snowcapped Rocky Mountains. The peaks looked crisp against a brilliant blue sky when Andy and I walked across the parking lot to meet Dave and his partners at The Other Side.

"This could be cool," I told Andy, who cautioned, "Melissa, don't get too excited. They are asking for a lot in rent." Andy knew restaurant numbers better than I did. He had managed venues for a large restaurant group in the Front Range before coming home to Estes and buying the

Dunraven. "You're right," I agreed. I had worked at The Other Side for three months between Ed's and the Dunraven. "Plus, it is terribly dated," I said, adding to the list of downsides.

When we walked in the door, I saw that not much had changed from my short working stint more than seventeen years earlier. There were trout on the wallpaper, and the restaurant layout was centered on a large buffet room. Not exactly my vision. My dream didn't involve sneeze guards or wildlife on the walls. The developers wanted to work with us on updates, but this needed more than a fresh coat of paint and new curtains.

I walked out less cheery than when I'd walked in. Everything seemed off. As we walked across the parking lot, I gestured at the gorgeous mountains.

"It's so bizarre that this beautiful view of the Rockies is not visible from the restaurant," I said. Andy agreed, adding, "Why did they design the dining room to face that boggy pond and the RV park?" We agreed this was not the place.

Pulling out, we stopped at the red light at the corner, and Andy pointed to an even older restaurant across the intersection. "That's the property you want," he said.

It was the Sundeck, a longtime landmark adjacent to a motel, the last commercial properties before you entered the national park.

"Great location, and with the view," he said.

I'd heard the owners had been trying to sell for years, but it was on the same lot as the hotel, and they were attempting to sell the hotel and restaurant together.

Andy's right, I thought. *That is a nice location.*

Chapter Twelve

When One Door Closes, Don't Yank

Estes Park, Fall 2016

I walked into our local bank for my scheduled meeting with the new loan officer who'd recently taken over the loan for Adam's Tree Service after the previous banker retired. I wanted to remove our house as collateral for the Tree Service loan to free up assets as I searched for a landing place for my restaurant. We only had about $20,000 left on the Tree Service loan, and our equipment assets far exceeded that number.

While some may think of banks as big and impersonal, in my case, in my adopted hometown of Estes Park, it got very personal—in the best way. Everyone was a friend, or a friend of a friend, creating a comforting small-time vibe.

Usually, that is.

The new loan officer seemed bemused by my arrival. He didn't stand up to say hello or shake my hand, just rocked back in his chair and looked at me as if I was interrupting something.

"Hi," I said. "I'm Melissa Strong, here for our one o'clock meeting about Adam's Tree Service."

"Oh, right," he said, scanning his desk and shuffling his papers. "Hold on—I don't know where your file is," he said, standing and walking past me, out of his office.

Wow. This wasn't cool, or professional. *He didn't even introduce himself or shake my hand.*

When the loan officer came back in, I laid out my own papers, showing him titles, our good payment record, low remaining balance, our taxes, solid income, and the business's value.

I got to the purpose of my visit: "I would like you to switch the collateral for the loan from our home to the trucks and equipment."

He chuckled. "That's not gonna happen," he said, without hesitation.

I was dumbstruck. What is this creep laughing at? We were talking about $20k—less than the cost of a new car that any dealership would easily finance with no collateral. Was I not a big-enough customer for him? Was it because I was a woman? Wait, had I said $200,000? No, I'd clearly said $20,000. These thoughts whirled through my head while he just sat there, quiet and smug. The silent standoff ended when I asked, "Is there any way you would reconsider your . . . *hasty* decision?" He was shaking his head, closing the file, and saying "No" before I'd even finished speaking.

I felt insignificant and fought the urge to raise hell. He looked at his watch and I got the message. "Okay," I said, and stood up and walked out.

Making my way through the lobby, heart pounding, I saw familiar faces and awkwardly smiled in acknowledgment. I'd known the bank's president for years. *Maybe I should march into his office*, I thought, but decided I wanted nothing more to do with this establishment.

I left the building and gulped in fresh air as the doors closed behind me. It wasn't until I opened my car door that I let loose. "What an asshole!" I said, timed with slamming the door. Sitting there steaming, I gathered my swirling thoughts. I couldn't accept this treatment, or this answer.

Infuriated, I drove four minutes to the Bank of Colorado, walked in, and asked to speak with someone about a loan. The vice president of the branch, Phil Frank, stood up and shook my hand as I entered his office without an appointment. He listened to my story earnestly, reviewed the documents, and said I had plenty of assets with the equipment.

"We would be happy to take over the loan," he said, and retrieved the forms to move the loan and our accounts to the Bank of Colorado.

Was that so hard? As I filled out the paperwork I chattered away, telling Phil my idea about opening a restaurant. And he listened!

I talked about seasonally driven, quality fare, about the visionary dining experience I wanted to create for locals and visitors alike. "There is a culinary food movement happening in the Front Range," I told him, "and I want to bring it to Estes." I told him my immediate task: "I am on the hunt for the perfect location."

Back home, I dashed off a letter to the branch president of my former bank, explaining why I'd moved our accounts. I never received a reply.

With The Other Side restaurant a nonstarter, I contacted a local commercial realtor, Thom, with Verus Real Estate, who showed me a few available locations. One was on the fringe of downtown Estes, near a dated souvenir store that sold rubber tomahawks. I knew that downtown was a challenging location, having helped the Dunraven open a branch there. Tourists were there for knickknacks and taffy, maybe a burger, but not for serious dining.

Next was an old gas station that housed an extinct video rental store. I asked Andy to come and take a look, but he explained that he was going to pass on the potential venture. His hands were full with the Dunraven, he said, and he still had his own loan; he didn't want to overextend himself. I told him I appreciated his honesty. Now I knew for certain that I'd be taking on this project on my own.

Walking through the gas station with Thom, I dreamed aloud: "I can see adding a second story, maybe two different concepts: high-end serious diners upstairs and bar and burgers down." I had the vision but lacked the funds, and adding a second story and removing gas tanks would be a substantial undertaking.

I went back to see Phil Frank at the Bank of Colorado.

"Okay, Phil, I might have found a place—what do I need for a loan?" That was my naive question to my new banker. He rattled off a list, and I got to work on a business proposal.

My head reeled with facts and figures, pouring them into pages explaining why someone should support my dreams. The document included the big picture—exponential growth of the Front Range of Colorado, 4.5 million visitors to Rocky Mountain National Park—as well as the general concept of the place: upscale dining and approachable fare that puts a spin on comfort food. Call it modern mountain dining.

I pointed out that nobody else was doing this locally. I included profit and loss projections, break-even analysis, balance sheets. I even got into sample menus, an extensive wine list, and a whiskey collection. It was an abstract yet definite plan.

I'd periodically pause in the midst of this work: *Do you know what you're doing?* My answer was hardly confident, but the bottom line was *Yes.* My gut feeling and years of experience helped me push down the doubts. I somehow knew it would work. I put aside my uncertainty, double-checked my facts and proposed figures, and moved forward.

There were so many unknowns, especially for the gas station site. I knew this much: Removing gas tanks is a huge undertaking. "I like the location, but I don't think this is it," I told my realtor. I felt stuck, questioning every thought.

About a week later, Phil Frank called. "Melissa, the restaurant attached to the Alpine Trail Ridge Inn might be for sale, and I thought of you."

The Alpine Trail Ridge Inn? At first I thought he was talking about a restaurant at the other entrance to RMNP.

As Phil explained the situation, I realized he was talking about the Sundeck restaurant, the very one Andy had pointed out after our visit to The Other Side. Turns out the owners, who had run the place for about fifty years, had indeed been trying to sell the restaurant and the hotel as a package deal.

"We represent a hotel investor who is purchasing the hotel," Phil said, "but he is not interested in the restaurant." He said this investor would be willing to buy the whole thing if the town would allow him to subdivide the restaurant from the hotel.

"I hope it's okay—I took the liberty of mentioning you," Phil said, "and he would like to meet you."

Was it okay? *Was it okay?* This was great! Throughout this process, I'd had some brief highs and oppressive lows, and this was a paramount high. I was elated. This prime location, with fantastic views, was less than a mile from the main entrance to RMNP. It was already a restaurant, which was both good and bad. Having no gas tanks to remove was a plus, but rebranding can be a challenge. Everyone knew the place—it had a big retro neon sign on the roof proclaiming RESTAURANT. I had eaten there once, nineteen years earlier, and had found it rather dated even back then.

It was time for a recon mission, undercover. I asked Karla to join me—after all, she was a successful restaurateur, and I valued her opinion.

Before we got inside, I was already making mental notes. I whispered to Karla, "Why is there no seating on the patio, with that great view of the mountains?" The entrance took us into a bar dominated by knotty pine. A vast red wall formed the backdrop to a plain small bar, creating a dim space despite a high-peaked ceiling and west-facing windows. The cashier walked us into another room with a low, drop ceiling of popcorn tiles and beams framed by more pine walls. To call it dated was being kind.

We sat down and ordered a slice of key lime pie and glasses of white wine.

We looked at each other.

"This place needs a lot of work," I said quietly. I was somewhat deflated—this was hardly my dream space.

"Definitely has that mothball feel," Karla said. "And what is up with these floors—that varnish is so thick and shiny."

I looked down and could see my reflection.

But Karla kept scanning the room. "You can make this work," she said.

I continued my reconnaissance with a trip to the bathroom and got a glimpse of random storage rooms.

As we left and I looked at mountains, I was reminded of how special this location was, and I could see what was possible with the interior, even though it looked like an extensive—and expensive—proposition. I didn't focus on that, however, and left with a kick in my step. *This was the home for my restaurant.*

Over the next few weeks, I met with the investor who had purchased the property, Sean Keating. He wanted to see if I was the person he wanted to create and run a restaurant adjacent to his hotel. I explained my concept—fresh, quality food, casual yet sophisticated, and an open, welcoming feel. He seemed as enthused as I was. He introduced me to

Vic Horner, the man who had run the place for half a century and was winding down his last season.

Vic brought me in through the kitchen, where I noticed rags hanging on some pipes.

"Is that your drying line?" I quipped.

He chuckled. "I'm insulating the pipes with the rags. It's starting to cool off during the nights, and the building is not insulated. We close down for the winter next week. We're just trying to keep the water flowing for one more week."

My heart dropped. *Wow, not insulated.* "A lot of work" might be an understatement.

Out on the patio, Vic took me through the history of his family and the restaurant. The random nature of the Sundeck started to make sense.

"We added the bar in the 1980s," Vic shared, explaining the large sponge-painted red accent wall. "The dining room was built in the late 1940s. The original building is the kitchen—it used to be a hamburger stand in the late 1930s." I was warming to the quirky history of the place. "My family built this bit back here," he went on, "and we added the bathrooms and the storage area in the 1970s."

He admitted that the office was "a bit strange, with a bathroom, shower, and a cot." But there was an explanation: "That used to be a cabin that eventually became part of the building." The kitchen, even with rag-covered pipes, was spotless, and had some well-maintained vintage equipment. Thus, the odd layout was puzzled together over ninety years of history, which I could appreciate. He even explained the shiny floor, which he'd been re-varnishing every year for decades. It was part of Sundeck tradition: After a busy season, they would close, scrub the place, move all of the furniture out, and put a coat of bowling-alley finish on the floors, readying the place for the subsequent season of visitor traffic.

Learning the history I also came to a natural appreciation of Vic himself. Born and raised in Estes Park, Vic had never envisioned himself as a restaurateur. He'd been a ranger at RMNP and a ski instructor at Hidden Valley. Over the years, he'd acquiesced to running the family business. "I ran this restaurant for the past forty-six years," he said. "I am ready to be done."

He clearly loved the restaurant. "We had great times here. I cared for the place—it's all clean and in order, but undoubtedly needs updating, especially if you are going to run it year-round." The lack of insulation extended to the windows, which were not double-paned. I had to ask: "Why don't you use the patio for seating?" He said he'd wanted to, but the kitchen was already overtaxed keeping up with the tables inside. "I always envisioned putting in a bar railing out here that faced the mountains."

Good idea, I thought.

"The place is great," Vic said. "It just needs someone excited, someone starting out rather than finishing up." I hesitated to share my ideas, now that I knew I'd be tearing into someone's family history. But I told him, "I'd love to have an open kitchen."

Vic brightened. "This was all open, when it was Hap's Hamburgers!" It sounded like he wouldn't mind someone bringing it into the twenty-first century, even if it meant tearing down some of that history. "It's going to be interesting to see what you'll find in the walls."

I told him I was used to the unexpected here in Estes Park. "It can't be any more surprising than the .22 pistol we found dry-walled in our garage," I said.

We had a laugh, and I pretty much floated home. It was starting to feel like this could really happen.

CHAPTER THIRTEEN

Dollar, Dollar Bills
Estes Park, October 2016

SEAN KEATING CALLED WITH GOOD NEWS: THE TOWN PLANNERS HAD said the hotel and restaurant land could be divided. "We can proceed with the sale of the Sundeck," he told me. Over the next several days, we agreed on a purchase price. My dream of my own restaurant was racing toward reality.

There was just one problem—money. My hopes for a minimal refurbishment had faded after Vic's tour and meetings with an architect and contractor. The investment would be significant. If I wanted to keep within the building's footprint, I could only change it 50 percent, according to a local restriction. Anything more would mean demolishing the structure and building something brand-new and way more expensive. Our only option was sticking with its unique structure—three peaked roofs, echoing the mountains 8 miles away. Plus, I could only afford so much. What that amount was, I had no idea. First we had to figure out the cost of renovating and opening, then calculate how much I could raise or borrow.

I walked through the place with the architect and contractor, dreaming and talking.

"We want to tear down that red wall," I said, "and would like a horseshoe bar. I want it as open as possible. Then we need to remove the wall that separates the dining room—and can we get rid of the low ceilings in the dining area?"

The architect and contractor knew that anything was possible—if you're willing to pay for it. They tugged a bit on my reins. "You never know what we will find when we start ripping into it, and that will change as we go," the contractor said.

The architect agreed it would be a fluid process. "We'll get a good idea of scope as we dive into the plans," he said, adding that with the lack of insulation, "it would be extensive." Also expensive, obviously.

The contractor, who had years of experience with old Estes Park buildings, had another warning: "Odds are there will be asbestos that will need mitigation."

The architect was Steve Lane, who had founded a firm called BAS1S Architecture + Design, which seemed well matched to my thinking. I wanted to give Estes Park something new, a comfortable modern vibe without being too edgy. "Modern mountain rustic," I called it. Now I was talking with a team that could make this happen, and it was thrilling. They could take the vision out of my head and, sketched into notebooks, translate it into what was possible, run it through 3-D graphics, and get it all down on paper. I was stoked.

Reality checks were frequent. I reevaluated the business plan with an eye toward remodeling cost and anticipated capacity. Karla and Andy, both restaurant owners, were a tremendous help as I learned about gritty details like workers' comp, liability insurance, utilities, grease traps, keg lines, and the cost of everything from flooring to flour. This crash course in the restaurant business made one thing very clear: I needed money, and a good amount of it.

Furniture, fixtures, equipment—everything added up fast. Although most of the kitchen equipment had been well maintained, it had served its final years. Ethan Brown, who would become my business partner and chef, did spy something he loved: "This vintage white refrigerator with latch handles is so cool," he said. "It needs to be in the spotlight. And it still works!" We all agreed.

I definitely wanted to get rid of the mountain cabin vibe while still keeping a few reminders of this old building, honoring some original pieces, such as some of Vic's kitschy signs, like "Coffins Made to Order." I figured I could keep the old pine tables and chairs, and elevate the knotty-pine look, sanding and somehow updating them to fit into the renovations.

I had the location, the concept, and the business plan. Next, I hit the streets to find investors. I asked anyone I knew if they might be interested, and requested that they ask anyone *they* knew. My best offer was from a restaurant group, $350k, and they wanted 65 percent ownership. This offer wasn't worth exploring, as that figure was a small fraction of what I needed. Also, I was constructing the restaurant of my dreams, and didn't want to be indefinitely beholden to an absent entity telling me what to do.

I wanted partners who would split the work and contribute their expertise. I knew I could run a restaurant, no problem. I liked cooking but was by no means a chef. I knew about wine and cocktails after years of bartending, but more important, knew my knowledge was limited. I was not a sommelier (yet); my only experience outside of Estes Park restaurants was two months of busing tables as a teenager in Massachusetts. My goal was excellence, not mediocrity. While I felt confident in my front-of-house skills, I knew I had tons to learn about running a professional kitchen.

I called John Witmer, a restaurant manager, sommelier, and friend who had worked for years in Estes before moving to Steamboat to help a restaurant group open a new location. "Remember I said that I would tell you if I was going to do my own thing someday?" I said. "Well, I'm doing it."

It took John a few weeks to think about it, but eventually he said he was in. He would direct the wine program and have a heavy hand in front of house and hospitality, working with me. Another friend, Jimmy Kush, a whiskey expert, also joined the team.

Who would execute these menus I was dreaming up?

"I know a chef who would be great if we could get him," John said, putting me in touch with Ethan Brown, then chef at the St. Julian in Boulder.

Ethan and I met at a coffee shop in Lyons and hit it off immediately. I explained the concept of ingredient-driven, seasonally changing menus and showed him what I'd drawn up.

Ethan was intrigued. After some time and coercion, he agreed to become a partner and executive chef. My soon-to-be partners had talent and excitement but none had capital to invest, outside of $10,000 from Jimmy Kush's parents.

In addition to their labor, I asked my partners to invest in the concept: Believe in me and work with me, and when we get our loans paid off, we'll all be official owners of the business (as opposed to owners of the loans). I told them if they wanted to leave before then, they could walk away and relinquish the shares given to them.

They were in.

We had countless decisions to make, big and small. One of the fun ones: "What are we going to call it?" John asked one day at a meeting. I had a list of possible names that I'd been jotting down and started reading it. Ethan stopped me after "Isabella's."

"Who the heck is Isabella?" he asked. "And why would we name our restaurant after her?"

"Good question," I said, ready with a little history lesson. "It's a bit of Estes Park and Western history. Isabella Bird is a historical figure, a real lady from the 1870s who traveled around the world on her own, making it up to Estes Park, where she became determined to climb Longs Peak. On her way into town, she runs into a local character called Rocky Mountain Jim."

"Rocky Mountain Jim," John echoed, nodding to Jimmy.

"Yes, Mountain Jim, a one-eyed trapper mauled by a bear—Estes Park's Revenant, you might say. You know, Leonardo DiCaprio and the movie."

My partners seemed captivated, so I continued.

"He helps her get up Longs Peak, even carries her part of the way. And"—I paused for effect—"there was an alleged romance." I knew this (many people did) because her letters were compiled in a book called *A Lady's Life in the Rocky Mountains*. I added the next twist: "After Isabella left Estes and continued her travels, Mountain Jim was shot in the head. Lasted three months, then passed. Supposedly Lord Dunraven ordered his murder because he wanted to keep Estes as a private hunting reserve, and Mountain Jim opposed him."

By now I probably sounded pretty passionate. "This resonates with me because Isabella traveled the world alone, against the constraints of society. She had unique adventures and experiences that Victorian women were not exposed to. I find her inspiring."

It was Jimmy who said it: "Well, why don't we just call it Bird and Jim?"

And right then, in our minds and hearts, every one of us knew that Bird & Jim was the name of our soon-to-be restaurant.

While the team was coming together, finding the money to remodel and purchasing the building fell to me. We couldn't close on the purchase until February 2017, when the plans to subdivide would be finalized by the town of Estes Park. I wanted to be open by the time the busy season hit, in June. Sean was willing to let us start asbestos mitigation and construction before the sale, pending the town's approval of the amended plat. Since we'd technically be building on someone else's property, lawyers had to get involved. There was no time to waste; the plans came together quickly, and the contractor had us on his schedule. We had a lot of work to do to open for the summer season.

I borrowed money from my parents to start asbestos mitigation and interior demolition, beginning in January. I didn't have to be there, and Adam and I talked about getting away to Hueco Tanks. I'd missed last winter with the knee injury, and once Bird & Jim opened, I probably wouldn't have the luxury to slip away. This could be my last season to escape the winter and climb. So we did our usual and headed to Texas. *Another perk to bringing in partners*, I thought. *Maybe one day, I'd be able to get away in the slow season.*

Before we left, we rented two shipping containers. We emptied the contents of the Sundeck into the containers, not knowing what we might need. Maybe we could sell off excess items in a spring yard sale, but for now, we needed to clear the building.

In Hueco, I continued to work remotely on the restaurant plans and funding. My parents were the only investors not expecting majority shares. After several stressful conversations, they came to the rescue, but it got complicated. While my parents owned nice houses and had investments, they weren't sitting on piles of cash.

For my part, I couldn't justify spending too much time climbing. I was just happy to regain some strength and climb a difficult boulder problem ten months after ACL replacement surgery. Satisfied with the challenging boulder problem (Wooden Mushroom, then V10, now down-rated to V9), panicked about finances, and wanting to check on the contractor's progress, I decided it was time to return to Estes Park. In February, I loaded up our old white Lab Cassidy and even older cat Fiona in a rented car. I paused, looking back at the entrance to Hueco Tanks, tears rolling down my cheeks. This was typical; it was always heartbreaking to leave this special place.

If I had known those would be my last days to climb with all of my fingers and thumbs, I would have cherished each day and stayed longer. Instead, while Adam stayed behind to finish his vacation and close our place for the season, I did the responsible thing, returning to Estes Park. I needed to be there to make Bird & Jim happen.

By the time I got back, a specialty crew had mitigated the asbestos and the contractor had begun demolition of the interior. The work revealed some cool wood features and beams under that old popcorn-tile ceiling. I paid the contractor with cash borrowed from my parents because the loans were still not secured.

My parents had funded the project to this point, putting a strain on them. My father went to his bank to line up a loan, but that bank had declined. He wouldn't give up. He withdrew all his money from that bank and found a bank that agreed to finance his daughter's dreams. He put me in contact with his new bankers and told me to call them.

I did, and it was devastating.

My voice quivered when I called home. "Dad, the guy said no—they would not secure the loan."

My dad thought I was mistaken. "You just didn't understand him," he said. "He assured me it would not be a problem." I told him what the bank had told me: "No, Dad, for real, the banker said they would not secure the loan because of an eight-year-old disputed credit charge of $246 that you contested and refused to pay."

He was flabbergasted. "You don't know what you're talking about, Missy. I talked to him yesterday, and he said it was all set."

"I don't know, Dad—this is what he told me," I managed to reply. "I just hung up with him. Please call him."

We hung up, and I lost it. I sank to the floor, sobbing uncontrollably. When I stopped crying, I started screaming.

My phone rang. "Missy, I called the bank," my father said. "You're right. Your mother and I cannot believe it. They are saying no over a $246 fraudulent charge. So I called Rockland Trust here on Cape Cod, and they want my business. We will start moving accounts and assets tomorrow, and then they will secure the loan."

He told me that in the meantime I should call Phil Frank at the Bank of Colorado. "Ask him if they would secure the loan with my Amazon stocks," he said.

I hung up. Despite my father's reassurances, I felt bewildered, dejected, and skeptical, wondering if anyone would make this work.

Phil's response: "With that much Amazon stock, we can make it work."

Still not believing it, I rang my parents. "Dad, Phil said he could make it happen. Can you please call him?"

It looked like Bank of Colorado would come through, and seemed likely that Bird & Jim would become my reality someday.

Still, I wondered. While the loan stress appeared to be over, it was still hard to believe after all the false hopes.

Chapter Fourteen

Lichtenberg
Estes Park, March 2017

When Adam got back from Hueco in early March, three weeks after I'd returned, he found our garage stuffed with tables and chairs from the restaurant. In another cost-saving move, I hoped to somehow make the old pine furniture look hip, to fit better with the other renovations. The knotty pine had yellowed over the decades and looked like it belonged in a mountain cabin, not a new restaurant. I'd pulled them out of the shipping containers and carted them home to stay out of the way of the construction.

First, I sanded down a handful of tables and chairs and went back and forth to the hardware store for paint samples. I was hoping to discover and define the new look of Bird & Jim.

"This isn't capturing the change I've been hoping for," I told Adam one afternoon.

"What are you trying to create here?" he asked.

"I'm not sure," I admitted, "but painting them makes it seem like I'm covering something up. It's not the look I'm going for."

We had creative friends. I'd hired one of them, longtime climber and artist Daniel Yagmin Jr., to design our logo for Bird & Jim. He'd come up with one showing Mountain Jim on his horse with a bird flying above, silhouetted against the moon, to represent Isabella Bird, all against a backdrop of the East Face of Longs Peak. It was perfect.

I told Adam I was going to order wood-burning tools and try to burn the logo into some chair backs, and maybe make some designs on the table legs. I reminded him of a restaurant in Boulder that also had old pine tables. "The tops were somewhat charred-looking. I think I can lightly burn some of the wood with a blowtorch and put a clear-coat finish on top. That'll keep the wood its natural color and not turn yellow." It would certainly be better than painting them.

The wood-burning pen worked well. I showed Adam when he was home for lunch one day. "The logo looks good on the chair backs, but this is going to take forever," I told him. I was headed back to the garage when Adam called me back into the kitchen. "Check this out—this looks cool," he said, pointing at his computer to photos of thin, black, vein-like lines burned into wood. "It's done with electricity," he said.

"That does look cool. It looks like rivers on a map," I said. "I like it! How do they do it?"

He said it was called the "Lichtenberg" technique, and clicked on a video. It showed a black metal box with wires coming out, with small clamps at the ends like jumper cables. One clamp was attached to a piece of wood, and the other to a nail hammered into the opposite side of the plank. When the machine was turned on, black lines began forming between these two contact points on the wood. The guy narrating the video referred to it as "fractal burning."

"Can you make that machine?" I asked, excited.

Adam said he could: "All we need is an old microwave. I can rip out the transformer, hook up cables and clips, and wire a plug." Of course, the Internet provided plenty of how-to videos. This would be great, I told him. I thought the patterns would look cool on the table legs, and I could do some light scorching on the tops. It'd be artistic but not fussy, and better than covering everything with paint. "This'll add some light touches that people will notice," I told Adam excitedly. "This is exactly what I want to capture."

Now I needed a microwave. There were several in the storage container at the old Sundeck. After a meeting that day with chef Ethan, he dug one out and I proudly took home my prize. *At least we'd get good use out of it*, I thought—there would be no microwaves at Bird & Jim.

I was still working at the Dunraven and planned to continue as long as possible until our opening. Andy and the team there had become a family over the years. They supported my new venture, giving me advice and numbers for my business plan, and helping me believe.

One evening at work, my phone buzzed. Adam had sent a video of a test burn he had made. He had taken the transformer out of the microwave—a harmless-looking plain metal box about 6 by 8 inches, weighing maybe 8 pounds. Adam had attached a power cord to one part of the transformer, and the mini jumper cables came out the other end. In the video, the clamps were attached to nails he'd hammered into each end of the table leg, and the machine's power cord was plugged into a wall outlet.

The current flowed into the clamps, into the nails, and magically began burning the pattern onto the surface of the wood. Amazing!

I proudly showed the test video to some coworkers who were into my design ideas. They'd been at the house that day, helping to create rusted metal panels that I hoped would form a backdrop for the bar shelves.

"Wow!" they said as they watched Adam's video.

When I got home late that night, Adam demonstrated in person. He had the rig set up in our garage, the machine sitting on a chair and a restaurant table lying on its side. He held up a cup filled with a hazy fluid and a paintbrush in his other hand.

"This wasn't in the video I sent you, but first you have to paint baking soda and water onto the wood—then you fix the mini clamps to each end of the table leg and plug in the machine." Which he proceeded to do.

We watched. It seemed like nothing was happening, but then a buzzing noise emanated from the transformer. The metal clamps attached to the nails in the table leg sparked a bit. The buzzing grew louder. Then—*Wow*—black lines materialized on the surface of the wood. The charred lines emerged from the points of the connection, creeping down the table leg and branching into smaller veins, like river tributaries. The humming amplified as the grooves grew into each other, filling in gaps and becoming more defined. Glowing embers clung at the edges of the newly burnt lines as little blue flames danced along the scorched rut.

Holy crap.

"This is perfect!" I exclaimed, watching the show.

Adam unplugged the machine. We did a few more burns together. *Got it*, I thought.

Before we called it a night, Adam warned me: "This is very dangerous," he said. A microwave transformer converts the household current from 120 volts to 2,000 volts. "Whatever you do," he said, "don't touch these leads when the transformer is plugged in. I didn't put in an on–off switch. I think it's safer this way. The only way to turn it on is to plug it in."

I understood. "Okay," I said, "that makes sense."

Chapter Fifteen

Amped Up

Estes Park, April 2, 2017, 6:00 p.m.

My to-do list was overwhelming. There was snow outside, I had too much on my mind, and the prominent sharp pains from my elbow tendonitis put a hesitant edge on my desire to make outside climbing plans. I could barely focus on anything except getting the loan papers finalized and reassuring the contractor. Plus, we were flying to the islands to visit my family in a few days, so time was precious. I still needed to stay fit in the meantime, though, so I opted to use our garage climbing wall.

I impatiently jammed my feet into climbing shoes. The wall would be a safe playground for my knee, as well. My knee, elbows, and entire aging body could use a break from carrying a crash pad up a trail and enduring uneven landings; plus, the trails were still snowy. I pushed through the wall session with my mind on everything but climbing. When I finished, I asked myself: Was it time to relax—or maybe get more table legs done?

The restaurant work won out.

I had burned designs onto a few table legs without Adam and found it was working well. It was getting late in the day, but I wondered how some burns would look on a chair back. I found some homemade stew in the freezer, so knew we'd be set for dinner. It was only six p.m.—plenty of time.

Adam had just returned from fixing one of his wood chippers at the lot where he kept his equipment, which had increased over the years as he grew his business.

"Are you okay with leftovers for dinner?" I asked.

"Works for me," he said.

It was pleasant enough outside, so I opened the garage doors and moved the furniture and supplies into the driveway. I plugged a long orange extension cord into the wall and stretched it out. I had placed the transformer on a chair outside. The extension cord didn't quite reach, so I dragged the chair a bit closer to the garage doors and plugged the transformer into the extension cord.

Usually there was a spark when I plugged it in, but not this time.

Weird, I thought. *Bet the outlet's GFI had tripped.*

Just then, I realized I had forgotten the baking soda and water mixture. I dropped the power cords and went into the house to mix some up.

I returned with a cup of the slurry, ready to go. I painted the mixture onto a chair back and bent down to pick up the mini clamps so I could attach them to the wood. When I grabbed them, one in each hand, I instantly realized my mistake: I hadn't unplugged the machine from the extension cord. My body was now connected to the power.

I was part of the electric chain—and could not let go.

A tingling started in my hands and panicky thoughts flashed.

I'm trapped!

I tried to scream but couldn't. I couldn't even open my mouth. I had the resolve and the desperate desire to screech as loud as possible, but my will and vocal cords were helpless under the mighty control the electricity had over me. I'd had similar nightmares where I desperately needed to call out for help but couldn't. Difference was, this time I knew I was awake.

The prickly, pulsing wave amplified, gripping my arms with an unfathomable force that seemed to come from the inside out. It forced an intense connection to the clips.

Shake them free!

No go. I stood, frozen. I couldn't move my arms. I couldn't move my legs.

A grim reality revealed itself to me: I was cemented to the ground, helplessly staring at the power source that was frying me. My mind whirled with escape plans that failed. The electricity seemed to gain strength and control over me within seconds. Now the tingling radiated up my arms and the transformer buzzed louder. My body betrayed my will.

Fall over! Maybe that'd dislodge a clamp.

That was my last idea for escaping.

I gave up my feeble efforts. *I guess this is it. I am dying.*

My last thought was a pathetic whine: *I don't want to die before I get to open my restaurant.* Then, darkness.

Chapter Sixteen

The Forest

Estes Park, April 2, 2017, 6:05 p.m.

I opened my eyes. I was standing in a lush, dense, breathtakingly beautiful forest.

I looked to my left and saw textured brown tree trunks jutting up to a vibrant green canopy high above. Dappled rays of golden sunlight cascaded through the branches, illuminating thick beds of ferns and grasses.

Is this a dream? I asked myself.

I'm a vivid dreamer, but I think it's really happening.

I turned my head to scan the landscape, and a dark tunnel appeared. Abruptly gone was the peaceful comfort of the enchanting woods. The tunnel was framed by the woods and somehow suspended in air. It was massive, large enough to walk through, with cobblestones rimming the passageway. Inky shadowy figures floated before the entrance, which loomed before me.

Fuck! If this is really happening, I want to get the fuck out of here.

If I can get back to Adam, I can get help, I thought.

I knew intuitively that I was no longer in the world of the living, and that I desperately wanted to find a way out. I understood that I needed help badly, but first, *I had to get back.*

As this frantic desire flooded through me, I felt myself being rapidly pulled away. I was leaving the stunning forest and the ominous tunnel and—

Bam!

My eyes opened to a dramatically different scene. I took a sharp, deep breath, and blinked to focus.

Miracle is a weighty word—trust me, I've thought about this—but how else do you approach my experience? I died a little bit and then came back to life. Maybe my physical body wasn't compromised to the point of no return, and I was granted this choice. Perhaps it was sheer will. Or was it a decision at all? Maybe it simply wasn't my time to die. Maybe it was everything all at once, or none of the above. I didn't understand, and there was no time to ponder.

Nonetheless, I'd gotten my wish—I was back in the living world. At least I thought so.

Am I back? My eyes began to focus. I saw small rocks less than an inch from my eyes and felt stones pressing into my cheek. I was on the ground. Yes—this was my driveway. It took few moments to unravel the two worlds. There was no doubt I'd just been in a forest very different from the Colorado pines surrounding our house, but now it seemed I was back.

Baffled, I blinked some more. I still didn't comprehend exactly where I was, and I was apprehensive about dipping my toes into where I might have landed. Slowly my logical brain rebooted, and I accepted what I was seeing.

That's when reality reasserted itself: I was lying on the pea gravel of our driveway, next to a machine but not touching it. I felt ready to coexist with myself now.

Yes, I am here. I am back.

Realization flashed: I must have fallen, and somehow I'd let go. My eyes and brain slowly reengaged and I deciphered my situation. I was lying facedown in the driveway.

I am alive, I am back, and I need help.

The shouts that had been trapped in my throat by the shock now erupted in shrieks.

"Adam! Adam—*Adam!*"

Chapter Seventeen

The Scream

Estes Park, April 2, 2017, 6:10 p.m.

There was no reaction to my screams, which dissipated in the cool mountain air. The trees stood silent. Somehow, I had died a little bit and come back to life; nothing had changed, yet I knew everything had changed.

I managed to stand up. I caught a glimpse of my hands but willed myself not to focus on them, or on the forest and tunnel I'd just experienced, or on how the hell I had gotten there or gotten back.

Keep moving. Get help.

I took about five steps to the front door and screamed again: "*Adam! Adam!*"

After a few moments, the door popped open. I held up my mangled hands. "Hospital—now!" I said, before going limp in his arms.

Adam scooped me up and carried me to his pickup, a white diesel Ford. He managed to open the door and place me in the passenger seat, then ran around to jump behind the wheel. In just those few seconds the nauseating stench of my burned flesh and smoldering bones filled the truck cab. The opening door triggered the *ding, ding, ding* warning that the keys were in the ignition. (That's where we kept the keys—such is life in the woods in a small town.)

Adam rolled the windows down to try to clear the air.

"Fuck the glow plugs!" I spat out, referring to the few seconds he'd normally take to warm up the diesel engine before starting.

Without hesitation, he cranked the key and threw it in reverse. We were on our way.

Only then did I force myself to look at the horror at the end of my arms.

I smiled and greeted the young couple as they entered my restaurant, Bird & Jim. I checked their reservation, grabbed menus, and walked them past the bar and through the lounge with its couches, picture windows, high-tops, and happy customers. I made the usual small talk. "Is this your first visit?" Yes, the woman answered as they settled in at a window table, adding "We're your neighbors, actually. We live up on Enchanted Rock Drive."

"Oh," I replied, "just a few streets up the hill from us. I love it in Little Valley. We're on Ptarmigan Lane."

I wondered how they knew where I lived. There was an awkward pause, the kind of silence I'd become attuned to. They seemed a little solemn and then came the question.

"How are you doing?" the woman asked.

Ah, there it was. The silence, their somber tone with an edge of concern. I had become accustomed to reading a vibe and putting people at ease.

"I am healing up," I said in my cheery, optimistic voice, and with a smile I held up my hands.

There they were, right in front of them, in front of the world: my hands. A constant reminder that *yes, this happened. It was as gruesome as a horror movie, but it really happened. The young woman in the story was me.*

People knew about the accident; the local paper had published a lengthy article about Bird & Jim and my accident and recovery the week we opened. Reactions varied. Some people would steal awkward glances at my hands, while others would grab them and examine them up close. I knew they were all well-meaning, so I'd assure them, "I'm going to be okay." I'd thank them for their compassion and then try to change the subject to the restaurant or the menu or the weather.

This couple was slightly different.

"This is odd," the man said hesitantly, "but we are just happy to see you and know you are okay, because . . . well, we heard you that night—the night of the accident."

Wow. This is a new one.

"We were in our hot tub and heard you screaming," he went on. "We didn't know what to do—whether to call for help, or try to help ourselves—but before we could process it all, we heard a car speeding off, and more screams as it was going away."

I was astounded. Near witnesses to the day that changed my life. My routine responses didn't come to me and I stood there speechless, feeling exposed. Then my years in hospitality kicked in reflexively: I felt bad about disrupting their evening. *I am so sorry,* I almost said, but stopped, quickly realizing how absurd that sounded.

Knowing they had heard my desperate screams, such intimate details of my pain and suffering, connected me to these total strangers and left me dumbfounded. It was the middle of dinner service and I wanted to return to the host stand. This was my safe environment, but vulnerability had crept in. I hadn't realized that my ghastly cries had echoed through the valley that I loved so much. I thought about the screams that nobody heard, the screams that were trapped inside of me as electricity seized my body.

I finally snapped out of it and said to the couple, "That's really crazy. I never thought my cries had traveled that far." I felt sorry that on such a beautiful evening, my tragedy had invaded their night, shattering the peace, sending the fragility of life into the atmosphere. Amid the convivial buzz of my dream restaurant, I was reminded how grateful I was to be alive.

Later, Adam would tell me he'd been preparing some bills at the kitchen counter, sitting in front of our old forced-air propane heater, its loud fan muting my first screams. When he finally heard me at the door, he said, "I thought Cassidy was getting dragged off by a mountain lion." That was our old Lab. But when he opened the door and saw my hands, he instantly knew what had happened.

Now we were racing down the road, windows down, wind whipping through the cab. I had to face the mutilation, the smoldering carnage that was once my hands. I didn't want to face this—I wished I was unconscious.

There was no escape for me.

I looked down at my hands. Where my fingertips once were, charred, pointed, jagged bones jutting out of melted skin remained. I could see right through my thumbs. The inside skin of my thumbs was gone. It had been incinerated, vaporized—exposing jagged bones that were black from combustion. The tips of my thumbs were unmarred, looking like erasers on chewed-up pencils. The carbonized bones were held together by the backs of my thumbs. The remaining skin was pulled away from the scorched bones. Waxy layers of white, yellow, gray, and black descended into pits where my palms once were.

There was no blood. There was no pain—yet. Some fingers did not show any exposed burnt bones but were gigantically swollen, blistering tubes which appeared seconds away from combustion.

I took in this gruesome scene and a horrified reality sank in. I didn't know how to act or what to feel. *How am I going to make it to the hospital?* It was only minutes away, but I needed to endure and I needed a release. I took a deep breath and found my answer. It would be my voice.

The screams that erupted were far louder and more desperate than my first shouts of Adam's name. I was comprehending the tragedy and confronting the scope of the damage, and the wretched screams came from a depth I'd never known. It was as though the screams that had frozen in my throat in the driveway burst out, amplified.

In retrospect, it's no surprise that people in the neighborhood, including that couple soaking in their hot tub, heard me as we sped down our dirt road. Adam later told me that other neighbors heard me and called the police to report an apparent kidnapping. The shrieks continued throughout the 3.6 miles to the hospital. A "This is your speed" sign flashed 75 mph as we blew through a 45-mph zone. At one point, unbeknownst to me, a wheelbarrow bounced out of the pickup's bed.

My screaming was just primal noise at first, but eventually I formed words.

"This isn't happening!" But it was, and it was real.

"I have no hands!" was my next scream, and I repeated it over and over as the awful truth washed over me.

Adam did his best to reassure me, glancing over as he flew down the road. "You still have hands," he said.

The banshee beside him reacted to him, to Estes Park, to the world: "*I have no hands!*"

Then another kind of anguish found expression: "I will never climb again."

To that, Adam said nothing.

As we approached the hospital, Adam said, "Do I turn in here?"

My screaming suddenly stopped and I calmly answered, "No, keep going around to the emergency department, the next right." My normal reply helped me understand that I could stop screaming.

The truck jerked to a stop and Adam jumped out, ran around the truck, and opened my door to pick me up and carry me into the hospital.

But as soon as the door opened, I hopped out and headed through the automatic doors at a brisk pace. Adam was at my heels, the truck left at the ER entrance.

Chapter Eighteen

Helicopter, Please
Estes Park, April 2, 2017, 6:15 p.m.

Estes Park Medical Center is our town hospital, a modern but somewhat modest facility compared to a big-city or suburban hospital. After all, Estes Park is a town of only about six thousand people, with just eleven thousand in all of Larimer County. Estes nearly triples in size with summer residents, and of course thousands more arrive for day visits to the town and park. It has to handle everything from cardiac arrests and car accidents to injured hikers and visitors thrown from their horses.

But this was early spring, and one thing was clear to me as I walked through the doors: Someone had to call a helicopter, as I knew our small hospital wouldn't be able to handle my injuries. Still, I was relieved to be out of the truck and in an emergency room.

Until I looked around.

Surprisingly, there were no people in sight, from staff to patients. Cubicles where patients check in and the waiting room stood empty.

"What do we do?" Adam wondered.

"Push the button to open the doors—let's keep going," I said, holding my hands up in the air. Through these next doors, it looked more like a hospital: a nurse's station and gurneys, but still empty.

"Hello? Can someone call me a helicopter, please?" I yelled as we walked further into the emergency department.

Slowly, people emerged.

"I need a helicopter!" I called out again as nurses and EMTs approached.

One nurse said "I need you to lie down on a gurney" as she guided me over to one. "What happened to you?" she asked.

"I need a helicopter," I repeated, holding my hands high.

"The doctor is the only one that can call the helicopter," she said. "What happened to you?" she asked again.

"I electrocuted the shit out of myself," I answered.

As the nurse helped me onto the gurney, I felt pain for the first time. The shock and adrenaline were wearing off.

"Could I still be burning?" I asked, gesturing to my right rib cage with the back of my hand. Another person with a large pair of scissors began to cut through my clothes: one Adam's Tree Service sweatshirt, one Lululemon shirt, one Patagonia sports bra.

As the clothes came off, other large burns were exposed. Under my right breast was a crater similar to the ones on my palms. Pink, yellow, and white skin with a dark center, down into my rib cage.

"Am I still burning?" I asked again, horrified.

At that point, of course, I was ignorant about electrical shock damage and exit wounds. I was beginning to understand that the electricity that had entered through my hands had to come out somewhere. (*The only way out is through*, I thought. What poem is that from?)

After they cut the sleeves off my left arm, I looked toward another locus of pain on the left side of my chest and saw more holes on my left shoulder and under my left breast.

A doctor walked around the corner and we made eye contact. My first words to him were familiar by this point: "Can you please call me a helicopter?" He turned without a word and picked up the phone. Seconds later, he told me my ride was on the way. The doctor—I would learn his name was Meyer—assured me they would be there in about twenty minutes. He instructed a nurse to start an IV with pain medication.

For the first time since my eyes had opened to the gravel driveway, I felt like I could relax—sort of. Help was on the way, and some of the EMTs were comforting familiar faces.

"Can you tell us what happened?" Dr. Meyer asked.

It had only been about fifteen minutes or so since the accident, and I was still unsure. I thought about it. "I touched two live leads and couldn't let go," I said. "Then everything went dark, and I must have fallen, because when I came back, I was on the ground."

That was obviously the short version. But as I focused, more details swam into my recall: the machine, the forest, the tunnel. *How did I break free? Why did the electricity shut off?*

I looked at my charred hands and wondered if maybe enough of my hands had burnt off that the clamps lost connection with my skin. *Seems logical*, I thought—and then I remembered that the machine was still plugged in, and live.

I said to Adam, standing at the end of the gurney: "You need to go home and make sure the machine can't hurt Cassidy or anyone else." I imagined our old Lab sniffing around and making a connection to both leads. Or our friends, tree crew guys staying in the apartment over our garage—what if they came home and tried to pick it up? I was surprised that my mind was still processing clearly; the drugs had not overtaken the adrenaline yet.

"Adam, the machine is still plugged in," I said urgently. "You have to go home and unplug it. While you're home, get what we need to spend the night and head to the Greeley hospital—I should be there before you can get there," I instructed.

He was torn, wanting to stay by my side, but finally admitted, "You're right." Knowing I was getting help, with more on the way, he left.

Within the safety of the hospital, surrounded by professionals and with drugs starting to take hold, the whirling of my mind slowed. Despite the IV, more pain crept in, and I started thinking of myself. I didn't want to do that—it would involve accepting the state my hands were in and contemplating a future without them. I was still trying to process the forest and dark tunnel—with no proverbial light at the end.

I looked up at the EMT at my side. It was Guy Besley, who I'd known for years. I had worked with his two children at the Dunraven Inn, watching them grow up and go to college. I felt the weight of my utterly changed world collapsing around me. I turned to his familiar friendly face and looked into his compassionate, sorrowful eyes.

"Guy," I said, "will I ever climb again?"

Tears welled up for the first time. Even as I asked the question, I knew neither Guy nor anyone else knew the answer. It was unfair to ask, and the odds were clearly not in my favor. *Why the heck are you putting this on him?* But the words needed to come out.

Now a nursing team was wheeling me off for a CT scan. The nurses explained where I was going, but I was confused. "I was electrocuted. Why are you scanning my head?" I asked. "Because you said you fell," they explained. The CT scan was good, and the EKG showed my heart to be okay. They checked everything they could, ensuring I was stable and ready for transfer.

The helicopter arrived. On the hospital roof, I was determined to stay present, but the drugs were heavy-duty, and they hadn't skimped. I tried to fight the loss of consciousness I had yearned for earlier. I wanted to know where I was going, to be aware. They strapped me in and the helicopter lifted off. I could look down at our little town and follow the road heading into the canyon along Highway 34. Adam would be driving down that same canyon, absorbed in his fears, sick about almost losing me, and uncertain of my fate.

As we made our way over the foothills, I slipped into unconsciousness.

Chapter Nineteen

No Light at the End of the Tunnel
Banner Health, Greeley, April 2, 2017, Nighttime

Memories of that night come in flashes. *The tub room, briefly coming to. A rubberized gurney, water flowing by me. Nurses gently cleaning the remains of my hands.*

Ah, I knew about this place. My friend Lisa Foster was here once. She too escaped death, surviving an avalanche, exposure, and severe frostbite. I visited her in this same burn unit. Somehow, despite my state, I recalled her talking about the tub room.

Out again, who knows how long.

Then I was in a hospital room. As I blinked the scene together, Adam came into my vision, accompanied by his sister, Vicky, and her teenage son, Aiden. Even in my drugged stupor, I knew my hands were unbandaged. There was no escaping the gore of melted flesh and burnt bones where fingers and thumbs once were. The terrifying reality was inescapable. The uncertainty and despair were overwhelming.

In an instant, anguish flooded my mind. *How can I live like this, with no hands? Is there any hope of recovery?* I looked at my scorched bones: *How can anyone help with this?*

Slowly I realized that chest pads and wires had me connected to a heart monitor, and a tube to a catheter just added to my pathetic state. I felt utterly helpless and devastated. I looked up at Adam, big tears welling in my eyes and spilling down my cheeks. My unsteady mind was a slow, thick, sloppy soup of grief and terror.

Adam leaned in. "You are going to be okay," he said. "The doctors did tests of your heart and your brain, and they look good." He went on, explaining that they'd be monitoring my kidneys. Recovering from burns puts stress on them, he said, but I wasn't really following what he was saying. I just let more tears flow. Heart and brain—*That's a relief, I guess.* But the feeling overall was misery, for myself and for Adam.

Adam looked at me with reassuring love, but trepidation and torment were heavy in his eyes. The depth of my sorrow was like nothing I had ever felt, not just for what I'd done to myself, but for what I'd done to us—to our future.

I took a breath, choking out, "Did they say anything about my hands?"

"Not yet," Adam said, "but the head of the burn unit was gone for the day. She's back tomorrow."

Vicky and Aiden shared their love and their relief that I was alive. Soon they were on their way back to Colorado Springs. Vicky said she'd be back soon, and that Adam's parents would arrive in the morning. Adam and I were now alone in the room. It was quiet.

"I died," I finally said, weakly. Adam looked like he wanted to say something but I kept talking. "When I was trapped by the electricity, I knew I was dying. And then I did."

He looked skeptical but stayed quiet as I told him what happened next.

"I landed in this beautiful forest. At first, it was this peaceful captivating scene. But then I turned and saw the opening of a huge tunnel. It was just . . . hanging there, in the middle of the woods. It was dark inside, and all around the rim there were these big stones. I didn't know what was going on. I just knew I wanted to get out."

Adam nodded slowly as I kept going.

"I had this overwhelming urge to leave and get help. I knew if somehow I could get to you, I'd get help, and I'd be okay."

He looked steadily into my eyes. "You didn't die—you are here."

He was right.

Now he was digging in his pocket, saying, "Check this out. I took this picture when I went home to unplug the machine." He held his phone up so I could see. My thoughts were hazy; why was he showing me a picture of our breaker box? I was talking about a mysterious tunnel and he was showing me a photo of a nondescript gray and black box.

"This saved your life," Adam said.

He zoomed in on the photo: One circuit breaker was flipped to the off position.

"You tripped the breaker. You didn't die—you surged the power. The breaker saved you."

"So that would explain why I am here," I said slowly, "why the electricity stopped. I thought maybe enough of my flesh had burnt off that the clamps lost contact," I said, pausing for a moment. "But I did die a little," I insisted. "And I decided to come back. I wanted to live, and there were shadowy figures floating in front of the tunnel entrance—between me and the tunnel. I was scared, and I willed myself to live. *I died.*"

Then I told him something distressing that I'd been afraid to share.

"Adam, the tunnel was dark," I said. "I wasn't going to heaven. There was no light at the end of the tunnel." There it was, laid out to my husband—my Catholic cultivation of heaven and hell spilling out. My two looming fears: the future of my hands, and the knowledge that I was going to go to hell.

Adam was shaking his head calmly. "That was a fictional scene that your mind created as you were going through the trauma," he said.

"I was there, Adam!" I contended. "At first, I questioned it myself. I went from frozen, trapped in the electricity, to the forest. I *saw* the shadowy figures. I think I *knew* them. I had this sense that they did not want me to go into the tunnel." The more I contemplated the experience, the more detail was filled in. "I think the figures were my grandmothers and Phil," I said, referring to our recently deceased longtime friend and climbing buddy. "I felt their presence." They were putting out energy to stay away from the tunnel.

Adam wanted to move on. "We should call your parents," he said.

"Do they know?" I asked, thinking of how distressed they would be. They were across an ocean, escaping the New England winter on the

Cayman Islands. My sister and her family were flying there that week to visit them on spring break; we were supposed to fly out to join them at the end of the week.

"Of course they know—I called them," Adam said, dialing his phone and putting it on speaker.

My parents were relieved to hear my voice.

"They say I'm going to be all right, but they haven't talked about my hands yet," I told them, my voice thick as I continued talking. "There was no light at the end of the tunnel," I said.

"What?" my parents asked, perplexed.

"I died and saw the tunnel—there was no light. I am going to hell."

Adam shook his head and leaned toward the phone. "I told her she's being ridiculous," he said.

"What are you talking about, Missy?" my parents questioned.

I explained the bright, beautiful forest and the darkness of the unnerving tunnel. Without hesitation, my mom said, "It was not your time. And it was dark because you were not supposed to go into the tunnel." That actually made some sense.

"You're right, Mom," I said. "It wasn't my time to die."

We concluded the call and assured them we would call tomorrow.

"We love you so much, Missy," my dad said.

"I love you too," I sobbed back.

For once in my life, I accepted my mother's argument without pushback. She was right: Evidently, it was not my time to die. *You are alive*, I told myself. I vaguely understood that I was doing myself a disservice to focus on death when I was alive, but I needed to process the trauma.

No light in the tunnel meant it was time to live.

I was not supposed to die. Those figures were family and friends steering me back to the living. It was time to put the tunnel away and be happy I survived.

I had plenty of other things to think about. I had to put this away.

As I lay there in the hospital bed, I tried a mental tactic that I'd used in the past. In my imagination, I opened a door to a large walk-in closet. I stepped inside and took a sizable circular box down from a shelf. I removed the lid and carefully laid the tunnel in the box. I replaced the lid and put it back on the shelf. *I can revisit this later*, I thought. Knowing that the forest and tunnel would always be a part of me, I peacefully accepted my role in the land of the living as a generous gift.

Some thoughts were harder to stash away. The thought of climbing, for instance; the uncertainty of what our future would look like; plus flashes of anger, like *I cannot believe I did this to myself.* These dominated my brain. *Back to the closet*, I commanded myself. The imaginary doorknob still felt warm from my grip. I turned the knob, shoving aside an intrusive thought: *how the hell can you turn a real doorknob with raw flesh and burnt bones.*

I entered the closet and spied a weathered leather antique traveling trunk, substantial in size. I tried to stuff climbing into the trunk—the years of pure enjoyment, joy, effort, training, triumphs, levels achieved, projects left undone. I struggled to close the lid on the trunk. I knew I couldn't get the latch to click or the straps buckled even if I sat on it. I hurried out of the closet and closed the door, trying to leave my passion and dreams behind.

Nodding off, I willed myself to focus on being alive.

You survived. You get to live. Be grateful to be among the living. You fought to come back—you fought for this chance.

Could I dare to hope? The desire to reach help had brought me back. I was still waiting to find out whether anyone would—or even could—try to help me. The carnage at the ends of my arms made it difficult to summon anything other than despair.

Chapter Twenty

Forgiveness

Banner North, April 2, 2017, Late at Night

THIS IS WHAT ELECTRICITY DOES WHEN IT SURGES THROUGH YOUR body: It finds a way out—crudely, powerfully, no matter what is in its way. In my case, it entered my body through my hands and left it by punching three holes in my chest. These were the exit wounds.

The most significant hole was 3 by 4 inches, below my right breast, the one I'd felt burning in the ER. The second largest was on the underside of my left breast. The third exit wound burned a large circle near my left shoulder, under my clavicle, looking as if someone had stubbed out a cigar in my flesh, twisting it deep into the dermis. The edges of all the exit wounds were a yellowish ecru, sloping down to dark centers. Electricity cauterized the wounds, so there was no blood. Just layers of my skin—my body—open, on display.

Nurses monitored me closely. Dale, the nurse on duty that night, did one last check-in. She explained that the catheter was to monitor my urine, and it would remain in place. "We have to make sure your kidneys are flushing the burnt tissue without damaging the organs," she said. "Making sure that you are okay comes first."

I knew she wouldn't have answers, but I had to ask.

"Do you know anything about my hands?" I said glancing at the blackened, protruding bones.

"It's too early to tell," Dale replied. "Electric burns are similar to frostbite. The injury is still declaring itself. The doctors will visit tomorrow morning to discuss potential paths forward with your hands." She paused. "The nurses' station is right outside your room. If you need anything or are in any pain, call us. Someone will be here all night," she said.

I thanked her as she left.

"Hold your hands up," Adam told me. He was aiming his phone. I hesitated, unsure. Usually, you smile for a photo. In this case, I was just trying not to cry. I wanted to protest, but didn't. I looked up awkwardly, feeling ashamed and pathetic. Did I want to commemorate the worst moment of my life with a photo that would outlast me? I knew Adam wanted to share our new reality with my family. They'd been reassured that I'd survived, but were obviously troubled over the state of their baby, the youngest of three children.

He snapped some photos, capturing for posterity the results of my grave mistake.

The inescapable truth of this nightmare was that I had done this to myself. I was mortified, and had no one else to blame. I had picked up the leads when the machine was live, exactly what Adam had told me not to do. It was a destructive, monumental mistake that would define me for the rest of my life. And the evidence would be on display, attached to me forever, an arm's length away. It was a billboard announcing my catastrophic mistake.

Photos done, I gently and awkwardly lowered my arms, trying to find a resting position for them while protecting the damaged flesh. Adam settled into the reclining chair where he would sleep by my side. At least we would face the future together.

This is so unfair to him. I did this to myself, but he would also suffer the consequences. The guilt, the pity for myself and Adam, the self-loathing—it consumed me. *What have I done?*

I started to spiral with anguish and self-condemnation.

What if I hadn't forgotten the baking soda and water? Why didn't the cord spark, alerting me that the machine was on? Why did I have to work outside? What if I had never heard of the Lichtenberg technique? Why had I asked Adam to make this death machine? Why wasn't I more focused?

I was entering another world, a dreary, melancholic, harsh space. It was lonely and isolating. *Will Adam be able to bear this, and stay with me?*

Will I be able to endure this? I don't think I am strong enough. Are we strong enough?

I knew that what-ifs and laments were obstacles to forward momentum and healing. But everything about this was dark.

There were two options: I could let myself slip into a harsh world consumed by grief and regret, or I could forgive myself. That night, I was on the edge of a pit of despair that I could consciously slip into. *You cannot live here, Melissa. You cannot live in a state of self-loathing.* My logical brain knew that defining myself by my blunder could not be my path, and that forgiveness was crucial to healing. *Am I capable of that?*

I understood that life came with challenges and tragedies that alternated with contentment and triumph. I knew about fears and obstacles, and—more important—how to overcome them and push through. I knew about being careful, about facing a problem and figuring it out, in climbing and in life.

One thing was sure that first night: I did not want to be a victim; I did not want people's pity, including my own. I told myself the only way to get through this would be to try harder than I'd ever tried in my life. I knew I would have to fight for myself and for anyone who chose to support me. I wanted to come back. The hard part was just beginning.

I understood deep down that replaying the accident, tormenting myself with "if only," I would trap myself in a scenario worse than the one I was sitting in right then. Even though I comprehended all of this, ahead of me were myriad unknown challenges that I had to confront to survive. There was no room for defeatism. One clear thought came to me: I had only myself to blame—and only myself to forgive.

I remembered what my friend Liesl told me when her husband Dave passed away following the avalanche: "I will not be defined as a widow." I had marveled at her strength. I realized now that I would be doing a disservice to the life I'd lived up to this point if I allowed the accident to define my existence. During that first night in the hospital, in the dim light of my room, I decided to exonerate myself, right then and there.

Later, Adam asked in a caring, concerned tone, "How do you think you'll cope with this?"

"It was a mistake," I said. "This was not my choice. It was an accident, and accidents happen all the time." I chose forgiveness. I promised myself to let go of the what-ifs.

Of course, this left plenty of other questions: Would others forgive me? Would they judge me? Would Adam forgive me? Would my parents forgive me for hurting the person they'd protected all through childhood? Hopefully, I would be so strong that no one but me would have to forgive.

Still, I knew I wasn't strong enough to let all of this simply evaporate into the ether. There was sufficient room in my imaginary closet of woes. I needed to compartmentalize; there was only so much physical and mental baggage a human being could carry at one time.

Wearily, I entered the closet in my mind and took another box off the shelf. Into this I placed the anger at myself for making a mistake. I put the box back on the shelf next to the climbing trunk and the tunnel box. The forgiveness box was adorned with a heart.

That night, I resolved to forgive and be open to self-love, even though I knew the anger and sadness might travel with me for an undisclosed period, until the poultice of time would lend a hand in healing. For now, the walk-in closet of my mind gave me comfort.

I lay there in my hospital bed, impossibly tired. I wasn't the same person who'd woken up that morning, physically or emotionally. An athlete and businesswoman, a whole person, full of energy and optimism. A woman who'd scaled her climbing wall that morning with strength and confidence, clinging to holds with powerful fingers, lifting herself higher.

I drifted toward sleep, terrified and sad. And yet deeply grateful.

You lived. You are alive!

It was time to live the chance I'd been given.

I felt Adam's presence beside me as sleep descended.

Chapter Twenty-One

Four Fingers

Banner North, April 3, 2017, Morning

Someone talking. Movement. The activity in my hospital room nudged me slowly out of a deep sleep.

I opened my eyes to see a woman standing over me, scanning my body, then looking up at my face to see that I was awake. A kind face, about my age.

"Hi, Melissa. I am Dr. Deeter, head of the Greeley burn unit," she said.

I blinked away the morning blur, quickly remembering my new reality. I muttered a reply and tried to listen. Burn unit. Right—I've been horribly burned. *My hands.* This is my life now.

I forced myself to look at my hands, and then over at Adam. He gave me a reassuring smile.

The doctor was talking. "I know you're concerned about your hands," she was saying. "I need to be honest with you. I'm sorry to tell you this, but here at Greeley, we will not be able to save your thumbs, and probably not any of the damaged fingers. If you continue treatment here, you will only have your index fingers and pinkies."

Her words seemed to stop time. *Index fingers and pinkies? No thumbs?*

I struggled to keep my composure and not look horrified. But I was on the verge of crumpling. I looked at Adam.

Dr. Deeter was continuing. "We will transfer you to UCHealth Anschutz in Aurora," she said. "With your approval, of course. We sent pictures to the burn unit there. The doctors there agree with our assessment, but they have more resources."

I would soon learn that UCHealth in Aurora was the University of Colorado Hospital just outside of Denver, the biggest and best in the state. Right now I was in Banner North Colorado Medical Center in Greeley, 20 miles north.

"There is a plastic surgeon there that's apparently done wonders," she said, pausing. "But I will caution you: He saw the pictures and is not optimistic."

Pictures, I thought. *Well, I guess it's the thing to do. How else can you accurately share this damage?* Doctors had been looking at pictures of my hands, of the holes in my chest. I wondered how they'd reacted.

Dr. Deeter explained that they could manage the burns here in Greeley with debridement, helping to stave off infection. I felt a familiar rush of desperation, the same feeling that had flooded over me when I faced the tunnel: *I need to get out of here—now!*

"Okay, yes, transfer—that's great," I responded robotically.

I was starting to shut down, walling off the emotions roiling inside, undoing the mental progress I'd coached myself into the night before. If staying in this burn unit meant no hope, then I was done. I wanted to get away from statements like "no thumbs" and "four fingers" and hear someone say the opposite or at least someone willing to try.

Dr. Deeter's message had been professional, succinct, realistic, and solemn. The depressing future she'd outlined had pushed me toward despair. Pinkies and pointers but no thumbs, no fingers in between? Forget about climbing; how could I even function in daily life? I thought of all the things I did at work, all of which required my fingers. *Everything!*

The more I thought about it, the more "How will I be able to . . . ?" came to the surface, with no answers.

The prognosis reverberated throughout my being, threatening my sanity and my very existence as I knew it. I hoped for better news at the next hospital, but my mind relentlessly returned to Bird & Jim. Carrying plates to a table? Opening a bottle of wine and serving it? Hell, would I even be able to turn a doorknob with two pinkies and two index fingers?

And climbing? That just slipped through the cracks. *Come on, Melissa—really?*

I slammed the lid on that trunk. Survival trumped climbing. *How will I even take care of myself?* A void of sorrow pulled at me. When I'd faced death, I intensely wanted to live, and I got my wish. But now, anguish for my future trampled the security of being alive. I was scarcely able to draw a breath.

I looked at Adam. His face lacked expression, which told me that his internal terror matched mine. And yet, his eyes flowed with love. I could feel it. I knew he was playing out a similar nightmarish future with a wife who had four fingers, but he wouldn't reveal his fears. I knew his stone-faced expression was resolute support—for me, and for us.

Dale entered the room as the doctor left, stifling my words of despair from exploding into the room. She knew what the doctor had said, knew why we were stunned and silent.

She put her hand on my leg and looked me in the eye. "They can do wonders," she said. Her simple statement, not followed with "but" or "however," sparked a light flicker in my heart. She had the determined look a mother might give a fearful child.

I nodded and offered a crooked smile, trying to hold back a flood of tears and emotion. Deep inside, her words ignited the growth of a tiny reservoir of hope that I desperately needed.

I decided to focus on hope rather than the alternative. *I cannot accept four fingers right now*, I thought. While honesty and obligation drove the doctor's ethical message, I needed to grab onto something positive. No matter how minuscule that hope might be, I let it in.

Dale's compassion was my first glimpse of how vital the nursing teams would be in my recovery. Her words of hope kept me on the right side of sanity.

As preparations continued for the transfer to Aurora, another nurse entered. "You probably don't remember me, but I remember meeting you," she said. My narcotized, distracted brain couldn't place the face. "We were in Rocky Mountain National Park, bouldering," she said. "I was out climbing with my friend, who knew your friend Lisa. I remember watching you climb. You were so strong!"

I couldn't believe what I was hearing. First, the small-world-ness of it blew me away. Then, even my foggy brain noticed that she used the past tense. Affronted, I thought, *How could she even say the word* climbing *to me?*

Then, I redirected my thoughts. *No, that's not it. She is giving you a compliment.* I was someone she looked up to in the climbing world.

There was a huge lump in my throat, and I could feel tears about to spill, but I forced the edges of my mouth upward in a weak smile. I looked down at the blackened, charred bones jutting out from raw flesh where fingers once were.

She was right: I was *a strong climber.* Strange how I finally accepted this, now that I couldn't climb. *Gee, Melissa,* I told myself, *you never gave yourself that accolade.* I'd always been so hard on myself: *Try harder, you're not good enough, train more.* It was as though the lid on the climbing trunk had burst open like a jack-in-the-box. The sweet nurse had unknowingly cranked the handle.

I looked at her blurrily through my tears and mumbled an awkward "Thank you," finding no other words.

She left the room and I rested my head back and shut my eyes. The tears rolled down—tears for my four fingers, for climbing, for everything.

After a few breaths, I turned to Adam. "I really was a strong climber," I sobbed.

"I know you were," he said.

Another deep breath. *Not now,* I resolved. *You can't feel sorry for yourself about climbing right now.*

I shoved climbing back into its trunk, realizing I'd be doing this repeatedly. I returned it to the shelf in my mind.

Do not shatter. Focus on hope.

Confront the reality, and endure whatever comes next.

Chapter Twenty-Two

Net Worth

Banner North, April 3, 2017, Mid-Morning

The initial shock of the accident was morphing into a bleak reality. I couldn't help but see a future of despondency, for me and for Adam. I pictured an exceedingly melancholic woman moving morosely through life, fumbling with four fingers. Strangers would heap pity upon her. She was a wretched revenant, someone who would recall the past bitterly, facing each day sullen and ill-tempered, fumbling through life. Worse, maybe love itself was dying for this woman—love for herself, love for life, love for and from her partner.

I felt like one foot was already hovering over a deep, ruinous pit, and I was teetering at its edge. If I stumbled in—or dived in willingly—it would utterly consume me. But I also knew I had no other choice than to draw on my inner strength, and that more mental tactics were needed. I had forgiven myself and used that imaginary walk-in closet to compartmentalize my fears about survival. I had filled the boxes and trunk with distress and heartache, setting them aside while I focused on recovery, knowing I would have to encounter them in time.

I knew more trauma was inevitable, that the agonizing journey ahead had an uncertain outcome. I put my imagination to work again to envision a net over this oppressive abyss. It would have to be strong and durable. I began to weave my net and discovered some of the fabric was already present. Tragedies previously encountered in life were instrumental in constructing the fabric that would span this expansive chasm.

Some of it came from witnessing how my friends had navigated their own pain. I had a sweet friend and coworker, an exemplary Christian mother, who'd lost one of her five children. I recalled her standing in the pulpit at her son's funeral, making the congregation feel better through her resilience and faith. My friends Lisa and Liesl taught me firsthand what fortitude in the face of unfathomable tragedy and what loss looked like. Lisa survived an avalanche, while her climbing partner, Liesl's husband Dave, perished.

I thought of 2013, when torrential rains had flooded the town and washed out roads, wrecking our community's infrastructure and throwing us into isolation and uncertainty. I remembered helping my close friend Leah get back into the home of her dreams, which she'd narrowly escaped. We picked our way through the moldy, skewed house, which also included her ceramics studio, resting sideways in a riverbed, trying to save family treasures and memories.

I had stood by all of these women, offering friendship and love. Witnessing their perseverance helped me create a personal reserve of resilience that I could draw from. Their fortitude formed the foundation of my net, long before I knew I would need one for my salvation. While it saddened me to think their suffering was now giving me strength, I was nonetheless grateful for the lessons they had taught me. These were the threads I clung to.

Desperately searching for survival tools, I continued exploring within myself, discovering more that were ingrained at a young age. My doggedness came from way back, and from deep within. My New England family never accepted excuses or endured whining. If I put on my "pissy pants" and started squawking, they'd tease me with something like "We'll get you a bumpah stickah that says 'I'd rather be crying' instead of 'I'd rather be skiing.'" With my family, it was *Get up, stop whining, try again.* If you wouldn't, they'd laugh you into it. My mom and dad created threads that became cords for my life's net. They did not tolerate excuses. They taught us that we were in charge of our destinies. How we approached each day helped lay the course for our future.

My parents were born at the tail end of the Great Depression in borderline poverty. Raised in the Irish section of Cambridge, my mother was mostly reared by her grandmother because her own mother was working. My mom often witnessed drinking and fighting in the home, but they made the best of a life filled with adversity. They laughed, sang, and stuck together while scrapping for everything they had. My father's parents moved to America from Italy, landing separately in Cambridge. My grandparents were thrown together in an arranged marriage at ages sixteen and seventeen. The youngest of three, my dad put himself through college and law school, much to the chagrin of his parents. They wanted him to be a truck driver, since his dad was a Teamsters organizer. Lawyers were crooked, they thought.

My parents' family closets were full of hardships, and skeletons. What they endured gave them the strength to weather adversity and raise three children capable of the same grit. Their resilience and faith were at the heart of my net's infrastructure.

Despite all the love and privilege I grew up in, we had difficulties. My brother was an addict. His first exposure to painkillers was the result of a high school sports injury. He was prescribed OxyContin during the pill-frenzy era spawned by the Sackler dynasty. After that, he did whatever it took to find his next prescription. My parents corrected and steered, provided him with parental and medical support, and cleaned up his messes. They loved their only son and did not want to see him fail.

Despite all of their efforts, Paul slipped further into a lifestyle of manipulation and addiction. His fabricated stories and manufactured excuses were a never-ending cycle that meant a life of lost opportunities and blame. He went back and forth from living at home to being "independent." As he fought to be clean—"opiate-free"—doctors gave him different prescriptions, which he then abused. He was in and out of hospitals and treatment centers, sometimes leaving addiction centers with girlfriends, eluding help his whole life. Still, no one in our family ever gave up. We never stopped loving Paul, and always believed he could change; there was so much potential for a bright, funny young man who got lost.

My brother's story allowed me to weave more webbing for my safety net. I had a small understanding of what it was like to live in darkness, because that's where my brother resided. He never got free from his pit. Eventually he found solace in religion, and made peace before he left the world suddenly, prematurely, dying from a heart attack three years after my accident. As the younger sister, I had worshipped my big brother, wanting to emulate him, which annoyed the heck out of the teenage boy. I never knew exactly who or what I wanted to be, but through my brother's suffering, I knew what I *didn't* want to become. That was a gift, and further strengthened my net.

Love. I was fortunate to have it in my life. The love I gave to family and friends, the love I received from them, and my community, plus my love of life itself, comprised many strands of my net. While I could still see myself slipping through these strands, I was off to a good start with some foundational fabric.

Vividly remembering the horrific electrocution was a strange gift that left me fully aware of how fortunate I was to be alive. I couldn't throw this second chance at life into the darkness. The threads had been woven into cords that I fastened above the pit—love, family, resolve, the gift of life. Experiences, forgiveness, self-love, and faith, all of it lashed together with resilience and gratitude. I added hope to this assembly, praying that it wasn't absurd.

I breathed deeply, thankful for what I had, and somewhat positive that my net was strong enough to hold me up. For now.

"I don't have what it takes to go through what you did," a friend told me later.

"I would have said the same thing if the roles had been reversed," I replied.

We humans can do amazing things that we'd never dream possible. Tragedy taught me that some of the tools I required to get through were with me already. I had to dig deep, be open to the light, acknowledge the good, and turn away from the darkness. My net was in place and I was ready for the next step.

The door opened and two wiry men entered, pulling a gurney into the room. They looked me over, checked my chart, and then retreated to the nursing station.

When they got back, one of them explained: "We asked the nurses to up the drugs for the ambulance ride. It can be a little bumpy." They administered the medication, transferred me to the gurney, and whisked me down the hall and out into the cool air where a paramedic opened the ambulance door.

"Your chariot awaits," he said.

Chapter Twenty-Three

Tiny Pools of Hope

UCHealth Anschutz, Aurora, April 3, 2017, Midday

The paramedic had an unexpected question. "Do you want the lights on?" he asked before shutting the doors. "It costs more," he added. He meant using the flashing lights of the ambulance for the drive south. "No lights, thank you," I said.

He wasn't lying about the ride—it was bumpy. I was jostled quite a bit; they seemed to have just one speed, though this wasn't a typical emergency. I felt like a pinball and worried about getting in a wreck. Fear of tragedy was a close companion those days.

Adam attempted to follow the ambulance, but lost us as we zipped through I-25 traffic.

We arrived safely at UCHealth Anschutz in Aurora. My gangly stewards unpacked me, and we roamed the halls, looking for the burn center. My gurney-level glimpses revealed the enormous size of the complex.

At one point, they stopped to ask for directions. Finally, they rolled me into an exam room of the Burn ICU, got me settled, and then dashed off to their next assignment.

I sat alone in the room, wondering if anyone knew I was there, who I was, or if I was in the right place. A nurse eventually entered the room and unwrapped my hands. The swelling had increased overnight, and the fingers that hadn't burned looked like they might burst with a touch.

"Dr. Anne Wagner, chief of the burn unit, will be in shortly," she told me.

Dr. Wagner came into the room soon after and examined my hands. "Honestly," she began, "there is not much we can do for you, as I'm sure you heard in Greeley. We can care for your burns and clean up the tissue as the injury progresses."

Even in a narcotic haze, I knew this wasn't encouraging. *Sounds familiar*, I thought.

She spoke again: "We're waiting for the plastic surgeon to finish up in the operating room. He knows you are here and will stop by when he is done."

Plastic surgery? All I could think of was boob jobs.

"His name is Dr. Ashley Ignatiuk," she said. "He specializes in hand reconstruction."

She must have read my mind. Hands—that makes sense.

"He might be able to make something happen," Dr. Wagner said. "If anyone can, it would be him. He is very talented, and I've been impressed with what I've seen him do. Still, there are no absolutes in this case."

She left me to wait for my miracle, the minutes ticking away with nothing to look at but the charred, jagged remains of my hands.

"This place is a maze!" It was Adam, relieved to find me, his parents and Karla behind him.

I felt naked sitting with the carnage of my wounds, my raw reality on exhibition. They had only heard about the damage, so seeing it firsthand was shocking. I saw trepidation and sorrow in their devastated looks, eyes heavy with anguish and rimmed with tears.

"Oh, Mel," Karla exhaled sadly. I could tell she wanted to embrace me, but, afraid to cause any pain, she gently settled her hand on my shoulder instead. The familiar faces brought a new layer of visceral realism, as though being seen verified my tragedy, bringing unescapable tangibility. It was a no-words moment, just somber faces and awkward head tilts.

Encouragement was not on the table, just love and support. I felt like a slab of crude meat, helpless and hopeless yet desperately wishing for both help and hope. I could tell that seeing me in person eased their minds: I was alive, and I could feel their love and relief, which soothed my edginess. I told them about the plastic surgeon, the hand specialist who was on his way.

"The burn unit treats burns, but they but can't change anything," I said. I paused, then added, "Supposedly, he can do wonders." Maybe repeating this statement would build some optimism. Then it was small talk about insignificant matters. There were no words for the weight of my situation.

A nurse came in, but only to rewrap my hands, saying the doctor was delayed in surgery, and that it was a priority to keep the burns covered and moist. Two nurses applied multiple layers of ointment, Xeroform, and gauze, then a final gauze wrap that covered all the fingers except the only one untouched by burns: my right pinkie. It took about thirty minutes to do all of this, as wrapping the skin, bones, and palms was a delicate process,

Of course, Dr. Ignatiuk showed up shortly after they'd finished.

My nervous husband met him outside the door. I craned my neck, trying to hear, and got my first glimpse of the surgeon. *So young*, I thought, a bit disappointed. *Well, youth might mean inexperience but also innovation.* He was tall, with salt-and-pepper spiky hair and a round, pleasant face covered in stubble. *How long had he been a doctor?*

As he moved into the room, he was engaging with my gatekeeper, Adam.

"There are many things we can do for thumbs, including taking the big toe off and putting it on as a thumb."

"You are not going to take her big toe off," Adam interjected (later telling me he thought I'd have enough trouble without fingers; he didn't want to add a missing big toe to the mix).

"Adam, let him look at me first," I said, my voice feeble with exhaustion.

The doctor introduced himself and inspected my hands, from the burnt palms to the exposed charred bones of my thumbs, which held up the fleshy remains of my thumb tips. He made a face you don't want a doctor to make—squinting, pursing his lips, tilting his head. It was a look of doubt. "Get a needle," he called to a nurse. Then he looked at me.

"The damage is severe, but if there is blood flow, we can try to save the thumbs."

The nurse handed him a needle and time stopped. We all held our breath. He carefully pricked the flesh of the thumb pads, right, then left. This deciding moment meant everything: A tiny (yet monumental) drop of blood would determine the future of my thumbs and whether anyone would try to help save them.

I stared intently. What would my future look like? Would I only have my index fingers and pinkies left? My throat constricted as my mind whirled. Through the tears that blurred my vision I could see tiny pools of blood. For the first time, the tears were of hope and relief.

Ignatiuk moved his intense regard from the pinpricks of blood to my eyes. "No guarantees," he said firmly, "but there is blood flow, so I have something to work with. I'll try to save your thumbs."

That was all I needed—someone who would try. I swore to myself that I would do everything I could to assist him, to be the best patient possible. I can't say my spirits soared, but they definitely lifted as I stared at my new hero.

He proceeded to explain. "Thumbs are the only digits that have arteries on the back, and they are still delivering blood, which means at least we can try." That was the crucial word I yearned for: *try*. "This will be a long journey," he cautioned, "with many surgeries and no guarantees the thumbs will be able to overcome the damage." I understood; how could there be any guarantees with this carnage?

I didn't want to push my luck, but had to ask: "What about the rest of the fingers?" They were just burnt bones with no fingertips.

"Burns are like frostbite." Ignatiuk explained. "The injury needs to declare itself still, but we will save everything we can along the way." In other words, I would learn, the injury wasn't complete yet; a burn can take forty-eight to seventy-two hours to finish causing its damage. At this point, it had only been about twenty hours since the accident.

I felt every muscle unclench. The scenario of life with two pinkies and two pointers eased a bit. I was in good hands, so to speak. Young, old, it didn't matter; this doctor would help, and there was hope.

"If you save my thumbs, it will be a miracle," I declared.

Without hesitation, Ignatiuk looked at me and said, "If I save your thumbs, it will be science."

I nodded. The miracle had already happened. I'd survived. Now, I needed all of his training, knowledge, and gumption.

"The burn team here represents some of the best," he said. "They'll get you settled and take care of you. We have to give the injury some time before we take any action." He said he'd be checking on me, then left.

Fully aware the road ahead would have plenty of bumps, blocks, and detours, I still wanted to cry with the relief he had provided. *Maybe I could be one of Dr. Ignatiuk's wondrous works*, I thought, adding a layer of hope to my net, vowing to comply with whatever strategy lay ahead.

Chapter Twenty-Four

New Home
UCHealth, April 3 and 4, 2017

After Ignatiuk left, the nurses checked me into Room 4 in the Burn ICU.

Dr. Wagner, head of the Burn & Frostbite Center, stopped by to say she'd be stepping aside. "Dr. Ignatiuk will be your main doctor," she said. "You're in good hands with the Plastics team, and we have a top-notch staff that will take care of your burns and needs while you are here."

I settled into the foreign atmosphere. My bed was adjacent to a wall of glass with sliding doors, my new home for now. I felt like I was in a vast, clangorous fishbowl hooked up to beeping and whirling machines. Buzzing and ringing alerts were continual throughout the ward. It was loud and hectic but reassuring, knowing that all of the people and machines were there to help me and the other patients. There was a bathroom in the room, a recliner, and a bench that could double as a bed for Adam to stay.

The plan involved no immediate action or surgery, just watching and waiting. The staff filled me in on life in the Burn ICU, where I'd be staying until the injury had fully declared itself and we could contemplate next steps. They let me know they were there to treat my burns, observe the progression of the wounds, monitor my overall health, and keep me comfortable and out of pain. I was still hooked up to a catheter until they were sure my kidneys were processing the internal burnt tissue. Because I was so shocked and drained from absorbing the electricity and understanding the extent of my injuries, first diagnosis, and transfer, I forgot it was "just" my hands I could not use.

The second evening after the accident, my first at UCHealth, I had to remind myself I could still walk. Lisa came to visit, and the three of us, with my IV tower and bag of urine, took a turn around the burn floor. Feeling weak and self-conscious, I suddenly noticed the draft on my backside.

"Adam, would you see if you can cinch my gown down?" I asked. Another patient passed us and I felt a little less self-conscious. "At least I'm not the only one walking around with their ass hanging out."

Items from home arrived with friends: underwear, our toothbrushes, and other necessities. Adam held up a pair of my underwear.

"Nice," I said, "but not the coverage I'm looking for."

Visiting friends knew I was in for a long haul, and delivered small comforts, including our hot water kettle, my favorite loose-leaf tea from the Tea Spot in Boulder, a diffuser, essential oils, a hairbrush, contact lenses, face soap, and creams. I was grateful to see these familiar items, but wondered how I would use them. Adam was here, and we would figure it out. *I guess he'll brush my teeth.*

I'm not a sedentary or patient person, and a multitasker by nature. Restaurant work suited me. In one sense, I was a lousy manager at the Dunraven because it was always easier to do something myself than to explain what needed to happen.

Same thing at home. When we first met, Adam would ask "Are you ever going to sit down?" I'd reply, "Sure, after I finish doing . . . ," listing the stuff I needed to get done. Adam had a business to run, so I rarely asked him for help; I went to the grocery store, cleaned, cooked, pulled weeds, and tried home improvement projects on my own. I was stubborn and resolute, but I got things done.

Now, sitting in my hospital room with no way to help myself, I knew I needed to reset my personality. Not so easy. Simple self-care was hard enough—using the bathroom, drinking water—let alone addressing a zillion things about daily living, and the restaurant. I needed to find patience and learn how to ask for help. There was no negotiating this; I had to accept being dependent, incapable, and vulnerable. This would have to be part of my vow to be the best patient ever.

Simple things required patience, and help from anyone available, from the staff, who had a unit full of patients, to family and friends.

"Can you please get me some water?" I'd ask, and then try to sit up and get the straw in my mouth. It wasn't just acquiring the water and food, but also getting it in me, which required another step. I learned quickly that I'd have to request help, and be gentle with my care team, and myself.

This was a whole new world. You don't realize how much you use your hands until you don't have them. I even needed them to see. I have horrible vision and usually wear contacts, taking them out only to sleep. Adam had grabbed an old pair of glasses with an expired weaker prescription, but they would do since I could only see blurred blobs of color until someone put them on my face.

Everything required help: brushing my teeth, urinating, brushing my hair, ordering food, eating. (Fortunately, the opiates constipated me, resulting in infrequent requests to wipe my bottom.) The occupational therapist had encouraged a new skill: turning pages on my iPad using a pen she put my mouth, the goal being to read my Kindle. It proved to be a futile and frustrating exercise, trying to read with a pen in my mouth and applying pressure to the iPad propped up on pillows. With both hands bandaged and immobile, the limitations felt overwhelming.

We Skyped with my parents, which was rather amusing on occasion, considering the situation. They got to meet Dr. Ignatiuk and learn what had happened to my body, and what might yet happen. To me, my injuries were alien, nothing like the strains you endure as a climber. To Dr. Ignatiuk, these weird craters and burnt ends were familiar. Challenging, severe, and numerous, for sure, but familiar.

"Bone density has the highest resistance of any body tissue," he explained to me and Adam, with my parents on Skype. "So it generates the greatest amount of heat when exposed to an electrical current. Thus, the areas of greatest thermal injury are often the deep tissue surrounding long bones. This results in periosteal burns, destruction of bone matrix, and osteonecrosis."

Our blank looks told him to shift gears.

"You were burning from the inside out," he said. "Like a hot dog in a microwave—the bones burned first, because they are denser."

Well, that makes sense, I thought, since I was using a microwave transformer and my hands were fried.

"What would have happened if the breaker didn't trip?" I questioned.

"It would have been a gruesome find for Adam," Dr. Ignatiuk said.

We were getting a crash course in skin grafts and other surgeries. We all had questions, including my dad.

"I just saw on the news that this guy had a penis transplant," he said. My mom looked mortified. "I told you not to ask that, Paul."

Ignatiuk chuckled. "Organs transplant better than skin," he said.

Then my father offered *his* thumb.

"Grafts from the individual are better," the doctor said, "and full finger transplants from a donor have never been successful." He mentioned the big-toe transplant idea, but said, "Because there is blood flow, we will explore salvaging the thumbs first."

After he left, my mom mentioned how young he was.

I told her I'd had the same thought at first. "But his youth might mean innovation," I said. "And he said he would try to help, which is better than what anyone else has offered at this point."

I came to understand that if I'd had a traditional surgeon, I would have sat in the Burn ICU while they trimmed away tissue, leaving me with just two index fingers and two pinkies.

The next morning, April 4, 2017, I learned how early rounds started for the plastics team.

Dr. Ignatiuk stopped by at four a.m. with a group of young interns. He gently woke me, my bandaged hands nestled in large blue foam blocks to elevate and protect them when sleeping. He put my eyeglasses on, and gave me an update.

There was no rush for surgery, he said, but "We don't want to wait too long." He said I'd be having my first operation that afternoon, "a simple debridement surgery, cleaning off some of the dead tissue and taking a look. Basically poking around while you are knocked out."

Adam and I waited for several hours before I was wheeled into the operating room. Time for some poking around to see what my future might hold.

I don't remember asking the question, but Adam definitely does. I was in the recovery room, coming out of anesthesia in a groggy fog, and saw Adam there. I was able to form one question: "Do I still have my thumbs?"

"Yes. Yes, you do," he said, exhaling with relief.

Well, that's good, I thought drowsily.

"They made it through the dead-tissue cleanup, and . . ."

I didn't hear the rest as I drifted back to unconsciousness.

Back in my room, my hands felt somewhat safeguarded for the first time. They were nestled in small half-plaster supports, secured and padded with multiple layers of gauze, and wrapped in elastic bandages. I noticed that a burnt bone, once the tip of my right middle finger, poked out of the cloud of gauze.

So maybe more had survived than just my index fingers, pinkies, and (possibly?) my thumbs.

I had questions.

Adam said the surgeon would be stopping by. Also, his parents and his sister would be coming. "They asked if you wanted anything."

"Oh, better underwear would be nice," I said. "Maybe some briefs, like little shorts, so when we walk around the hospital, it's less drafty."

"Good call," Adam said, texting his sister.

We also asked a friend who was coming for a visit to stop at the house and get some joggers and rummage around for short-sleeved tees with wide armholes. I figured that with my hands bandaged, once I was free of the catheter that they planned to remove that day, I could go for a walk, fully clothed.

A hospital social worker stopped by the next day to ask some basic questions, including, "Do you have health insurance?"

"That's one thing I don't have to worry about," I replied, explaining that we'd had a scare a few months earlier when our coverage was canceled. The news had come via a snail-mail letter that got buried in a stack of mail, lost in the shuffle after being gone for our winter climbing session. No phone call, no e-mail, just a letter stating that if you had a preferred provider organization, it was ending.

When I called the company, they said they couldn't help me because we'd never responded to the letter. We were saved by a technicality (the date of the notification letter made it an improper cancellation, enabling me to sign up with a different provider outside of open enrollment), and by March, we had insurance again. I was relieved to be able to tell the social worker that we were covered (barely!).

The social worker also asked about my mental state.

I told her that I had nightmares about the accident. I would wake up shaking my hands, trying to drop the electric leads. I also told her about opening the restaurant and my hopes of returning to rock climbing. Much later, I was able to read the notes she made in her report from April 5, three days after the accident, and the day after that first surgery:

The patient has a goal to be able to return to her highest level of independence with working at her restaurant and returning to enjoy life and hobbies such as rock climbing. The patient is realistic and aware that some adaptations may need to be made due to her hands, but displays strong motivation for healing. Patient appears to have a strong insight into her sense of self as well as the long road to recovery ahead of her.

All true. I had, and still have, a strong sense of self. But in the dimly lit hospital bathroom that night, I wasn't so sure who I would be on the other side of all of this. I sat on the toilet, head down to avoid looking at the nurse who'd gathered up my hospital gown and draped it over my shoulder. I got situated on the commode while she waited on the other side of a cracked door. I looked down at my legs and hips.

"This is strange," I said.

She peeked in. I looked up and told her, "I am tan all over." She looked confused.

"I haven't been to a beach or sunbathing in forever," I said. "In fact, I was supposed to be flying to the islands today, to visit my parents. Somehow, I'm bronzed everywhere, with no tan lines. Could this be from the electricity?" I asked.

"Honestly, I have no idea," the nurse answered. "It's rare to see people survive electrical burns this severe."

Chapter Twenty-Five

The Way

UCHealth, April 5 and 6, 2017

Dr. Ignatiuk came into my room looking exuberant.

This was good, right? I hadn't seen him since the surgery the previous day. I wanted to hear something encouraging, and he came through. He told me he had scheduled another debridement surgery for the next day.

"We are going to go in for a closer look," he said.

Closer look? How could they get any closer than literally working *inside* my hands?

He read my mind. "We are going to use something we've never used for this application before—we call it SPY."

Okay then. This sounded . . . interesting.

He explained about a dye called indocyanine green (ICG), used in angiograms to check on blood flow in the heart, liver, eyes, and elsewhere in the body. Ignatiuk wanted to use it in my hands.

"We will inject the ICG intravenously," he said, "then use a near-red infrared laser to watch the blood flowing in your hand. That way, we can see what tissue has enough blood and what doesn't. The dye is the SPY." It was a way to gauge the extent of the damage.

"With this, we can see the future of the injury and make a plan, instead of waiting."

Yes. This was the passion and innovation I'd hoped for. He said the SPY would "give us a living map of salvageable matter." He was clearly excited to try this.

Ignatiuk then brought up a bit of information that was both disturbing and encouraging. He told me that one of the reasons extreme electrical burns like mine are difficult to treat is that there's not a lot of useful case studies.

"Why is that?" we asked.

"Because people typically don't survive," he said calmly.

Gratitude flowed through me and into my net.

"The character of electrical burns this extensive is unknown, so it will be great to get a look from the inside."

I knew that my case was quite unusual. I'd gathered that from every nurse in the burn unit who'd seen my wounds. After all, this was the Burn & Frostbite Center in Colorado, a land of high altitude, cold winters, campers and skiers and hunters, snowfields and remote canyons. Lots of chances for exposure, frozen extremities and lightning strikes, which caused injuries more similar to mine. My intense connection to a mammoth source of electricity was a different extreme.

During one afternoon visit Dr. Ignatiuk asked me about the accident. "I want to understand more about what you were doing when this happened."

I explained the Lichtenberg technique, asking him to navigate my phone so he could scroll through pictures as I talked about the machine and the artistic burns it created on furniture.

"This is crazy!" he exclaimed, going into his own phone to show me the arm of a lightning-strike victim who had Lichtenberg marks on their skin.

"Wow!" I said. "Too bad I just didn't get a cool design."

The medical team's grim statements about people not surviving shocks like mine oddly reassured me. Being alive was a phenomenon, which meant it was possible other wonders could follow. I had beaten the odds by surviving. Now, I hoped to beat the odds by saving what was left of my hands.

As I was getting prepped the day of the SPY surgery, April 6, a new surgeon popped in.

"Hi, I'm Dr. Seth TeBockhorst," he said. "I'm interning with Dr. Ignatiuk, and I'll be assisting with this surgery." He was concluding his plastic surgery residency, and following Ignatiuk's path, planning to head to Texas to specialize in hands when he finished at UCHealth in a few months.

He wondered if I had any questions.

Sure, I had lots of them that I knew nobody could answer. But I asked him one that I suspected he might actually understand. The man was tall and lean, looked strong, and was wearing a light blue Arc'teryx jacket. He looked like any number of climbers I knew. *He looks like a climber*, I thought, *might as well*.

"I do have a question," I ventured. "Do you think I'll ever climb V10 again?"

Right to it. Why not? This was the first time since the Estes Park emergency room that I'd asked anyone about climbing again. But I wanted my medical team to know that I was a serious rock climber—and once, a really good one.

"You've climbed V10?" the doctor replied, looking surprised.

"She's climbed harder than that," Adam said.

"Are you a climber?" I asked him.

This proved easier for Dr. Seth to answer than my first question.

"Yeah, I love climbing," he said. "I was a boulderer, but after graduating and becoming a doctor, I don't have much time for it. Plus, being a surgeon now," he added, holding up his hands, "I have invested so much time and effort into these hands that I feel like I should preserve them rather than risk climbing."

I managed a smile. "Adam and I are both sponsored rock climbers," I told him. "Boulders predominantly, these days. We divide our time between Estes Park, climbing in Rocky and volunteering with the climbing rangers, and Hueco Tanks. We also operate a guiding concession in Hueco, to help with access."

My throat tightened as I talked about climbing. I told him we'd traveled the world to climb. "Climbing is our life," I managed to say, without breaking down.

"I love Hueco Tanks!" Dr. Seth said. "My last big climbing trip was when I graduated med school. I took a reward vacation to the Rocklands in South Africa."

"The Rocklands are amazing," I said. "We visited in 2005 and can't wait to get back." I caught myself. "Well, at least that was our plan, before this." Despite my emotions, this was positive for me—one of my surgeons sounded like one of us, and understood the passion involved with climbing rocks.

We continued talking about climbs, climbing areas, and mutual climbing acquaintances. I told him what he could already tell: For us, climbing was not a hobby. It was what we ate, slept, and worked for. "We eat smart, train on our home wall, lift weights, strengthen our fingers and core, and do cardio—all to excel at climbing," I said. I told him about training with coaches in Colorado, Utah, and the UK over the years.

I nodded at his jacket. "We're sponsored, so clothing companies have given us free gear or discounts, and they've helped out with some funds for climbing trips," I said. He nodded as I named companies that supplied us: Organic Climbing for crash pads, Friction Labs for climbing chalk, Kilter Climbing for holds, prAna for clothing, 5.10 for shoes.

"Climbing isn't a diversion," I told him. "It defines our way of life." Our livelihoods—the tree service and restaurant work—were secondary to climbing, no matter how much it hurt our savings. "Climbing is our life, our past, present, and future. At least it always was our future." I stopped myself. We all knew the future was unknown. It all hinged on time, healing, and what the doctors could conjure.

Seth got it.

I told Adam I loved him and would see him later.

The anesthesiologist injected the Versed sedative into my IV.

As I was wheeled off, I wondered what the SPY would reveal about my future.

Chapter Twenty-Six

I Dream of Jeannie

UCHealth, April 6, 2017, Late Afternoon

When Dr. Ignatiuk came into Room 4, he seemed as excited as a kid on Christmas morning.

He took out his phone and held it up for me. (Reality thwarted any reach-out-and-grab urges I might have had.) On the phone I saw images from CT scans of my hands from that morning. They appeared veined with green blood. It looked like the SPY had completed its mission—those glowing tributaries of vascularity would now determine how much tissue could be saved.

"The bright areas are the dye lighting up blood flow, and the dark areas are where the dye could not reach, meaning no blood supply," Dr. Ignatiuk said.

I looked closer. The thumbs were the worst, showing little to no blood flow. But he had an idea for that. He wanted to bring a steady blood flow to my charred hands by attaching the hands to a healthy part of my body and its blood vessels. That way, he explained, "We can introduce the bones and tissue to good vascularity by sewing your arms into another part of your body with a flap of healthy skin." The technique was called "bilateral flaps," a way of bringing a piece of skin and its blood vessels from one part of the body to another—in my case, my thumbs.

"The skin flap will hopefully connect with the vascularity of your hands, allowing me to create grafts with this skin that your body will be less likely to reject," he said. "The flaps will provide us skin for your thumbs and a chance for the thumb tips to survive."

"Doctors have used this flap technique for ages," he told me, "but we would be covering new territory with bilateral flaps." (Later, Adam's Internet searches revealed that the basic procedure had been used as far back as 600 BC!)*

Okay, but what part of my body would provide the donor skin for my thumbs?

Dr. Ignatiuk explained his proposal: "Your elbows will be bent at an angle, with your thumbs sewn into your tummy," he said, standing next to my bed, arms bent and hands on his own abdomen. "When we separate them, we will use the tissue from your stomach to make thumbs. And I'll give you a little tummy tuck," he added with a chuckle.

While excited to hear any news about forward progress, when I tried to picture it, I was actually horrified. I looked at the position Ignatiuk was mimicking, trying to imagine my arms being sewn to my stomach. It was already difficult to cope without the use of my hands. If we tried this, how would I even get in and out of bed?

He asked to see my torso, lifting the hospital gown. He let out a disappointed *Hmmph* upon seeing my abs—the result of years of sit-ups, crunches, ab rollers, you name it.

"Well," he said, "you don't have enough tissue to work with."

I replied, "A strong core is key to climbing."

He stood there thinking. In the years since this moment, we've had a long-running friendly debate about how we decided to proceed. He claims it was my idea. Maybe it was how I was naturally sitting in the hospital bed. My hands, bandaged from the SPY surgery, were folded across my lap on top of one another—protecting my abdomen from the thought of my thumbs being sewn into it.

I wouldn't put it past me. I might've encouraged him to come up with another idea rather than risk slowing his excitement and momentum. The doctor claims I said, "We could sew my arms like this," referring to the

---

* "Classification and Principles of Flap Surgery," *Medscape*, https://emedicine.medscape.com/article/1284474-overview.

pose I was in at the time. In my recollection, Ignatiuk said, "Well, another idea would be to sew your thumbs into your opposing forearms."

"Like *I Dream of Jeannie!*" I said.

Both of us recall some smiles and optimism breaking out at this point.

"How long would I be like this?" I asked.

"Two weeks," he answered.

I summoned some outward confidence even as I was melting down inside. "Well, if it's going to help save my thumbs, let's do it."

He mapped out the plan. The operation—what I called "tethering surgery," and he called "bilateral flaps"—would start with another SPY look: "We'll clean away what we know we cannot save, including amputating the burnt bones of your fingers," he said. Next, he'd perform the bilateral flaps, adding that it would be "a long surgery." He said Saturday, April 8, would be good, giving my body a few days to recover from the earlier surgery.

"I'll check on the operating room for the eighth and let you know. In the meantime, feel free to get outside for a walk—it's beautiful out," he said, then left.

I turned and looked at Adam. "What the fuck?!" That was all I could muster for several minutes. "How am I going to get through this?"

"You will," Adam said. "*We* will."

More fears charged into my mind. I already couldn't do anything for myself, besides walk. How would I sleep, sit up, take a shower, have someone put clothing on me? My mind reeled. Sewing my arms together ... Could I mentally endure it?

"We will get through this," Adam said again, meaning he would be there for me. He'd been at my side for the past four days since the accident. We both knew he had to start working again at some point. His crew kept the tree service going with the town contract and scheduled residential jobs, but messages and new requests were piling up. And his birthday was four days away, on April 10.

Adam had been my main care provider, although I relied on the nurses and aides for taking care of my showers. Adam was not a fan of water, or even getting wet. Hot tubs, pools, lakes, and oceans were off his list. Showering me—with my open exit wounds and bandaged hands—was a delicate and challenging task best left for the professionals. This was decided after a few attempts left me in tears. "Adam, you are showering me, not hosing down the dog," I tried to coach.

Thus far, Adam had only left my side for brief periods, to get food and coffee, and to bring stuffed animals from the hospital gift shop that resembled our pets. Our plan was that before the *I Dream of Jeannie* surgery on Saturday, he would drive home to check on our dog and cat, as well as work and home routines with the foreman of the tree service crew (who was staying in the apartment over our garage), only to turn around an hour later to make the two- to three-hour drive back.

The next phase was two weeks with my arms sewn together.

"I know you can't stay here the whole time to take care of me," I said, as Adam put pants on me. "That'd make three weeks in the hospital. If I think this is bad," I said, holding up my giant bandaged mitts, "how am I going to function like this?" I folded my arms on top of each other. "What am I going to be able to wear?" I said, holding my arms back up so Adam could put my T-shirt on.

Adam thought we should take Dr. Ignatiuk up on his suggestion to get some fresh air and a change of scenery. As he brushed my hair, I told him the new terror that had just hit me: "You know that nightmare where I'm trying to throw the leads down? What if I wake up trying to pull my arms apart?" I asked, my voice rising in panic.

"Well, you won't be able to—you will be sewn together," Adam said rationally. "Come on, let's go out; it will be good for you to get some sunshine."

We left my room, stopping at the nurses' station to let them know the doc had cleared us to walk around the campus.

"Oh, it's beautiful out," the nurse responded. "It's good that you're getting some vitamin D." She chuckled and nodded at us. "Did you realize that you two are dressed the same?"

I looked—indeed, black pants and Kelly green shirts. "I blame that on him; he dressed the both of us," I said, laughing.

As we descended the stairwell, Adam ahead of me, just in case, I held my arms up to prevent the thunderous pain of blood rushing into them if I lowered them—something I hadn't done since the accident.

"Maybe your sister could get me a tube top or something," I thought out loud. I realized that would be impractical—if it slid down, I'd have no way of pulling it back up. I already felt naked and exposed in a hospital gown as it was. The boy shorts Adam's sister Vicky had brought were a big help, and a nurse's aide, hearing that I was uncomfortable in just the thin gown, had constructed a halter bra for me out of roll gauze.

We stepped through the door and into the warm spring air. The sun was bright and piercing, a welcome change from the fluorescent lights.

"I'm going to grab something to eat," Adam said. "Do you want anything?" We were near a sandwich shop next to the hospital.

"No, thanks, I'll just stay out here. I can't even stand to smell food right now."

I settled in at an outside wire-mesh table. The opioids the nurses gave me were doing their job in terms of pain relief, but they also resulted in constant nausea and occasional vomiting. They were trying to help me keep food down with anti-nausea medication and seasickness patches, but it was still a struggle.

It was spring down here in mile-high Denver. Up in Estes Park, at 7,250 feet, spring meant aspens struggling to bud between frosts and snowstorms, dry brown grass, and clumps of snow. But the grounds of the UCHealth campus were beautiful shades of vibrant green. The trees were budding and displaying early flowers, swaying in a light breeze, and tulips and daffodils pushed forth from the carefully mulched beds. Nursing and medical students milled around or whisked by in a hurry. Seeing healthy people living their day-to-day lives created a surreal juxtaposition against my suspended state of existence.

"These people know exactly what they are doing today, tomorrow, and next month," I told Adam when he sat down, unwrapping his turkey club.

"Yes," he replied calmly, "and *you* know what *you* are doing and *will* do when you get out of here. You will open your restaurant."

Ah, the restaurant. Good distraction.

"Yeah, the bank should finalize the loan papers this week," I said. All that stress about the loan seemed tangible yet distant in the shadow of my injuries. I told Adam: "It's hard for me to imagine how I will function in the restaurant. It's such a hands-on business—pun intended." Then again, "It doesn't matter—the building is purchased and gutted, and people have quit their jobs to work for me. I have no choice. Thank goodness I have partners. At least I can rely on them to be my hands. But still, it's just hard to imagine."

The refreshing breeze blew Adam's napkin across the table. I reached up and put my bandaged hand on top of it—*See, I can still be helpful*—and tried to slide it back to him. As I did this, the protruding burnt bone of my right middle finger grated across the wire tabletop, sending a shivering distant pain through my body, followed by another wave of nausea. I swallowed hard.

"Was that your *bone*?" Adam asked.

"Yes," I gurgled.

"Gnarly," Adam said, visibly shocked. We sat in silence a bit.

"Look at those banners on the light posts," I said. "Looks like there is some sort of art display. That would help kill some time." I thought ahead to the post-surgery period, thinking if I could wear clothes and get out, maybe I could attend this art exhibit. *But how with my arms tethered, harrumph.*

Adam's phone buzzed. "Bronson's here," he said. "Do you want to go back to your room, or can I text her to meet us outside?"

Bronson was my first climbing partner and a vivacious close friend who always lifted me up and cheered me on. I knew my days outside might soon be limited.

"Let's stay out and meet her at the pavilion with the picnic tables," I said.

Seeing Bronson would be simultaneously great, and challenging; the thought of catching up with a climbing friend was hard. Our friendship went beyond climbing, but that was our common love. I knew people were stopping their lives to drive hours to see me. I felt guilty for taking up their time, but grateful for the distraction and love.

Bronson had flown in from her job at the time as a scenic pilot in Moab. When we met at the pavilion, Bronson took me in her arms and hugged.

"Oh, Melissa, it's so good to see you. I am so happy you are alive."

"Me too!" I agreed, laughing snot and tears as she released me. It was an intense reminder that my near-death had profoundly impacted those who loved me.

We sat down and chatted—about her life and new flying job. For the time being, we did not mention climbing.

I told her about the upcoming *I Dream of Jeannie* surgery and shared my fears about being sewn together, about simply existing and being able to take care of myself. Knowing that Adam had to leave terrified me, and we told her about his plan to commute to the hospital.

Bronson immediately devised a plan: She would fly back on her few days off and stay in the hospital with me so Adam could go home to work, not having to make a return trip.

"I couldn't ask you to do that," I said.

"It's all set; I just texted work," she said. "I needed to come back at the end of next week anyway. It will work out perfectly." She looked at the calendar on the phone. "I will be here on the fourteenth for a sleepover. We'll make it fun!"

Good god, how did I get such amazing friends?

I thanked her. Friends wove threads of support, stability, and purpose in my safety net, fortifying the inner strength I knew I would need to face the upcoming challenges.

Chapter Twenty-Seven

Grapefruit Pellegrino?
UCHealth, April 8, 2017

April 8 finally arrived. Dr. Ignatiuk had said the surgery could take up to eight hours; he had another operation that morning, and would spend the rest of the day on me.

Waiting is hard. And waiting to have your arms sewn together, and the burnt remains of your fingers cut off in hopes of saving your dying digits—well, that was a slow, numbing agony. The fear of being attached, the fear of waking up in a nightmare trying to rip my arms apart, the fear of going through this and still losing my thumbs, the fear of infection, the fear of the future, the fear of just *being* was overwhelming. The tremendous amount of medication dulled the physical pain but also helped me sit with this grim reality.

I felt trapped in a horror movie, except the woman in the film was me. There was no escaping my reality, no fast-forwarding through the cringey moments, no pause, no covering my eyes with my hands and peeking through my fingers. I allowed myself to feel sorry for the scared girl trapped in this nightmare. I grieved for my loss and opened myself to the sorrow. I also encouraged myself to become fully aware of the tremendous strength I would need to summon for the next steps.

In my mind, I took out my safety net, knowing that I would need considerable fortitude, forbearance, and acceptance to endure my two weeks of tethering. I added threads of patience and resilience to reinforce the ever-growing net. I reminded myself that I would do whatever was asked of me in order to save my fingers and thumbs.

Adam and I sat in quiet dread throughout the morning and early afternoon.

Leah, my close friend (the one who'd lost her home and ceramics studio to the Estes Park / Glen Haven flood in 2013) messaged Adam about visiting. We told her to come on April 9, but warned her this would be a challenging day—Day One of waking up with my arms stitched together. She decided not to bring her five-year-old son to this visit.

Adam went about business as usual—got some coffee and breakfast and returned some customers' calls. For the better half of the day, I sat and stared at a grapefruit Pellegrino and a green apple on the counter. When lunchtime rolled around, I knew Adam must be hungry. I also knew he wouldn't eat until I was taken into surgery, in solidarity.

Around 1:00 p.m. he picked up the apple and I snapped, "Oh, no, that's mine!" Even though we both knew I wasn't allowed to eat, nor could I feed myself. He laughed and put the apple down, recognizing a woman on the brink of a hanger- and stress-induced meltdown.

Dr. Ignatiuk showed up after 2:30 p.m.

"Sorry for the delay. I just got out of surgery. It took me longer than I thought. If you are ready, we can go for it, but if you don't mind waiting, I'd rather we operate tomorrow."

My disappointment probably showed. He explained, "I want to be fresh and take my time. Plus, my wife, Jess, hasn't seen me in days, and we were supposed to go out to dinner tonight."

His honesty impressed me. Date night with his wife. Such a simple, commonplace reality, now so far from my world. My response was obvious: "Of course. I would rather you be fresh and ready to go rather than forcing the situation."

"Great. I'll confirm the OR for tomorrow morning."

Bonus, I thought. *I won't have to go through another hungry morning and afternoon of dread.*

"I hope you have a nice dinner with your wife," I said. As he turned to leave, I called out, "But don't drink too much!"

He smiled. "No way."

I was disappointed, of course, but relieved to have another day of independent arm movement and freedom. I proceeded to devour the apple, which Adam fed to me (I "gave" him a few bites), and happily downed the Pellegrino.

It was another beautiful spring day in Aurora, so we went for a walk. As I emerged from the dim stairwell, the warmth of the sun touched my skin, and the smell of flowers greeted me—reminders of the gift of life that I almost wasn't here to experience. I took a deep breath of fresh air and welcomed the gratefulness, then hustled off the path and into the bushes to puke up the apple and Pellegrino. The pain meds had struck again.

Walking beside Adam in my sedated haze, taking in the beauty, made the impending surgery and uncertainty less surreal and more factual. I decided to go into this with the best attitude I could muster. *Someone is trying to help you; you must do what you can to help them help you*, I coached myself. *This will be over before you know it. A poppycock cliché, but why not? You have to think of it in some way—it might as well be positive.* My internal dialogue was constant as we strolled and I soaked in the vibrance of spring.

We wandered the grounds. We walked under an art display of metal arches and sat on benches. I posed for a picture next to a gigantic stone orb, as though I was pushing this sphere. I thought of Sisyphus pushing his boulder up the hill. Life can be similar, I thought, constantly trying, only to try harder, over and over again.

I fought to keep the mood serene for myself, Adam, and anyone giving me care and love. They didn't need to see the cloud of fear, sadness, grief, and doubt that hovered over me. I did not want to bite the hand that fed me, literally and figuratively. I had to let light and positivity in to heal, face the next moment, and facilitate the love and support rather than pushing it away.

We were on a path lined with trees bursting with white flowers.

"Turn around, I'll get a picture," Adam said. He took several steps back, and I situated myself in the middle of the path and held my arms up high over my head in a V, matching the same stance with my legs. I welcomed in the gift of life that floated in the spring air, holding my bandaged hands up high, celebrating that they were freely moving at this point, the joy that I was alive, and that someone was trying to help me.

That evening Adam's parents, Charlie and Cheryl, and his sister, Vicky, visited. When Adam left the room to call back some customers, I asked Vicky if she could get me a Happy Birthday banner and some balloons to decorate the room for Adam's birthday. I felt utterly useless and hated asking for more. I told her we had a banner at home, that it was a small tradition to hang it for each other's birthdays.

"I know it won't be much of a birthday, but at least it'll be something," I said.

"Of course," my sister-in-law responded, and came up with a plan. Vicky would synchronize everyone's arrival, get them to lure Adam out of the room, and she would slip in to decorate. We would have a surprise birthday party for my husband in Room 4.

I wondered how I'd feel for this party, being sewn together.

Chapter Twenty-Eight

Beyond a Ten

UCHealth, April 9 and 10, 2017

Leah heard about the surgery delay but still came by early on the morning of April 9. I'd woken up that morning fretting and agitated once again, thinking it wouldn't help to have a visitor see me in this state. As it happens, it was the exact opposite. I was happy to see a friendly face and relieved to have a distraction.

Leah sat on the edge of my hospital bed in the quiet of Room 4, with Adam on the chair in the corner. "I'm sorry you have to go through this," she said.

I tried to explain my uncertainty. "I'm not sure how I'll get through it," I said, "but anything to save my thumbs. It will be bizarre, but it won't be for that long." I attempted to sound optimistic, even though I knew I was trying to convince myself.

"Sorry, I don't have much to contribute—except my fears," I said. "But I'm so grateful that someone is willing to help. My doctor is amazing."

Leah and I were snuggled in my bed chatting when the nurses came in. It was time.

"I'll text Adam and figure out a time to return," Leah said.

Adam snapped a picture of us, and we hugged good-bye.

I was grateful for the presence of someone so close to me, someone gentle and kind. I'd woken up cranky and didn't want to have to be a certain way, put on a face, or pretend I was stronger than I felt. Leah came into my heavy situation and gave me love. I was able to receive it, take it into my heart, and be grateful for the distraction. I allowed myself to be uplifted instead of weighed down by fear, to be true to exactly how I felt, still loved even with my fears and ill temper. I thanked the heavens for such great friends.

I said good-bye to Adam in the OR prep cubical, and the Versed concoction took me away.

The next thing I remember is waking up back in Room 4 in the evening. Adam and Becca, the charge nurse, came into view. With my return to consciousness came more pain than I had experienced up to this point, or anticipated. It was excruciating and actually audible—a high-pitched tone. I could barely hear what the nurse was saying. Her words were distant and muffled. Eventually, I deciphered her words: "What are your pain levels on a scale from one to ten?" she asked.

"Ten," I answered, my voice strained, panicked, far away. "Beyond a ten."

Becca called another nurse into the room. "We need to set up a Dilaudid pump for Melissa," she said, and began gathering plastic tubes and IV bags filled with opiates.

Normally a patient can self-administer painkillers by pushing a button. My case was different, obviously. "She can't use her hands for this pump," Becca said, pausing. "Let's set it up for her foot."

After some rigging, they had a system that included tissue boxes and other items secured to the bed's footboard, stabilizing the pump and bringing it close enough that my foot could hit the button. Becca explained that I was already on Oxycodone, but that the Dilaudid should help to manage the pain.

I nodded, terrified, finding it hard to believe that anybody could manage the intensity of this pain. She sensed my distress and rested her hand on my shoulder. "This is what we are here for—we will help you get through. Now let's see if this works; if you are ready, hit the button with your foot."

I extended my foot, clad in a bright yellow hospital slipper sock with rubberized sole, the smiley face on top beaming at me. The tissue boxes gave way a bit, but the rigging worked.

Becca busied herself around the room, waiting for the meds to take effect. Within five or ten minutes I felt the edge coming off the pain. Gradually, the high-pitched ringing toned down and the agonizing distress became a bit more bearable.

I felt naive. Before the surgery, I'd never thought about a pain increase. I was obsessed with the idea of being sewn together. Up until now, the most noticeable thing about my pain management was discomfort while sleeping and nausea from the opiates. Now I looked down at my arms and saw a horror show. Bloodstained bandages covered the freshly amputated fingers. It was clear my damaged fingers were now much shorter. This view, and the stabbing pain, was a brutal reminder that Dr. Ignatiuk had cut away the exposed, burnt bones of my fingers.

Come on, Melissa. Didn't it occur to you that cutting your fingers off and sewing your arms together would hurt more?

My fingers were now of varying lengths, covered in Xeroform and gauze wrap, with little tubes of fabric on them that held the bandages underneath in place.

They kind of looked like finger puppets. Yep, the drugs were working.

I was in a reclined position on the bed. Nurse Becca had propped my folded arms on pillows to elevate them and have them rest on my chest. I wished I could avert my eyes but this gory reality was in my direct vision—and was not going away anytime soon. I looked over at my right thumb, now resting on the top side of my left forearm. The skin from my left forearm stretched away from my arm and was stitched into my right thumb just under the tip and nail. The flap encircled most of the thumb where the flesh had burnt away.

The exposed burnt bone was now nestled in a taco of tissue, facing away from my vision, with the nail bed toward me. I saw that my right middle finger was almost entirely missing, amputated at the base of the first knuckle. The palm burns were exposed and resting on my arm. My left thumb was on the back of my right forearm. The raised skin flap pulled away from my right arm, covering the charred left thumb bone. On this side, the skin flap did not attach as neatly to the thumb tip and nail as on the other side, since there was more damage and less material remaining to secure the flap. The taut pink flesh extended backward and away from its former home on my right arm and covered the left thumb. The thumb tip was adorned with various patterns of stitches under the thumbnail that faced me. The left digits also resembled bandaged little finger puppets, two of them shorter than before.

Becca popped back in and asked how the pain was.

"Still intense, but less searing," I said. I found Adam's eyes mirroring the pain I felt.

"Once we manage the pain, it will become much easier on you," Becca explained. "Anything else we can do to help this situation?" she asked.

Actually, there was. "Can you wrap an Ace bandage or something around my elbows? Something to secure my arms besides just my skin? I'm a really vivid dreamer, and I'm scared that I'll try to pull my arms apart in a nightmare."

She returned with a bandage and wrapped my arms as I'd requested.

"We are going to start you on Trazodone right now, to help you sleep, and to help with the anxiety of having your arms sewn together," Becca explained. I didn't protest.

When she left the room, I asked Adam what Trazodone was.

He looked it up and told me it was for anxiety, insomnia, depression, and more.

"Well, that makes sense," I responded.

I was completely drained after the eight-hour operation and the intense trauma to my body. Adam tried to get me to eat something.

"Just water—I am so thirsty," I said.

The day before, Charlie had come in with an inspired idea: a Camel-Bak hydration pack that he filled with water and hung on the IV rack. Now, Adam put the tube in my mouth, and after some coaxing, he got me to eat a few bites of homemade granola, sent from our friends Julie, Paul, and Aaron in Tahoe. "It arrived when you were in surgery," Adam said.

It was perfect, but after a few bites, I just wanted to sleep. Adam reclined my bed and ensured I could still reach the Dilaudid pump. I was uncomfortable and the skin began pulling as I reclined, gravity pulling my elbows toward the bed. I looked at him, panicked, and explained. He propped a pillow under each elbow, and I realized that this was as good as my sleeping situation was going to get. The readjusting caused more pain, and I pushed the pump.

And I thought the foam blocks were uncomfortable. This was going to be a long two weeks. Then I slept, thanks to all of the medication finally knocking me out.

I woke the next morning, April 10, feeling like I'd been in a train wreck.

Dr. Ignatiuk and the team stopped by to check out his handiwork, a teaching opportunity for his interns. The doctor snapped a few pictures documenting the work and the skin flap color.

I looked over at Adam when they left. "Happy birthday," I said weakly. "Just what you want to do to celebrate."

He chuckled. "How are you feeling?"

"Not so great," I confessed. "The pain is pretty bad."

"Hit the pump," he reminded me, putting my glasses on for me. I pressed the button, then asked, "Can you help me up to pee?" He raised the bed so I could sit up and throw my legs over the edge. Adam placed a steadying hand on my shoulder as my smiley-face feet found the floor and walked me and my IV to the bathroom.

I sat on the toilet and whimpered. "Good god, this is going to be hard."

Later that morning, nurses Anna and Tom came in.

"We're going to clean you up," Anna said. "But it won't be a shower just yet. Right now, we're going to clean your wounds in the tub room," she informed me.

The pain was so intense just lying there—I couldn't fathom what level of agony this would bring. *I'll know soon enough.*

Anna read my expression. "There are two of us. Tom is joining to manage pain, and I will irrigate the wounds."

After transferring me to the rubber gurney, they started the water flowing. I sat rigid from the pain, anticipating the forthcoming suffering. Tom began to explain what he was doing, step by step, which I took to be legal protocol. He narrated constantly as he opened the fentanyl, measured the dosage, and began the injection. All eyes settled on me, and we waited.

In minutes, I acknowledged that I could feel the powerful drug hitting me; an intense, warm, relaxing feeling flooded my entire being. My pain became distant, the anxiety drifted away, and I became less guarded. *This must be what heroin feels like,* I said to myself.

Anna started removing the finger-puppet gauze coverings. Water cascaded over my stretched-out skin flaps and freshly amputated, malformed nubs, with raw hunks of skin flapped over the ends. My body tensed as pain penetrated the mighty opiate.

I looked pathetically at Tom.

"Opening second vial of fentanyl and administering to the patient," he announced.

The pain was now remote enough to become tolerable. In that moment, I understood addiction. My heart broke, thinking of my brother. I felt the power of these opiates used for good—relief for patients like me and others in overwhelming pain. Simultaneously, I understood the fraudulent fleeting security they delivered—their horrible side, luring people in and robbing them of their essence, commandeering individuals, stealing them from their loved ones, and themselves.

Somehow I made it through the rest of the session and back to Room 4, utterly drained.

Adam's parents came later in the afternoon. After a few minutes of catching up, Charlie asked Adam to go downstairs with him to carry up some coffee and snacks. After Adam left, Cheryl texted Vicky, who appeared a few minutes later with her husband, Brian, and their youngest son, Aiden, carrying a bunch of balloons and a cake. They quickly hung the big Happy Birthday banner. Adam's forty-fifth surprise birthday party in the Burn ICU was ready.

"Thank you so much," I told his sweet and thoughtful family.

Adam was surprised, to be sure. Vicky told him it was all my idea. As exhausted as I was, I tried to stay present. Adam's mom reached into her walker, which also served as a front-row seat by my bed, and took out about twenty cards from her church friends, all of whom were ardently praying for my recovery. She read each one aloud, adding them to the growing collection tacked up on the wall across from my hospital bed. They fed me a couple of bites of cake that I was scarcely interested in, and the subdued celebration continued as I nodded off.

Chapter Twenty-Nine

Surf's Up
UCHealth, April 11 and 12, 2017

Gradually, I began to feel more like a human being than a science experiment or a phantasm by Mary Shelley, thanks to the hospital staff and the medication.

My second day with my arms sewn together began with wound cleaning and a dressing change performed by the plastic surgery team, this time in my hospital room. The pain was less overwhelming, which I was learning was a matter of proper pain management. The pump was still at the foot of my bed, and the Dilaudid sufficed for wound care. A nurse's aide taped a plastic bag around my arms, under my armpits and above my elbows, covering my IV port, skin flaps, and hands, then carefully showered me. Afterward, I felt clean, refreshed, and thankful.

Adam was planning to resume a version of his former life. His commute to work—Aurora to Estes Park, 80 miles—would start the next day.

"It'll be fine," he told me. "I'll leave super early tomorrow, go do a few estimates, meet with the crew. Plus, I'll help with a tree removal. Then I'll go home, shower, and get the stuff from the house, and come back here. I'll be back in time for dinner. I can do this for a few days until Bronson gets here."

Before the tethering surgery, I'd thought that having anyone stay over was unnecessary; there was a capable team of nurses and a student nurse available twenty-four hours a day. I had been feeling guilty about the sacrifices people were making for me. After the surgery, however, I knew it was necessary. I feared being alone.

I was so grateful to Adam, and a little apprehensive about him starting his commute.

"I need to get a few things done while you're here today," I said. My brain moved slowly on opiates, so I had to take advantage of my helper while I had him. "First, let's Skype my parents," I said. We talked with them almost daily, but this would be a business call.

We called, and they told me the bank had finalized the loan papers last week. They had FedExed the documents back to the Bank of Colorado.

"We just got a call from Frank at the bank—they got the paperwork," Dad said.

My mom sat beside him at the kitchen table. "His name is Phil," she reminded him.

"Phil, Frank—either way, he got the papers," Dad said.

I thanked them for rescuing the loan situation.

"It's okay. You just focus on healing up and getting that restaurant going," Dad said. "This isn't a gift, it's a loan."

"I know," I said, "and I will, Dad, no problem." I chuckled a bit. "We will open the second we get inspected. I'm going to call the contractor next."

I told them that our chef, Ethan; our wine director and manager, John; and our whiskey expert and bar manager, Jimmy, would be at the hospital the next day to get on the same page with me and review our to-do list. Adam had helped me schedule appointments to look at point-of-sales programs, the system we'd use to enter orders and process customers' checks.

It sounded ambitious to my parents.

"I figured I might as well. I have time on my hands," I said, realizing my awkward choice of phrase.

"Make sure you take care of yourself," my mother said, and I promised I would.

The next call was to the bank to get the contractor a check for the past week of work.

Then Adam called the contractor, and put me on speaker.

There were niceties—"Glad you're alive"—followed by an admission: "I was unsure of what was going on with you in the hospital."

"I can imagine," I replied. "Which is why I wanted to call you and talk. No matter what is going on with me, we are moving forward with the restaurant, and I want to make sure you know that. I have a check waiting for you to pick up at the Bank of Colorado to keep construction going."

He sounded relieved, about me and the work. "Don't worry about us," he said, "just take care of yourself." I assured him I would, adding, "Keep going on the restaurant. There's no time to delay if we're opening in June." I tried to sound as positive as possible, to fuel him—and me.

"When will you be out of the hospital?" he asked.

"We're not sure yet," I said. "But I'm just a phone call away—someone will be picking up calls for me."

Just then my phone buzzed with an incoming call.

Adam ended the call and picked up the next, putting it on speaker.

"Hi, this is Kevin Sturmer with the climbing rangers." It was my volunteer supervisor and lead climbing ranger at Rocky Mountain National Park. Hearing a familiar voice say the word "climbing" made me freeze and choke up. In my mind, the door to the closet in my mind blew open and the lid flew off the trunk that held my climbing heart, and hopes.

"Hi, Kevin," I said, my voice thick.

"I just wanted to call and let you know we are all thinking of you," he said. "We hope you'll be home soon."

I managed to thank him, but I was crumbling inside. Thankfully, the call was brief, but as I was saying good-bye, all of my uncertainties about climbing again tumbled out.

"Save my spot," I said, my voice cracking. "I'll be back."

Adam hung up the phone, got me a tissue, and wiped my eyes.

"That was really nice of them to call," I said. Then, "I need to blow, please," and he held the tissue up to my nose.

"We really need to work on this nose-blowing part," I said, smeared in snot, but still grateful for the help.

I allowed myself a brief moment to think about climbing. *Maybe, just maybe, one day I might be able to climb some simple warm-ups.* That tiny thread of hope, plus my climbing memories, added to my net, keeping me out of the abyss of despair. In this way, I could pour everything I had into recovery. I told myself not to, but I needed to hope, but not to obsess—especially looking at the bloody shambles of my hands.

I shut the lid on the trunk for now, keeping the tiny light of hope in my heart.

On the third day following surgery, April 12, I awoke relieved to feel less pain. My body was beginning to adjust to the discomfort and binding. But the anxiety was high as Adam got ready for his two-hour commute. I tried to show independence by sitting up in bed using my core muscles, swinging my legs over the edge and jumping up.

"Look at you!" Adam said.

I allowed myself a little pride at this small accomplishment, but reality promptly returned. "Will you put my glasses on me? I can't see." I then pushed the bathroom door open with my butt. "Will you brush my teeth?" Of course he would, Adam said. "But I have to go," he reminded me. "Well, I have to pee first." He brushed my teeth and then stood by to dutifully wipe me. "Okay, I am out of here," he said. "I'll be back tonight."

"Wait," I said. "Can you just put in my contact lenses, please?"

Adam replied in a mild voice, "Ask one of the nurses to do it."

I understood he needed to go and was trying to wean me off of him as direct caregiver, but I felt frustrated and lost.

"No," I said, and tried to explain that I didn't want to bother them—I had my glasses—"but I want them in because I can see better."

Adam remained adult—"Then just wear your glasses"—while I responded as my six-year-old self: "I don't want to. They're not the right prescription, and I hate them!"

"Melissa," he said, "I have to drive two hours to work, go to work, and then come back. I've got to go." I knew he meant business when he addressed me as "Melissa" instead of his usual "Baby."

My bottom lip quivered as anger and frustration welled up. But I had no argument. I stifled any other words I wanted to say, reminding myself how good he had been to me.

"I love you," he said. "My parents will be here later this morning—you won't be alone."

"I just want my contacts in," I whimpered.

We both knew that turbulent emotions and a surplus of fears, frustration, and anxiety were behind this outburst that had focused on contact lenses.

"I love you," he repeated, kissing my forehead, and the door shut behind him. "I love you too," I said hoping he heard it.

Cheryl and Charlie came in as promised, wanting to ensure I was okay on my first day without Adam. They also had a long drive to get to me, a little over an hour, depending on traffic coming from Colorado Springs.

"How was it, your first morning without Adam?" Cheryl asked.

I confessed it was a bit stressful. "I know he had to leave, but I just wanted my contacts in," I added pathetically.

Cheryl offered to help.

"Have you ever put contacts in?" I asked.

"No, but how hard can it be?"

After several failed attempts and a fingernail jab to the eyeball, we aborted the mission.

"It's okay," I said. "It's hard enough to put them in your own eyes, let alone someone else's."

"If you want your contacts in, you should have them in," Cheryl said, and went out to the nurses' station.

"No, it's okay," I repeated, but she was already on her way.

I hated bothering the nurses with so many burn patients in need, but soon, a nurse came in happily. "This will be a first for me, but I can try," she said, and within a minute, I could see clearly.

"Mission accomplished," Cheryl said, and told the nurse, "If you can put that on the list for the mornings, that would be helpful for Melissa."

Adam returned later than expected. "Traffic was a bitch—I don't know how all of these people do it on a daily basis."

"Well, good news for you," I said. "Jennifer texted earlier that she would spend tomorrow night with me. Your parents were kind enough to read the text. And Bronson's coming the night after that."

He fed me dinner as we caught up on each other's day. Later, he was opening mail and paying bills on his computer—which used to be my job—when he announced, "We got a bill for your helicopter ride."

"Yeah? How much was it?"

"Thirty-four thousand," he answered.

"Are you kidding me? They know we have insurance, right?"

"How do I know," Adam said. "They're sending us the bill."

"Promise me you'll call them tomorrow on your lunch break and let them know."

"Okay, I will," he replied. "Don't worry about this stuff right now."

Even though we had insurance, I feared things would not get covered and somehow fall through the cracks.

After opening a few more envelopes, Adam looked up at me. "I was thinking," he said. "Maybe we can take up surfing."

"What are you talking about?" I said. I was stunned. This was a man who hated water so much that we could spend a week on the islands and he'd never enter the ocean, or the pool. "You hate the water," I said.

"I know." He shrugged. "I was just thinking it might be something fun we could do."

I saw what Adam was doing. He was mentally planning for a future with me that didn't involve climbing. Instead of lamenting that I might never climb again, he was looking ahead to a resolution.

"That might be fun," I said.

Internally, I quietly took out the climbing trunk from the closet in my mind and peeked in, wondering.

Dare I hope? I shut the lid. *Maybe Adam is on to something. Surfing, eh? I couldn't see it.*

Chapter Thirty

Snap On

UCHealth, April 13 and 14, 2017

"Knock, knock," said a quiet voice at the doorway later in the afternoon. It was Jonna, my friend and coworker from the Dunraven. She came in smiling, but hesitant.

"I've been wanting to come in to see you, but also wanted to give you time and space after this latest surgery."

I smiled back and welcomed her in. She represented a huge aspect of the life I'd abruptly left—my job at the Dunraven. We caught up a bit, me talking about basic functioning and Jonna telling me about our friends back in Estes.

Then she grabbed her bag and said, beaming, "I have a present for you."

She took out four T-shirts.

"I was talking with Andrea about your surgery and your concerns about not being able to get dressed or go outside," she said. Like so many of us, Jonna was an outdoor enthusiast, and thoroughly understood my need to be outside of the hospital, even if I was trapped in an urban setting and not playing in the mountains. Just being in the air, among the trees on campus, helped. She had visited prior to the *I Dream of Jeannie* surgery and compassionately listened to my lament about not being able to wear clothes after this tethering.

Now she shook out one of the shirts. "We came up with this idea from her daughter's baby clothes—the onesies with snaps on top of the arms," she said. "I went to Target and got her some T-shirts, and she turned them into this," she said, holding it up for inspection. "They have snaps on the tops of the shoulders and sleeves so you can wear them while your arms are sewn together."

I was blown away. My smile turned to laughter and then to tears.

"Saved from the tube top, which never would have worked!" I said. I was choking up, thinking about how my distress had reached friends in Estes Park, then rebounded back as love to the hospital in the form of a brilliant solution. The care and thoughtfulness were overwhelming.

"Well, let's try one out," I said, overjoyed.

Jonna put pants on me and unsnapped the buttons that ran along the shoulders of the shirt from the neck to the ends of the short sleeves, creating an open tube of fabric. We found it easier if I stepped into the open shirt. Next, she pulled it up over my chest and carefully under my folded arms, securing the snaps on either side of my neck to the end of the short sleeves.

Just then another friend, Jennifer, showed up to spend the afternoon and night with me, giving Adam his first night off from hospital duty since the accident, eleven days prior.

"Perfect timing, Jen. Look at these fantastic shirts Jonna brought for me," I said. "Let's go outside! I saw some banners about an art exhibit on campus. It shouldn't be too difficult to find."

Jonna and Andrea delivered so much happiness through these shirts. The kindness, the concern, the creativity, and then the construction. I was bursting with happiness. Their empathy and effort were *literal* fabric for the webbing that would keep me sane. It would hold me up, carry me through, and bestow the gift of feeling human, able to go outside and be among other humans. I still felt self-conscious and fragile, walking around with my arms sewn together by skin flaps. But I was on a medical campus, as safe as possible, I reminded myself as we walked through the doors into another beautiful day.

Proudly wearing my snappy new shirt, Jen, Jonna, and I made our way to the art exhibit. It was a short walk from the Inpatient Pavilion to a place called the Fulginiti Pavilion for Bioethics and Humanities, a newish building fronted by a spacious lawn. I had no idea what would be in this exhibit, but it was an outing.

Snap On

We walked into the gallery and I was utterly floored. Was this for real?

The cerulean walls were filled with masterpieces—Renoir, Cassatt, Degas. There was a Matisse; a Monet over there, a Chagall on that wall. Twenty paintings in all, plus a Rodin sculpture. *Is that a Picasso? Yes!*

Wait, these aren't reproductions, are they? No—they're the real deal, each and every one. What are they doing at a medical center? I would learn they were on loan from the collection of Morton Mower, a renowned cardiologist, and his wife, Tobia. Highlights from their art collection were on display for anyone looking for escape, for enjoyment, for emotional sustenance.

The three of us were enthralled, drifting apart in a daze and standing before each piece of art, soaking in these masterpieces from inches away. The wonders continued: Léger, Legrand, Morisot, Pissarro, Sisley, Soutine. The exhibit was public but felt very personal, like a private affair. We were the only people in the place apart from a security guard near the entrance.

After a while, we stood together, shaking our heads in wonder. Jennifer asked me if I'd seen the Matisse. "The sketch—did you notice?"

"Notice what?" I said.

She took out her phone and beckoned me toward a black-and-white drawing.

"Stand here so I can take your picture," she said.

I walked toward it, curious. Oh, wow. It dawned on me just as Jennifer was saying "She's in the same position that you are—arms crossed!"

She was right. "Oh, that *is* funny," I said. "I didn't even notice."

The woman's arms were folded across her torso, like me, like the TV Jeannie, except this woman had no shirt on. I leaned toward the label on the wall: *Seated Woman Arms Crossed*, 1925. I turned toward Jennifer with a smile. "You could unsnap my shirt to look even more like her," I joked as Jennifer took the photo.

Other works hit me differently.

"I love the Renoirs," I said, walking over to a painting of a woman holding her napping infant, after breastfeeding. The woman—*The Young Mother*, the title said—looked at her child adoringly. My heart ached, thinking of our fertilized egg that never made it. I was also reminded how much more challenging my condition would be if we'd had a baby.

"Renoir always reminds me of my mother," I told my friends. "When we were kids, she let me and my sister skip a school day to take us to a Renoir exhibit at the Gardner Museum in Boston. Such a special day."

Jennifer nodded, then pointed at the painting. "Look at the light, and the print on the fabric of her dress," she said. These were small yet stunning details I hadn't noticed. I thought to myself: I am going to have a lot of time to examine details like this, to shift my focus from objects and go deeper, into the brushstrokes.

"I like this Monet," Jonna said, as we moved toward *River and Mill Near Giverny*.

"I love how you can see a breeze with the movement of the trees," I said.

Jonna said, "That footpath looks like a nice place to walk." I agreed.

A Degas caught our attention: *Woman at Her Toilette*, an intimate pastel and charcoal of a woman at a basin, washing. "I love *The House in the Woods*," I said, nodding at a Pissarro. "It looks like a pleasant place to pass time."

One thing was for sure: This small gallery was a nice place to be.

"I cannot believe this is here—it's so wonderful!" I exclaimed once we'd left the gallery. "I'm going to come back every day." There were booklets at the exit. "Can I have one?" I asked a man standing there. He hesitated and held out a brochure and we both awkwardly realized I couldn't take it from him. I smiled and turned to Jen, who acted as my hands.

Back in the hospital room, looking over the brochure, Jen told me she thought we were supposed to pay for it.

I laughed, saying, "No wonder he was looking at me funny—I thought it was the arms."

Jen read from the brochure about Toby and Mort Mower, who had moved in retirement from Baltimore to Denver. "He co-invented an implantable defibrillator," she read. "They insist on living with their acquisitions," she read, so they could have continual contact with the art. "The Mowers aren't especially interested in filling warehouses with exquisite trophies that go unseen and unappreciated.'"*

"Wow," I said. "Imagine how incredible it would be to live with masterpieces in your house. I wonder if they just sit and stare, or if they get used to them."

"And which one is hung in the bathroom?" Jen joked.

Then it occurred to me: "In a way, I'll get to live with them for a while."

Jonna and Jen said they'd be back and would happily return to the exhibit with me.

I felt so lucky. What a treat—a five-minute walk to spend time with these masterworks each day while I was here, with or without visitors. Oddly, I'd been feeling bad for people who'd been coming to visit me— the long drive, and then just sitting in a hospital room with nothing to look at but me, in my state of disrepair. Now I had something to offer in return.

And I was thrilled to wear my new snap T-shirts, which enabled me to escort visitors to my secret world-class art museum. This privilege resonated deeply. The art gave me something to do, to look forward to. It helped me feel like an ordinary person, among everyday people living life, pausing to enjoy beautiful artwork. Sure, my arms appeared oddly crossed under the Ace bandage wrapped around my elbows, and my finger-puppet family was on stark display. But when I looked at the art, my arms and hands, and woes, briefly disappeared.

Every second my uncertain fate weighed heavy upon me. Daily, someone from Plastics changed my bandages. I couldn't avoid seeing the fingers disrobed, the bloody mess, the odd shapes created with each amputation, and the random pieces of salvageable skin flapped over the nubs. With each dressing change, they checked my thumb tips for life. The right thumb progressed well, pleasing us all. The team kept a close eye on the left thumb that had suffered more damage yet was showing signs of life, giving us all hope.

---

* For a scan of the pamphlet, visit https://www.melissaistrong.com/art.

Being able to take my walk and immerse myself in the profound beauty of the art helped to shift my focus beyond my temporarily small world, alleviating my fears and anxieties, even if just for a short time. The art transported me from my gruesome reality, thrusting beauty into my personal horror show, while at the same time, weaving distinctive threads into my safety net. By immersing myself in beauty, I opened up to strength. What a gift!

In subsequent years, I was twice transported back to these healing moments gifted through art. The first happened in 2018 when the Denver Art Museum hosted an exhibit called Her Paris: Women Artists in the Age of Impressionism, which I attended with my friends Jen, Marsha, Kathleen, and Quinn.

I turned a corner and *Bam!* I was stopped short by a familiar painting of a young girl, dressed in blue, in a blue room, seated at the piano, looking serious and somewhat melancholy. It was *Lucie Léon at the Piano*, by Berthe Morisot, one of the paintings that had been at the hospital exhibit.

"Marsha, I remember you saying it looked like the girl was pouting," I said, "being forced into practicing, as if it was the last thing she wanted to do."

"I remember," Marsha confirmed, "and it really does."

Seeing it now was unsettling. Facing this painting out of the hospital setting rattled me deeply. It had once helped me heal, but now it transported me back to the pain and uncertainty of nine months and four surgeries ago. I allowed this vulnerability to wash over me. I challenged this sorrow by welcoming it as a memory.

Around the next corner, I found my friends standing before another painting we all remembered from the hospital exhibit: *Woman with a Fan*, by Mary Cassatt. We took pictures and visited with our old friend, and instead of clinging to the sadness I initially felt, I pivoted to embrace a chord of profound strength and the healing progress I'd made since my hospital days.

The second encounter happened in 2019 in a sea of 120 Monets at a Denver Art Museum exhibition called Claude Monet: The Truth of

Nature. This time I revisited *River and Mill Near Giverny*. Instead of feeling vulnerable, I instantly felt the warmth of a loving hug.

This Monet seemed to greet me and say *I see you. I see how far you have come.* It saw the strength I'd gained—tall and strong like the poplars that lined the river. I took a deep breath and thanked my old friend, for being there for me, for distracting me from pain and sadness, for allowing me to see beyond myself and my misery, for letting me live in its restful landscape. And for reminding me that life is beautiful.

I caught up with the others. "Did you notice the Monet from the hospital?" I asked.

They had.

This intimate connection with the paintings will be with me forever as threads of beauty, of other worlds, of history and appreciation. Countless times over the years, I've silently thanked the Mowers for letting me live with their paintings. I never met them, but when I read that Dr. Mower died in 2022, I welled up and thought of his widow with gratitude.

During my time at the hospital, I never tired of the exhibit, nor did my friends. The day after I'd first visited, I returned with Bronson.

"Melissa, that Matisse drawing looks like you, with her arms crossed!" she said.

I laughed and agreed, posing for another picture with *Seated Woman Arms Crossed*.

CHAPTER THIRTY-ONE

Spinning My Wheels
UCHealth, Mid-April, 2017

THANKS TO THE OVERNIGHTS BY JENNIFER AND BRONSON, ADAM was able to spend his first nights in Estes, giving him a reprieve from hospital life and letting him go back to work, and to live—including going climbing. Just because I couldn't did not mean he had to stop.

Others visited daily. I was surprised by each new face and blown away by the benevolent and thoughtful nature of everyone. Mary Ellen, a longtime Dunraven customer who became a friend to all of Estes with her charming husband Walt, showed up, saying, "I don't have a lot going on, so I'm happy to keep you company." She was so helpful. She dialed numbers for me, fed me, navigated the computer, met my parents via Skype, and helped me accomplish tasks for building the new restaurant. Then Brooke, a local business owner and esthetician, showed up, saying, "I thought you could use a facial."

"I cannot believe this," I said, overwhelmed by their compassion. After my facial, we all walked over to the gallery. It was a hot day, and I was wiped out by evening. After dinner, Bronson and I settled in to watch a movie, but first I told the nurse about some terrible itching under my Ace wraps. Upon inspection, it was just a heat rash, and she gave me a Benadryl.

"Are you sure I'm not going to overdose with all of these drugs?" I asked, playful, yet laced with a bit of concern.

She reassured me, quipping, "We also have Narcan, so don't worry."

The Benadryl conked me out fifteen minutes into the movie. Adam called while I was asleep. Bronson asked if she should wake me. "No, don't bother. Just tell her I called, and that I love her."

The next day, Dr. Navin Ganesh, a future cardiologist on rounds with Plastics, changed my bandages and inspected my thumbs. The dressing changes were still painful, and the nurses tried to time my pain meds to precede wound cleaning. I no longer needed the Dilaudid pump, as oxycodone was managing the pain. The timing was challenging, since we never knew precisely when the doctors would show up. The doctors on rounds recorded notes such as, "Hands wrapped in gauze and Ace wrap, crossed across chest with bilateral pedicled forearm flaps to bilateral thumbs, left thumb improving, flap intact."

When Dr. Ganesh asked me how I was passing the time, I told him about my visitors, the art exhibit, the long-distance restaurant work. I mentioned that Lisa and my Dunraven friend/boss Andy would be coming by later that day.

"Well, I guess *former* boss," I said, "since I probably won't be going back to the restaurant I worked at before the accident."

"Oh?" he asked.

"The next time I go to work, I will be at my own restaurant."

As I talked about hospital life, and the walks to the exhibit, he said, "Some days I practically live here, not finishing up until midnight. Since I have to be back at four a.m., I stay on campus rather than go home. But I found an exercise bike on the sixth floor in the waiting room to get some movement in."

"Wow, those are some long days," I said, then asked, "Do you think it would be okay if I tried to ride the bike, like this?" I added, nodding at my hands.

He cocked his head and shrugged. "As long as you're careful, it would probably be good for you, especially since you were so active before."

"The sixth floor?" I asked.

"Yeah. I wish I could tell you where—it's a maze. You'll have to walk around and look for a waiting room that overlooks the entrance."

I told him I'd check it out the next day, excited to add more movement to my long days. I wondered how it'd work with my arms sewn together.

That evening, Saturday, April 15—thirteen days after the accident, and six days after being sewn together—I felt more confident about being alone (with an entire team of nurses and aides). I discovered that I had one usable finger—my right index finger. I could tilt my arms, pointing my right elbow up in the air, which directed my right index finger down, and I could use that finger to navigate the computer keyboard. This finger's only visible damage was a burnt circle on the tip where the bone had started to burn. The left index finger had lost skin from the middle of the fingertip to the palm and was less user-friendly.

I used my computer independently for the first time that day, quite an improvement from when my hands were bandaged separately. The touchscreen of my phone did not respond well to the large round scab, but with persistency, I could create a short text or make a call. I laughed. Using one finger on a keyboard was massive progress toward a little independence.

I told the night nurse of my plan to try the stationary bike the next day.

"Did you run that by Dr. Ignatiuk?" she asked, wisely.

"Good point," I acknowledged. "I'll text him."

She gave me a sideways look. "Text him?"

"Yeah, he put his number on my phone and told me to text him with any questions or concerns."

She was surprised. "Wow, that's great. I've never seen a doctor give out his cell number."

I texted Ignatiuk and got two thumbs-up emojis in reply.

(The next time he saw me, he looked tickled. "Did you get it? Did you *get* my text?" he said. "Two thumbs up—that's what we are creating, two thumbs for you." I laughed, assuring him the emojis did not go over my head.)

The nurse returned to the room and I showed off my handiwork, navigating my phone with one index finger.

"Looks like you are cleared," she said. "I'll make a note for the others and let them know so they can dress you and get you ready in the morning."

I was excited and scared, ready to at least try to find the bike and look it over.

The next morning, April 16, the nurses dressed me, brushed my teeth, put in my contacts, put my hair in a ponytail, administered my meds, and sent me off for my big stationary bike adventure.

At the elevator, I utilized the newfound power of my one index finger and pressed the "up" button. On the sixth floor I wandered in circles, on the hunt for this elusive waiting room and its exercise bike. I wondered if someone would question me as I repeatedly walked by patients' rooms and nurses' stations. But with my arms tethered and wrapped, I guess I didn't look out of place. Corridors and blocks of rooms that resembled each other kept me wandering.

After a length of time, I looked down a long, narrow waiting room lined with glass and saw, at the far end, two ancient stationary bikes. I was thankful no one else was in the room, so I didn't have to explain myself.

I approached the bikes and chose the one that looked like I could rest my arms on the handlebars. *I guess this could work.* I kicked off my clogs, thinking barefoot would be better, straddled the bike and rested my arms, then inched my butt back to touch the seat. *Okay, you're doing this.* As my feet found the pedals, I suddenly wished that someone else were in the room in case I fell.

I started pedaling, slowly. An Atari-like screen came to life as red bulbs lit up, indicating my movement and the basic resistance setting. I tried to hit some buttons with my right index finger, but extending and tilting my arms threw me off balance. *Just keep pedaling,* I told myself, and I did. I had no idea how much time passed. It wasn't a real cardio workout, but I moved, I broke a sweat, and I felt my blood pumping. I stared down at my thumbs and willed the blood to flow into the tips.[*]

Back in my room, a nurse greeted me with a paper cup full of pain meds, and my friend Mary Ellen was there.

"So I have news," the nurse announced. "You are going to have to move."

"Move?" I asked, unsure of what she was talking about.

---

[*] In 2023, after I spoke at the Evo sporting goods company, a man stood up to say he'd worked at UCHealth Anschutz when I was there. "Most everyone in the hospital knew who you were, or knew of you—the patient with her arms sewn together, riding a bike. You were a hospital legend."

"You're getting more independent, and we need the ICU beds," she explained patiently. "We called upstairs, and they have room for you on the seventh floor."

I was surprised, but understood that new burn patients needed ICU care more than I did at this point.

"Okay, I get it," I said. "You all are just so great . . . I'm afraid to start all over with another team."

She assured me there were great nurses throughout the hospital. "We let them know about your unique situation."

I felt a swirl of emotions, from fear of change to abandonment. I had grown secure with this team and felt like I was getting kicked out, even though I knew this was irrational.

"Any suggestions on how to move all of this stuff?" I asked. I'd accumulated countless cards, flowers, and items from home.

The nurse looked at Mary Ellen and said, "I'll get you a cart."

I told Mary Ellen how glad I was that she'd chosen to visit that day. "I truly need a set of hands. I'm sorry this is falling on you," I said.

"Happy to help," Mary Ellen said, and began gathering up the items.

She loaded up the cart and then unloaded my belongings—and me—into Room 765.

I met Grace, the charge nurse for my wing. Mary Ellen sensed my fragile state and told Grace, "With no notice, this is a little jarring for Melissa."

"I understand entirely," Grace said. "Melissa is going through a lot, but she will be more comfortable on the seventh floor with us. It's less noisy and hectic than the ICU. And there's a much better view."

I instantly realized I had a new caring team member—and friend—in Grace. And she was right: There was much less whirling, buzzing, and ringing. The wall was solid, not glass, and I had a door that shut. This change came just as I was learning to adapt, and I was a bit fearful. But the collectedness and motherly nature of Mary Ellen and Grace soothed me; more layers for my safety net.

And indeed, there was a lovely view out the large window, north and west to the gleaming peaks of the Rocky Mountains that cradled my home, Estes Park.

Chapter Thirty-Two

Straitjacket
UCHealth, April 17–20, 2017

The door clanged shut, echoing off the concrete.

Oh, crap. I was trapped in the hospital stairwell with no hands to open the door.

This wasn't how the day was supposed to go. I'd awakened that morning excited to ride. I'd set out from my new room on the seventh floor and walked down the hall, taking in the quiet morning scene. I realized I'd been silly to be afraid of leaving the ICU. My morning ablutions had gone easily; the aide nailed my contact lenses, and the nursing staff was less harried.

I'll take the stairs today, I'd told myself when I reached the elevator. The door to the stairwell was a push bar—perfect, I thought. I turned my rear end toward the door and pushed it open with my hip. Quite pleased with myself—stairs could be another little daily workout—I heard the door shut behind me with solid finality. *Click.*

Turning quickly I looked at the door and—uh-oh—there was no push bar on this.

Okay, then. Don't freak out.

I walked down the stairs to the sixth floor and weighed my options: wait for someone to come along, holler for help, or try to open this door. It had a lever-style handle, not a knob, which was great, as I had no hands to grasp and turn one.

I approached the door, placed my elbow on the handle, and tried to push it down to disengage the latch. No go. *Even if I turned the handle all the way, there was no way I could pull the door. That's all right. Someone will come along eventually.* I coached myself away from panic.

Minutes passed, then I heard a door shut a few floors below, and the chatter of voices. I moved as quickly as I dared down the steps to catch these people as they reentered the building. Not wanting to explain my situation, I followed them through the doorway as nonchalantly as possible. So much for taking the stairs.

I used my magic finger to press the elevator button, exiting at the sixth floor. I looked for the bike again and was vaguely alarmed at how difficult it was. My foggy brain wasn't retaining directions. I stood in a glass hallway, knowing I'd been there before but having no recollection of where to turn. I eventually found the bike and did a careful, slow workout.

When I returned to my room, I was sweaty and pleased that I'd gotten my heart rate up and been able to take some angst out on the bike. A nurse was there with my medication.

"Is this required?" I asked, referring to the pain meds.

She shook her head no. "You are an at-will patient," she said. This was a new term to me. "You can have more medication, or less—it's up to you."

In that case . . . "Less, please. I feel like I'm undoing anything good I may have done on the bike if I take medication after. My brain is like molasses, and I'm tired of being so foggy. I have to look for the bike every day."

The nurse said she'd make a note of my request. "We will bring the dosage down. Just let us know how you are doing with the pain."

I was fully with the program, eager to do whatever I was told. I'd never thought about asking for fewer pain meds. And up until the last few days, the pain had made this inconceivable. I was hyperaware of opiates and feared them, knowing that similar pills had ensnared my brother. The idea of lower dosages thrilled me.

I decided to wean myself off medication with the goal of being opiate-free before leaving the hospital. That was pretty ambitious, since I had another extensive surgery in my near future—my initial two weeks of the bilateral flaps and the "Jeannie" pose were coming to an end on April 23. There would be more pain, more trauma. The plan was to separate the bilateral flaps, use the skin to create thumbs, and take donor skin from various places of my body to reconstitute my palms and fingers.

But when Dr. Ignatiuk stopped by on April 18, a couple days after I'd moved to Room 765, he had discouraging news. My left thumb wasn't progressing as well as he'd hoped. (The notes from Dr. Ganesh said it looked "dark, dusky.") Dr. Ignatiuk wanted to wait and monitor it, potentially adding more time before the next surgery—meaning I'd be stuck in my tethered state longer than expected.

The *I Dream of Jeannie* pose was becoming a straitjacket. Even though I was using all of my mental net to remain positive, I was truly looking forward to getting out of this position and seeing how my hands were doing. The extended sentence and the darkening of the left thumb tip left me crestfallen. In addition, my shoulders were killing me from sleeping with my arms crossed; my body had grown weary of this prescribed hunched position. Still, I knew I had no choice—I told myself I'd made it this far, and could handle what lay ahead.

Walking back from the bike the next day, I felt more mentally alert with the lower opiate dosage. The movement and exercise was a new way of adding to my net. I felt privileged to have such great care, to be able to move, to enjoy the art exhibit, and to receive support from the community. The steady stream of visitors continued, including a friend who pedaled next to me on the second bike. Others dashed from the airport during layovers to visit, or took breaks from their business meetings in Denver to stop by. Gifts accumulated: healing stones and crystals, chocolates, flowers, and cards took over the counters and windowsills in Room 765.

With all of these external blessings, I resolved to do my part, to open my heart and stay positive, and allow these increasingly strong cords of support to keep me out of the pit. Did I think about never climbing again? Of course, daily. But I acknowledged the fears and then put them away. I also couldn't help but imagine working in my new restaurant, struggling to function with my disfigured hands, alarming customers when delivering food or drinks. These were heartbreaking, distressing thoughts, and each day, I closed the lids to these fears.

I had an acquaintance, Fanny, who had unique insight into my plight. She was the wife of one of our guides in Hueco Tanks, part of our Wagon Wheel guiding business, and a master prosthetic maker. In a phone call, I explained the stress I was feeling about my hands—both the physical limitations I would face, and the apprehension about having my disfigurement on display in the restaurant. I asked her about prosthetic fingers. She was thoughtful and kind, explaining that prosthetic fingers wouldn't provide the stability I'd need. She encouraged me to accept my new hands and assured me that people would be empathetic.

I was sure she was right. This had been a revelation in my new life—people were generous, kind, wonderful. This horrible accident had opened my eyes to the compassionate world around me, the friends, family, medical saviors, and total strangers who kept me going.

Later on, I would have a chance to review my medical records. A late April entry from Helen Lim, a member of the inpatient support staff, gave me a sense of how I appeared to others:

> *Pt [Patient] states that she feels "grateful" for the medical care and support that her friends, family, and community at Estes Park have provided. Pt believes that she may be here for another 2–3 weeks, and is trying to not "predict or know" what life will be like after her hands have healed from surgeries. Pt anticipates that she will have to be open to "new hobbies" and "new ways of doing things," and expressed that her injuries still feel "surreal." Pt states that she has been "taking showers every day, exercising on the stationary bike every morning, and appreciating the art exhibit in the old part of the hospital" to manage her mood. Pt was also actively sending emails on her laptop and waiting for a conference call during session as she works from the hospital to continue opening her restaurant.*

Grateful is right.

One day, passing the room next door, I overheard an older woman say, "But I can't afford the $20 Medicaid charge for the walker." It seemed the social worker was telling her the fee couldn't be waived, but that she needed a walker before she was sent home.

When a nurse came into my room later to help me clean up, I brought up Medicaid and asked if the hospital takes everyone, even without insurance. She said yes, the hospital takes all patients. Knowing this made me feel better. I'd felt fortunate to have a private room and such an elite level of care, and was thankful to learn this was available to all.

That afternoon, Vicky came to visit.

"Vicky, do you have twenty dollars I could borrow?" I asked.

She reached for her wallet without hesitation. "Can I ask what you need it for?" It wasn't like I was going to shop at the gift store.

"Yes, and I need your help too," I said, telling her what I'd heard earlier.

We went to the next room; the door was still open, and I asked if we could come in.

"Sure," said the voice I'd heard earlier.

I quickly explained what I'd overheard, not wanting to be too intrusive. "If it's okay, we would like to help with the twenty dollars." I knew I was catching this woman off guard and didn't want to offend her, but she smiled and said, "Well, isn't that nice of you? Thank you." Not a big deal by any stretch, but something small I could do, with Vicky's help, to share some of the love and support I'd received.

After the bike the next morning, I kicked a towel to the floor of my room, spread it out with my feet, and started to do some sit-ups.

In the midst of my workout, Dr. Seth—member of the Plastics team, and fellow climber—came in to change my dressings. (We'd tried to switch to the nursing team for this task, but the experienced regulars on rotation were quicker. Plus, they were "voluntold" by Ignatiuk, knowing they would get a close look at my hands and report back to him.)

Dr. Seth looked down at me. "Are you doing sit-ups?"

"Yeah, almost done," I replied. "I assumed it was okay since I'm riding the stationary bike."

He smiled and said, "Of course it is. You're probably the healthiest person in the hospital."

I finished my sit-ups and shrugged. "It's not much compared to before," I said, "but it helps me stay as positive as possible."

That afternoon I met Liesl and Becky outside and got to see my sweet thirteen-year-old white Lab, Cassidy. She was notorious for giving me the cold shoulder whenever I returned from an absence, and true to form, she turned away when she saw me that first time.

"It's all right," I told my friends, who were surprised at her behavior.

I bent down and let her smell my arms. After a few sniffs, she understood that her mom was not on holiday, but something bigger was happening. She nuzzled my leg and leaned into me. We walked her around campus, and she was allowed to join us when we visited the art exhibit.

Chapter Thirty-Three

Paws Before Hands

UCHealth, Late April and Early May, 2017

As compliant a patient as I was, I was also human. The days continued to pass slowly. Adam would come down periodically. Some days he would climb at indoor gyms to get in a workout, stopping at a nice restaurant for a menu change, bringing back takeout food and a bottle of wine. I could indulge in a sip or two, since I was weaning off pain meds.

Over dinner one night, he said, "Tomorrow afternoon, I think I'm going to Mount Evans, climbing," referring to one of Colorado's iconic mountains (now known as Mount Blue Sky). "I'll be back for dinner, so order something for us from the hospital."

"Okay," I said grumpily. I was never really jealous of him going to an urban climbing gym, but climbing outside on a beautiful day was different.

As the hours ticked by the following day, I told myself I'd better get used to this.

I was hungry, impatient, and feeling sorry for myself. An open bottle of wine left by Adam from a previous night beckoned to me from across the room. After another hour had passed, I said *Screw it*, walked over to the counter, and eyed the situation.

There were some napkins, tissues, and paper-wrapped straws on the counter. I used my elbow to slide the straw to the counter's edge and bent over to grab it in my mouth. I stuck the other end in my right armpit and ripped off the paper with my teeth, spit the top out, and pulled the straw free of the paper. Then I set the straw on the counter and moved to the wine bottle, its cork pushed partway into the top. I grabbed the cork with my teeth. Luckily, Adam had not pushed the cork too far in, and it fell easily from the bottle. Dropping the cork on the counter, I traded it for the straw, picking it up with my mouth and leaning over the wine bottle.

I really hope a nurse doesn't walk in right now.

Damn. There was less wine in the bottle than I'd thought. *I hope my straw makes it.*

I bent further over and found that indeed it did. I sipped some of my favorite Barbaresco, which tasted brilliant even through a straw.

With just a few small sips, however, I quickly hit the limit of my straw's reach, so I devised a new plan: With straw in mouth, I placed my folded arms over the wine bottle and tilted it slightly (and cautiously) toward me. After a few more sips, the straw fell from my mouth into the bottle, which seemed like a good conclusion to this escapade.

Later that night, when Adam poured himself some wine and a straw slid out, he said, "I can guess what you've been up to tonight."

"I got bored waiting," I whined,

The next day, April 23, Ignatiuk came in for a closer look, and dropped some heavy news.

"Let's go the full three weeks," he said. "I'll book the OR for May the first." he said, looking at the calendar on his phone.

Wait—what?

"What do you mean by three full weeks? You said two to start, and two weeks is today. I know you mentioned an extension, but another full week?" I said, alarmed.

"Did I say two weeks?" Ignatiuk responded.

"Were you planning three weeks this whole time?" I wondered aloud.

Apparently, all timelines were conditional. "I'd like to give your left thumb some more time," Ignatiuk explained.

I prepared for more days in my straitjacket.

The final week dragged on, but I had a visit to look forward to. My sister flew in from Massachusetts for a long weekend at the end of the month—the perfect way to get me through some of my last days, tethered.

"Well, at least your visit won't involve waiting for me to get out of an eight-hour surgery," I said to Alison as we walked around the campus, passing time.

On Alison's last day, Dr. Ignatiuk stopped by to explain the surgery, scheduled for the following day.

"We will divide the flaps, identify the salvageable portions of the thumbs, debride, and cover exposed palms, fingers, and exit wounds with full and split-thickness skin grafts." They would use a nerve block at my shoulders to try to stop some of the intense pain, in addition to other pain medication.

"What comes after that?" I asked.

"Well, you'll need to stay as still as possible for five to seven days, for the skin grafts to take," he said. "We will apply a wound vac to your chest graft to help the large area heal." He seemed to anticipate the next question on my mind: "There is the possibility of you going home after the first few days if you want."

Without hesitation, I asked if it was okay to stay.

"Not a problem," Ignatiuk said. "In fact, I prefer having you on IV antibiotics, and in a conducive atmosphere to promote stillness."

I was totally on board.

"I'm afraid to go home and lose the help I have here at the hospital," I told him, especially without the use of my hands and having to stay as still as possible. "Plus, I'm nervous about managing the pain and risk of infection." I was a seasoned patient now, advocating for what I wanted for one of the first times in my stay, which now numbered twenty-eight days.

I speculated out loud: "If you send me home on day three and I have to come back two days later—if it's okay, I'd rather stay. I won't have help or the option of a ride back until May tenth." I told him a friend would be flying in to help me transition back home, and he had tickets for that date. "Adam will have to work," I said, "and I won't have a way to come back until my friend is here."

I was surprised to realize that I was afraid to go home. Even so, we were making plans for my return. Mike, a close climbing friend who lived with Adam and me years ago, called and said, "I am no good at hospitals, but you are going to need help when you get home." He offered to stay with us because Adam would be working.

I agreed without hesitation, and with extreme gratitude. I had no concept of what I'd be capable of, or what state my hands would be in. Another friend wondered if I feared going back home because it was the site of the accident.

This surprised me. "No, not at all—my house saved me," I said, referring to the circuit breaker that had tripped. I told her my biggest fear: "I am terrified of how I will be able to function."

On May 1, three weeks and one day after the *Jeannie* surgery, Dr. Ignatiuk and Dr. TeBockhorst released the bilateral flaps. I woke not to the same agonizing pain of the prior surgery, but to a strange dead weight attached to my neck. The nerve block had worked. Still, considerable pain emanated from the newly covered exit wounds on my chest, and from the donor sites on my groin and thigh, used for the grafts.

I must've been a sight. A strange bandage resembling the paper lining for a package of freshly ground hamburger covered the patch of skin on my thighs where the doctors had shaved away layers of skin for partial-thickness grafts. The bandage drooped, heavy with coagulating blood. A little vacuum unit hung from webbing around my neck, with a tube that ran to the right side of my chest, covering the new skin on the exit wound.

Thick bandages and wraps shrouded my hands from fingertips to elbows, not a bit of skin exposed. Because they needed my arms to be still—unencumbered and covered—the surgeons had moved my IV port from my arm into my jugular vein. The IV dangled awkwardly from my neck, delivering high doses of antibiotics. Doctors ordered me not to get out of bed for twenty-four hours. When I had to pee, Adam and Grace hoisted me like a sack of potatoes—but carefully—onto a bedpan.

The nerve block started to wear off the next day, May 2. The pain was significant, but not as fierce as the flap surgery. I knew the following days were going to be long: no riding the bike, no use of my one finger, and no walking to the art exhibit. There was always TV, though. I turned to the streaming shows someone would start for me on my laptop. I'd never watched *Veep*, and episode after episode kept me distracted.

After staying with me on May 2, Adam headed to work on May 3.

I was rattled that morning when a new resident in Plastics stopped by to inform me I'd be going home that day.

Whoa, whoa, whoa. We'd already discussed this with Dr. Ignatiuk—I would remain an inpatient for five to seven days, until they removed the bandages. *Apparently she hadn't gotten the memo.*

I could barely cope with my current state—the emerging pain, wondering what my hands would look like—and now they were saying I'd be leaving that night? I didn't even have a ride; Adam was working and not coming back for a few days.

I tried to protest, explaining our earlier understanding. The new doctor seemed taken aback. Later, I would see her notes: "Very tearful, worried about support/resources if going home today. . . . Will assess patient's desire to stay in-house vs. discharge home in the PM. Patient feels very overwhelmed and nervous about 'ruining her skin grafts,' appears to be very anxious."

Well, she got that right; I *was* very anxious, and had been even before she'd delivered her shocking news.

Dr. Ignatiuk heard what happened and, with his kind nature and assurances, settled my fears. We were sticking with our original timetable, waiting the five to seven days, removing the bandages, and then assessing my discharge date. (I never saw that resident again.)

Still, my anxiety increased over the next few days as I resumed the path toward fewer pain meds. Each day, the nurses would lessen the doses per my request, with the goal of being opiate-free before I left the hospital, the date of which was still unknown. Coincidentally, my first day being opiate-free turned out to be the day before what Dr. Ignatiuk called "the Big Reveal," when they'd remove the bandages.

Each day, with less medication, I became more edgy, irritable, and itchy. I asked a nurse if these were symptoms of withdrawal.

"I don't know," she said. "I've never had a patient wean themselves off of medication while still in the hospital."

Fair enough.

Karla and Quinn brought Cassidy again on May 4, right to my hospital room this time.

"I'm glad you were able to get her in, since I can't leave," I said. "How'd you do it?"

"I took my sister's advice and just walked on past everyone like we owned the place, and no one stopped me," Karla said triumphantly.

Cassidy happily sat by my bed as I petted her with my feet, a great distraction.

Later that day, Kathleen and Marsha showed up for a visit. I'd tried to discourage them—I have to remain still, and they'd just be sitting in my room. "It's not that exciting," I said.

"We are coming to see *you*. We don't need to get out," they explained.

When they showed up, I had a request. "If you are okay with it, could you please wash me up and shampoo my hair?" It was finals and graduation week, so there were fewer nurses' aides around. I couldn't have a real shower until they'd removed my bandages.

"I feel disgusting. I haven't washed up since the day before surgery, four days ago. Plus, the smell of rotting flesh is getting to me," I said. "I'm hoping this will help."

By this point, so many people had seen me naked and showered me that I'd stopped caring. I sat in a chair with my arms held up as they washed me and my hair as best as possible, working carefully around the bandages and the vacuum attached to my wound.

After so many visitors the day before, I was anticipating a quiet day on May 5. Immersed in another season of *Veep*, I was surprised to hear a knock on my door. I wasn't expecting Adam back until that evening. *And why would he knock?*

"Hi, how aah yah doin'?" a large man said as he cracked the door.

"Sorry, I think you have the wrong room," I said.

The man backed out and the door shut. Then it hit me—I knew that voice, and the Massachusetts accent. The door opened again.

"Kevin?" I said.

My cousin opened the door, laughing. I hadn't seen Kevin Sheehan in about fifteen years.

"Oh my god, I can't believe you're here!" I said.

Kevin explained that he hadn't seen my post on Facebook until just a few days earlier.

"I had no idea about your accident. When I saw it, I said, Deboraah, get your stuff together. We're driving to Colorado." They had come up from Las Vegas. "Got a room at the hotel next door. We'll keep you company the next few days."

Another unexpected bit of support.

"Great!" I said, thankful for company as I counted down to the Big Reveal.

Later that afternoon, Dr Ignatiuk made the call. "Let's wait the full seven days, and plan the Big Reveal for Monday morning, May 8."

On May 7, a nurse's aide checking on me came up with an amusing way to distract me during the wait: She would draw paw prints on the outside of my bandaged hands. I sat nervously as she gently drew on the bandages with Adam, my cousin, and his wife watching. I wondered what my hands would look like after all this pain, patience, and suffering.

That afternoon, Dr. Ignatiuk stopped by with a beautiful blonde woman by his side.

"I wanted you to meet my wife, Jess," he said, introducing her to Adam and me. He went to check on some patients, leaving us to get acquainted.

"You must be a very patient person," I told Jess. "I bet it's hard with a husband so dedicated to his work—you must not get to see him very much, since he seems to be here all the time, including weekends."

She smiled. "I do wish we had more time; this is our date day!" she said, laughing.

"Oh my, you are an angel," I said, certain this wasn't the first time he'd pit-stopped at work during a date.

"It is challenging, but I'm proud of him," Jess said. "He is so talented and passionate."

We had time to chat a little more before Dr. Ignatiuk came back.

"Are you ready for the Big Reveal tomorrow?" he asked.

"Oh yeah, I'm excited to check them out," I replied nervously.

He told me the plan. "We will unwrap first thing in the morning. I plan to keep you tomorrow night, but it's possible you could go home the next day." Then, reading my mind: "You should be able to start using your hands."

"Wow, so soon—that's great!" I said, thinking about how they'd looked the last time I'd seen them, marveling at the thought of using my hands again.

When they had left the room, I told Adam, "If I can use my hands, maybe you should call Mike and tell him he doesn't have to come."

That night, my anxiety was elevated as Adam brushed my teeth. I shook away from him. "That's good," I said. "I just need to get out of the bathroom."

"What's wrong?" he asked.

"It's too small in here. I feel claustrophobic. I don't know if I'm just anxious about seeing my hands, or if it's withdrawal, or what. Sorry," I said.

"Probably both," he said.

Chapter Thirty-Four

The Big Reveal
UCHealth, May 8, 2017, 6:00 a.m.

This was it. The result of all the events and all the work of the past five weeks would now be seen. Everything since 6:00 p.m., April 2—from the circuit breaker tripping, to Adam carrying me into the truck, to the efforts of the EMS team and ER nurses, the chopper pilot, the burn unit nurses, the teams of surgeons on four operations, my visiting friends, and even me, trying to be a good patient for thirty-six days—all of it had led up to this moment.

Dr. Ignatiuk and Dr. Seth entered the room early waking us up with the question, "Ready for the Big Reveal?"

Adam got up from the window bench that doubled as a rather uncomfortable bed and stood witness in his pajamas with phone in hand to commemorate the occasion. The curtains were still closed as the doctors set to work removing the bandages. They raised my bed to an upright position and each took an arm, conveniently propped on my blue foam sleeping cubes, which had returned to my room after they'd separated my arms. They carefully snipped away layers and layers of dressings and gauze, revealing first my forearms, marked by long, stitched-together portions of skin, up to where my thumbs were affixed.

I was shocked. First, at the length of the incisions; I didn't say anything, but imagined that maybe during surgery they'd had to cut more than what was attached to my thumb. My right arm had a prominent long line of stitches that forked into two lines, toward my elbow. The left arm's stitches were about 6 inches long, and straight. The process slowed as they approached my hands and gently peeled the final gauze away.

Dr. Ignatiuk inspected his handiwork. "Everything looks good. The grafts are pink and are taking," he said in a satisfied tone. He reminded me that "Sometimes, the body rejects the grafts, and we have to do this again."

"I couldn't imagine," I was barely able to mumble. I was stunned, rendered nearly speechless at what I was seeing. And yet Dr. Ignatiuk was continuing brightly. "It was surprising," he said. "I had plenty of skin from your arms to make your thumbs."

I scanned my limbs. It made sense, what he said. "Yeah, look at how tiny my arms are—when I got here, I had a lot more muscle mass filling out the skin," I managed to say.

"Good point," he replied. "There is no sign of infection, which is great. We have a way to go with your left thumb," he said, gently holding up my forearm. My left thumb was a short little thing crowned with a charred black tip. He moved his head closer. "I had to lose length here, and cut off some of the bone," he said. "I couldn't save the tip—that portion had turned dark—but I fought hard to save the nail bed. As you heal, I hope the nail will grow, and if it does, we will have something to work with, to add length to your left thumb."

I nodded numbly but added nothing. Thoughts swirled, words were difficult to put together. I was on the verge of breaking down. I didn't want that to happen in front of two wonderful doctors who had been entirely supportive and so invested during this journey. They'd poured enormous work, knowledge, and talent into rebuilding my hands. And they were so pleased with the outcome! Even if my reaction was horror, I didn't want to show it to them.

"We will stop by later today and talk more about your going home tomorrow, or the day after," Ignatiuk said. "I would like to keep you for another day to monitor the grafts, if that's okay."

"Yes," I said, taking a deep breath and pushing my shock down as they started to leave. "Wait," I said. "You said I could start using my hands when I go home?" That didn't seem possible.

"Yes, lightly," he said encouragingly.

"Like, can I chop an onion?" I asked, trying to imagine how using these things would be possible.

He squinched his face and shook his head. "No, not yet."

"Can I wipe myself when I go to the bathroom?"

No, was his answer. "You want to be very careful. The worst thing that could happen to your left thumb would be infection."

When they left the room, I turned to Adam.

"Did you call Mike and say I didn't need him?" No, Adam said. "Okay, good, because this is fucked, and I am going to need a lot of help still." No tears yet, just shock. I stared at my hands, shook my head, and looked at Adam. "These things look like Frankenstein baseball mitts!"

My hands had ballooned with fluid from the trauma of the surgery, accentuating their vast size and making them quite a bit larger than they'd been when they were sewn together. My thumbs were even more swollen than the rest of the inflated mess, jutting out prominently. Various textures, coloration, and large stitches delineated the skin grafts. Deviations in surface patterns highlighted the fact that the skin came from different areas of my body.

The skin flaps from my arms that my thumbs had grown accustomed to had been cut away from their original home. The skin now encircled the compromised bones, forming two very uniquely shaped thumbs. This relocated arm skin was a darker color from more constant sun exposure than the other pieces of flesh used to create my reborn hands, and my new thumbs boasted light-blond arm hair.

On my palms was bright pink groin skin, showing a waffle print from something I assumed they'd done to prep the skin. The graft on my right middle finger, the smallest nub, was light pink and appeared draped over the stump. The edges of the nub were gooey with bright red and yellow ooze. My right ring finger was still oddly club-shaped and draped in light pink thigh skin. Large red holes remained open on the fingers left ungrafted, where skin was attempting to grow back.

Thick black stitches crowned with crusty dried blood emphasized the puzzle pieces of skin that had come together to blanket my new hands. "They're like a quilt of my own body," I said. "If he wasn't a brilliant surgeon, it seems like he'd be some weird serial killer character like in *Silence of the Lambs,*" I commented, submerged in awe over the gore at the ends of my arms and the bittersweet triumph Ignatiuk had accomplished.

The shock soon caved into horror, then avalanched into melting down, plummeting me into the pit. "How am I going to live with these things for my hands?" I said.

Adam and his sister Vicky, who'd recently arrived, tried to reassure me.

"This is only the beginning," Vicky said. "The healing has yet to start."

Adam came over to my bedside with his phone. "Look at these pictures," he said. "These are skin grafts fresh out of surgery, see? And here they are, months after."

My breathing slowed a bit. I was so affronted by the sight of my hands that this hadn't dawned on me. *The healing is just starting, even after all this time in the hospital.*

I repeated this thought to myself. Had I really imagined the Big Reveal would show me smooth, healthy hands? I'd put so much positivity and good intentions into my healing.

"Somehow, I didn't think they would look as bad as this," I confessed to Adam and Vicky.

Good god, I thought I was through the hard part. I had to pull myself together.

Right about then, I could feel additional signs that the opioids were out of my system.

"I have to go to the bathroom," I alerted the team. "Not a great time to start feeling free from the constipation side effect." I thought wryly that the drugs would have made it easier to face my hands.

Oh well, you got this far without medication. You're not going backwards. You will not use the meds as a crutch.

Embracing the prospect of future healing helped to assuage my fears, but thinking about functioning in life with these mitts did not. I didn't dare ask the question aloud, but the sheer sight of my hands crushed any optimism of climbing someday.

Everyday functionality was the bigger question. It wasn't just my fingers' incongruous new shapes and sizes that disturbed me; the doctors had fused my thumb bones because the electricity had blown away the flexor tendons. My hands seemed borderline useless, but I made a resolution: *I had to try. I couldn't quit now.*

"Ignatiuk said I should start using my hands," I said to Adam. "I think I'll try to write something." *Baby steps.*

Adam found a sheet of paper and a pen at the nurses' station. He put the paper on the tray that slid over the bed and I sat up, looking at the blank canvas.

Adam gently handed me the pen. I cradled it in my right hand as best I could, even though the colossally swollen fingers could barely grasp the pen.

It felt weird, and my sense of touch was distant, although there was shooting pain. What was once a natural, automatic motion—holding a pen—now felt foreign.

I forced my hand into muscle memory movement and maladroitly began scratching words.

Hello, my name is Melissa Strong.
These are my first words written with my new hands.
One day I will climb again.
I will probably cry a lot along the way, which is okay.

I didn't believe the words about climbing as I wrote them, but I was determined to try. There is no doing without believing. I had battled not to slip into darkness, and the doctors had fought to give me my hands back. My net needed to be reinforced—I knew it would have to catch me frequently. My will and resolve became the anchors of my net.

"Look at you!" It was Dr. Ignatiuk, reentering the room with Dr. Seth.

"I assumed this would be okay," I said.

He smiled. "This is great," he said. "Some patients shut down and won't even look at their reconstructed hands or fingers."

I could sympathize.

Dr. Ignatiuk confirmed that he wanted to keep me for another day, "to get some more heavy-duty antibiotics in you." The official discharge date would be May 10, with an office follow-up on May 16.

"That soon?" I asked. Somehow I'd thought I wouldn't see him for a while.

My left thumb was his main concern, and he wanted weekly visits. "After you heal some, we have more work to accomplish on the thumb."

No kidding. I looked down at the fat tube with its black tip. *I'm certainly glad this isn't the final look.* I wondered how a nail could grow out of this mess.

After the doctors left, I told Adam it was a good thing Mike would be around. "Someone will have to drive me back for my appointments." He agreed.

We talked about our new logistics. "What am I going to do at home?" I questioned. "Just hang out? I'll go crazy."

Adam said he was looking at getting me an exercise bike. "I know you'll need something to get your energy out, and there's no way I'll let you on the elliptical, with your hands," he said. "You won't want to be gripping any handles."

A nurse in the room piped up. "You should get her a Peloton; they're the best. There is a screen, instructors, and classes. I'm a cyclist, and I think it's the best training and the most authentic." I told Adam I loved the idea.

"I'm already on their website," he said, and minutes later, with a click: "I just bought you a Peloton. It will be there one to two weeks after you get back."

I thanked them both, then resumed obsessing over my hands.

The doctors came in the following day and asked if I had any other questions before going home.

I did, as a matter of fact. "I'm afraid I am going to be attacked by a coyote or some wild animal before I get into the house, because I reek of rotting flesh," I said. "When will that smell stop?"

They smiled. I didn't smell so bad, they said, and it'll fade. Okay, fine, but I had lots of other questions.

"What about the pubic hair growing out of my palms?" I asked next. "How can I bring food to the tables at the restaurant with hairy palms?"

It'll be taken care of down the line, Ignatiuk said. "After some more healing, we can get some laser hair removal sessions set up for you here."

"Thank you," I said and looked at my palms. "I had no idea the skin would still grow hair after it was moved."

"Skin has a specific DNA," he explained. "Even if you move it, the skin is programmed to be a certain way, and will not change." For instance, he said, when infants are born with their fingers joined together, the fingers are separated and grafted using skin from the groin. "At puberty, when they start growing pubic hair, it also grows on the grafts."

"That is crazy," I said.

He had more. "One patient needed skin grafted on her forehead, and the surgeon used skin from her abdomen. Years later, when they gained weight in their stomach, they also gained weight in their forehead."

This was all too surreal. I felt overwhelmed by the sight of my hands, and the prospect of leaving the hospital and the staff after five weeks. On the other hand (you might say), I was going home.

Chapter Thirty-Five

Home

Aurora to Estes Park, May 10, 2017

Longing and fear: That was me, getting ready for discharge. It was nerve-wracking. I wanted to return to my home and everyday life, of course, but I was terrified, not knowing how I'd be able to function, especially without a nursing staff around me 24/7. Moreover, what would I do all day? I knew the hours would be long, floating in a limbo-like abyss as I focused on patience and mending.

I'd be heading back into the mountains marred, reconstructed, forever altered—never to be the person I was before we'd sped away from the house thirty-eight days ago. The person I had been for forty-three years.

I was not afraid of my house, but I was fearful about seeing the apparition I'd imagined become a reality, learning to accept the new me after the accident. I knew functionality preceded this acceptance, and hoped I could learn how to love my new self.

Baby steps, I told myself again—my new mantra. Weeks of waiting and wondering had ended with the Big Reveal. At least now I comprehended the form my new hands had taken, even if they were disconcerting at first sight.

Adam brought bags to pack up our transplanted belongings. Did I want to bring the blue foam blocks to elevate my arms while I slept? Nah, I said. The plan had been to swing by the airport to pick up my new caregiver, Mike. But that morning my stomach took a turn, and the nursing staff had insisted on a blood test for C. diff (*Clostridioides difficile*), a bacterium linked to strong antibiotics that can cause diarrhea.

Another few hours of waiting, and the tests came back negative. They loaded me up with Bacitracin, Xeroform, gauze, and bandages so we could continue wound care, cleaning, maintenance, and making finger puppets at home.

Mike's plane was delayed, and he texted that he'd get to Estes on his own the following day. Some of the nurses ceremoniously wheeled me to the door, and I carefully climbed into the open passenger door of my 4Runner. I moved slowly, guarding my throbbing hands laden with stitches and areas that oozed through their protective bandages, Xeroform, and gauze, with cotton tubing holding the bandages in place. The stitches and raw patches at my donor sites added to the discomfort.

The nurses warmly wished me well and promised to come up and visit Bird & Jim when we opened. Adam buckled me in, and as we drove away, I gazed at the facility and felt the import of the transition.

"I am beginning my second life," I announced to Adam, and myself.

Adam smiled and placed his hand on my knee, giving me a reassuring squeeze.

As we slowly made our way out of metropolitan Denver and toward the mountains, through rush-hour traffic, I marveled, "I cannot believe so many people did this drive to see me in the hospital."

"I'll certainly be happy to come here less," he said.

You might expect a joyous reunion with our thirteen-year-old dog, Cassidy, and fifteen-year-old cat, Fiona, but it wasn't that simple. They greeted me excitedly, and while I was equally happy for the reunion, I experienced a rush of panic. *Germs!* I could hear Dr. Ignatiuk's words: Infection was the worst thing that could happen to my left thumb. I couldn't pet them, which broke my heart.

I awkwardly moved around my home, the place I'd lived so happily since before I'd met Adam. Now it was *our* home, for which I was deeply grateful. Still, I felt helpless: I couldn't unpack, I couldn't clean up, I couldn't organize. I found this idleness arduous.

What I *could* do, the doctors said, was wash my hands (gently!), reapply bandages, start wrist and arm movements, and wiggle my fingers. I hadn't really used my hands or moved my wrists and arms for nearly forty days. I sat bewildered, my elbows on the kitchen counter and my hands in the air as Adam brought in the bags and to-go food we'd picked up in Lyons.

"Do you want to eat?" Adam asked.

It was almost ten p.m. and I was exhausted. "I guess I should try to eat something."

He put a salad in front of me, opened the lid, and took out a fork to feed me.

I saw this as a good first test. "You eat," I said. "I will try to feed myself."

Adam held the fork up for me. Ineptly, I pinched the end of it with my right thumb and the side of my index finger, then gently stabbed at the greens. I tried not to put pressure on the wrapped-up, seeping nubs. My fingers strained to hold onto the fork, and it slipped from my feeble grip into the to-go box.

Seeing the food made me somewhat hungry, and determined. I clenched the fork again, better prepared for the stabbing force, and got some lettuce on the tines. I raised the fork to my mouth, not noticing that Adam was taking pictures. It was a milestone: the first bit of food I'd fed myself since April 2. I was both proud and annoyed that this was an achievement. It did require focus, determination, and considerable effort with each bite.

It'll get easier, I told myself.

After making a small dent in the salad, I gave up.

Adam brushed my teeth because I didn't want to spoil my clean hospital bandages. I took my contacts out—yay—learning that I could do this with my two index fingers.

"I am really tearing through life here," I said sarcastically. I told Adam I'd still need help opening the lens container and putting them in. I didn't want him getting any ideas that his days of helping me were over.

We headed upstairs to go to bed. He helped me into pajamas, pulled back the covers, and situated two pillows to elevate my arms, with Cassidy and Fiona looking on.

Although I'd seen Cassidy in the hospital, I hadn't seen Fiona since April 2. That first night home, she jumped on my chest as soon as I got into bed. Fiona never held a grudge; she was like Velcro, in constant contact. I'd had my cat and dog longer than I'd had Adam, and while I was comforted to see them, I froze when Fiona jumped on me and tried to nuzzle me.

Germs—infection! Somewhat panicked, I said, "Adam, I didn't think of this—I should've kept the foam blocks. They would have protected my hands." I knew I needed to shield them from Fiona.

"Tell me what you need," Adam said.

I thought for a moment. "Maybe the oven mitts." I chuckled half-heartedly, adding, "The only thing big enough to cover these mitts."

Adam returned with the oversized oven mitts and slid them over my hands. He was soon peacefully snoring away as I stared wide-eyed at the ceiling, terrified. There were germs inside the oven mitts, Fiona on my chest; these things weren't clean. My hands heated up with the insulation and panic. I shook the mitts off. I grasped at webbing in my mental safety net, thinking of friends who had survived worse. *You can do this*, I coached myself. *You are lucky to be alive, to have this chance to try again at life.* I pulled together the various strands of support and tightened my net.

The comfort of my own bed that I'd yearned for was lost to me, overridden by the apprehension of merely existing. Eventually, I drifted off, Fiona at my side.

Chapter Thirty-Six

The Slow Race

Estes Park, Mid-May, 2017

Waking up that first morning back home was disorienting, and for many mornings thereafter. I had to remind myself where I was, and then I'd reabsorb the fear of facing life. I'd breathe it in, confront it, and accept it. This became a daily self-coaching ritual upon waking up.

I recalled the work on my emotional net I'd done the night before, and hauled myself out of bed. Adam stayed at home on May 11, as Mike wouldn't get there until the afternoon.

Feeling misplaced and questioning how I was going to handle these first days at home, I announced a plan: "Adam, I decided that you are going to put me on the elliptical and hang out in the garage while I use it." He looked dubious. "I don't know about this." I insisted: "I have to do it. I have to move."

We went into the garage and he helped me up onto the machine. I slowly initiated the foot pedals, feeling off balance. I rested my wrists on the forked handles and slowly got a rhythm, picking up the pace a little. Adam opened the garage door opposite me, and I stared outside, to our deck and the Rocky Mountains in the background.

"My goal is twenty minutes," I told him, and he plopped onto the sofa in the garage across from the climbing wall. I felt frail, noodle-like, depleted. I questioned my decision but pushed on. After twenty minutes, Adam helped me off, and I stumbled out onto our porch, leaning on the railing.

"I'm super nauseous and dizzy," I said.

"I told you this wasn't a good idea," he said.

"No," I replied, "this is what I have to do. I have to push through this and get some fitness back."

Adam reminded me that the Peloton would be arriving next week.

Mike arrived in the afternoon and we talked about Adam going to work the next day. I had a bit of a problem to discuss with them, related to my lingering stomach issues.

"I really don't want Mike to wipe my ass," I said.

Mike quickly agreed. He mentioned that his mother had a unique toilet seat that converted to a bidet called a Toto. "They are great, actually. You just have to install the special seat and hook it up to water and power."

The guys checked the bathroom, and there was an outlet near the toilet. Adam ordered one on Amazon. "This one can be here by the day after tomorrow."

Although I'd grown used to people wiping my bottom and showering me in the hospital, this was different. I was home, and Mike was a close male friend, not a nurse.

"I'll just have to get through tomorrow somehow," I said.

Adam would be working nearby. "I'll come home if I have to." And he did.

Eventually, the Toto was exactly what my ego needed, giving me the independence to go to the bathroom by myself. It was not smooth sailing from the get-go, however; there were a few lessons to be learned. Adam stood by waiting for the report. Holding the remote and pressing the button proved slightly more challenging than I'd initially anticipated. I soon cried out for help, literally and figuratively. Adam came in to turn it off, as I was sitting there, with tears of frustration running down my face, unable to stop the stream of water without assistance.

On the second attempt, Adam shut the door behind me and stood by. All good with the Toto, but we soon realized as I called for help again that I could not do doorknobs. Eventually this got easier.

Everywhere I went in our house, I was surrounded by climbing. Photos of us and friends climbing throughout the world: Switzerland,

France, Hueco, the Rockies, Australia, South Africa. Our climbing gym was down a hallway strewn with climbing bags, climbing shoes, chalk, and tape. When I had gotten on the elliptical, I couldn't bear to look at the climbing wall, turning away in sadness. *I cannot even imagine.*

I turned away from the climbing area and headed in the opposite direction. I used my elbow and hip to open the screen door to our patio, stepping out into the sun and gazing at the mountains.

It wasn't just my hands that had changed. My arms had lost muscle mass and looked like spaghetti noodles. *What are the baby steps regarding these feeble arms?* I rotated my wrists, which had been immobile for nearly a month and a half. I was shocked at the effort required but continued the motion. Keeping my elbows bent and hands in the air, I tried shoulder shrugs. Even that feeble movement was taxing, but also felt like it was accomplishing something, at least combating the hunched posture the *Jeannie* surgery had forced my frame to hold.

"I cannot believe how weak I am," I told Mike. "This is going to be a long road to regain any type of strength."

Mike followed me around the house, acting as my hands.

"Let's see what's in the kitchen and make a list for the supermarket," I said on one of those first days back home. "You and Adam will have to cook dinner," I reminded Mike. He had an idea: "Let's make that soup with white wine, greens, and lima beans." Great; I looked forward to some home-cooked food and favorite recipes.

In my absence and with Adam's limited time at home, the house had gone from cluttered to messy. I decided we had to do some major organization, so we worked our way through the house: Can you pick that up? Can you put these things in the wash? Can you move that over here?

"What's that?" I asked, nodding at a bag in the hallway.

He opened the drawstrings and a heinous smell emerged.

"Wow, that's vile—what is this?" he said.

"Oh my god," I said quietly. I was suddenly swept back to the day of the accident. The stench of burnt flesh flooded the hallway, all these weeks later. Images of my burnt hands filled my mind.

I steadied myself.

Mike pulled something out—it was the top the nurses had cut off me in the ER. He picked through the bag, showing me the items.

"I guess we can save the prAna pants and socks," I said. "Throw them in with this load of laundry and toss the rest, please."

There was another priority for that day. "Before we hit the Safeway, can we stop by the construction site?" I asked. I was excited to see what kind of progress the crew was making on the restaurant. Mike buckled my seat belt, shut the door, and we drove to the other side of town. My heart quickened when I saw the retro neon RESTAURANT sign atop the building that would become my dream business.

As we approached the building, something seemed off.

"Weird—there's only one car here. It's a Friday, but still early. There should be a whole crew working today."

I managed to unbuckle myself (easier than buckling in) and waited for Mike to open the car door. We walked in through the back entrance.

"I cannot believe it," I said, looking around the gutted space. "It doesn't look like they've done anything the whole time I've been in the hospital!"

A man appeared. "Hey. I'm the electrician, Jerry."

Dazed, I started to introduce myself.

"I know who you are," Jerry said quickly. "How are you doing?" He asked this in a kindly tone, nodding at my finger puppets and gauzed-wrapped hands.

"Well, Jerry, I was feeling better until I got here. Where is everyone?"

Jerry said the contractor was building a spec house across town. "I suppose they're over there."

"Good to know," I harrumphed.

We walked around a bit, and during a quiet moment, Jerry said, "Being an electrician, I know what you went through. You are very lucky to be alive." He certainly knew what he was talking about.

"I guess what happened to me is your worst nightmare," I said. "Difference is, you know what you're doing. I am done trying my hand at any of that." We laughed. I thanked him for his work, and Mike and I returned to the car, where I called the contractor.

"Hi, I'm back in town, and just left the restaurant," I said.

"Welcome home. How are you doing?" he replied.

"Honestly, things are pretty rough," I said. "And it got worse when I saw the restaurant. It doesn't look like any work was done while I was in the hospital. What's the deal?"

He didn't deny anything. "It's tough right now. I'm stressed, and have to stretch the crew—I just can't find people to work."

"Well, what do you need?" I asked.

"Framers," he said.

I swallowed my frustration and told him I'd reach out to some friends. Using my two index fingers, I sent off desperate texts, then messaged the contractor with some phone numbers. I let him know that I expected him to hire my friends and that I'd see a crew there next week.

Adam came home from work, wanting to unwind, but I wanted a shower. As he sipped a glass of wine, I told him about the state of the construction, and then we got in the shower. (We figured it'd be easier to shower together until I could use my hands.) I stood under the water, hands unbandaged, letting the shampoo rinse out of my hair as Adam washed himself.

I drifted in thought. I hadn't put my arms down at my sides since the accident, even when sleeping. I wanted to keep the swelling down. *You'll have to do this at some point*, I encouraged myself. I took a chance and slowly lowered my arms for the first time in months.

Pulsing waves of blood pounded past my wrists and into my exposed hands, causing thunderous surges of pain with each heartbeat. I leaned my head forward and cried onto Adam's shoulder. I sobbed for my hands, for what I had to accept and learn, for the struggle ahead, and now for the construction site that was supposed to open as a restaurant *in six weeks*. At this last thought, I choked and sobbed harder.

Everything seemed bleak: my hands, the loan, my future.

Thump, thump, thump went the pain and blood. The pressure was so intense I thought my stitches would burst.

Later, Mike and Adam performed some slightly inebriated nursing care. It took forever for them to apply layers of Bacitracin, Xeroform, gauze, and tubes to my hands. They moved slowly and carefully, afraid of hurting me. I'd watched the professionals do this countless times, so was able to walk them through it. I sat patiently, restraining myself from barking orders. After all, these two had taken care of me all day and would face the same duties tomorrow, and for weeks beyond.

When we started the bandaging process the next day, however, I said, "All right—it took you guys forty-five minutes yesterday. Let's see if you can set a new speed record."

Chapter Thirty-Seven
Out with the Old, In with the New
Estes Park, May–June, 2017

The Peloton took a little longer than we'd hoped for, arriving after my second week back home. I was thankful, and so were Adam and Mike, because it meant the end of elliptical watch duty.

I opened boxes from my imaginary closet and worked out my frustration, anxiety, fears, and sadness on the bike. The Peloton system seemed perfect for me—you log on and work with instructors (from anywhere in the world) who lead classes and offer encouragement, all from the screen in front of me. Some days, the instructors' uplifting messages penetrated; other days, I wept while pedaling.

I gravitated toward certain instructors who I knew as Robin, Cody, Allie, and Emma. I visited with them daily, pedaling while pouring my heart out to a screen and to people who couldn't hear me. This was what I needed, and ideal, since I couldn't offend them with my anger or burden them with my sadness. As I got into the core biking classes I quickly realized how little effort I'd expended in the hospital on the antique stationary bike.

A late-May snowstorm dumped several feet of spring snow, grounding the tree crew. Adam was home, climbing in the garage. Mike sat with me in the living room, recovering from a climbing shoulder injury.

When Adam came back in the house and heard my laughter, he walked over, happy as could be. He sat beside me, smiling, and said, "I am so glad you're happy."

I snapped. I turned to face him and retorted, "Just because I am laughing, do not think I am happy." He looked at me, wide-eyed. "I am far from happy, and completely unsure whether I'll ever be happy again." I tumbled into my sadness. "I am just trying as hard as I can to not be an asshole."

I knew I'd hurt him and felt terrible about what had just flown out of my mouth, but I couldn't stop. And then I went there, opening up misplaced, thoughtless emotions that had been boxed up since the accident.

"This is your fault. *You* found the idea on the Internet, and *you* made that machine."

Now Adam was shaking his head. "Oh no, you don't get to say that," he said evenly. "I told you how dangerous it was, and I made it very clear never to touch the leads when it was plugged in."

He was correct, and I knew it. He wasn't culpable, but despair had gotten the best of me. Still grappling with my anger at damaging myself beyond repair, I retreated to a cowardly stance and tried to assign blame where it did not belong. I felt bad for him and disappointed in myself for letting the forgiveness box explode open. I'd labored doggedly, taking steps forward, healing physically and mentally, only to plummet into anguish.

Adam understood my desolation and decided it was best to let it go, leaving me be for the moment. He turned back to the wall to finish his session.

Getting into bed that evening, I apologized again.

"I am sorry," I said. "You didn't deserve that."

I thought back to my first days in the hospital, when I'd exonerated myself, and also pledged to be kind to anyone helping me through this. Of course I was still angry at myself for making a grave mistake, and I'd let my frustrations be misdirected. I had faced this already, on night one, when I realized I couldn't live in a world of blame or self-loathing. Like many other things I'd put in my closet, I learned this box wasn't locked. It would take years of revisiting and additional hard work to heal.

"I can only imagine the mental anguish you're going through," Adam said, letting me know he understood, adding, "I love you."

Out with the Old, In with the New

"Thank you for loving me. I couldn't have endured this without you," I responded.

Today I'd taken steps in the wrong direction, but there was always tomorrow.

In a couple of days, I would see my parents in person for the first time. During our Skype calls, they had said they wanted to leave the islands—their getaway from New England winters—to come visit in the hospital. We all agreed they should wait until they were back in the States. It was harder for them to get around these days, with knee, back, and hip issues, and there was no rush to see me in the hospital, where it was just a waiting game.

I persuaded them it was better to come and visit once I was home. That way they could return to Massachusetts first, to pack for the snowy Colorado spring; bathing suits and other island attire wouldn't cut it in May around here.

"I hope some of this snow melts before my parents get here," I said.

Adam said that some would, but "42 inches will not melt fast."

"I thought everything would be easier for them to visit once I was home, but this snow will make it a pain."

Mike and Adam assured me it would be fine.

We continued our home organization project. As Mike moved some items around in the garage, he lifted a tarp and there it was: the microwave transformer—the powerhouse that had pumped electricity into me.

I froze, and for a moment, floated back to that day when the electricity had pulsed through me, stealing my hands, and almost my life. The cables were no longer attached, but the power cord was still connected to the box.

"This is the machine, Mike. This was the source of the electricity," I said.

"Do you want to keep it?" he asked.

I thought for a second and quickly came up with a resounding "No! Let's throw it away."

Before he picked it up, I reached out and gently touched the box. The cold metal seemed to vibrate even when unplugged. I followed Mike out of the garage to the trash cans, needing to affirm that it was gone. That odd moment of contact lingered with me the rest of the day.

When Adam came home later, I said "I found the machine in the garage."

He raised his eyebrows. "You did? I had stuck it under some stuff, not knowing what to do with it."

"Well, we threw it away."

Adam nodded. "Good," he said.

When my parents arrived, they held me tight and all three of us cried. I felt layers of sympathy and comfort in their arms, and used this to reinforce my net. I held my hands out, which were encased in compression gloves that I'd been given at one of my first checkups.

"I couldn't believe it when the lady at the doctor's office jammed these tiny compression gloves onto my giant hands. It killed! I'm getting used to them, though, and I hope maybe they will make my hands smaller." I chuckled, glad they were spared the sight of my swollen hands. "Under the gloves here, and on the nub of my thumb, I still have open scabby wounds, which I guess is obvious with the black tip," I said, pointing out the unavoidable. "Dr. Ignatiuk says I am healing up, and if this nail grows, I can get more length with additional surgeries."

I felt a bit like a child again as I bragged about my progress, like coming home from kindergarten and proudly announcing that I could tie my shoes. "I can pull up my pants now but can't do buttons or zippers. I also can brush my teeth, shower on my own, fold clothes, and kind of make the bed. Sometimes I have to use my teeth for help, and everything takes fifty times longer." My mom shook her head. "Be careful of using your teeth, Melissa." They took my hands in theirs and inspected the new shape. "Oh, Missy" was all they could say.

That night, I stood by and watched while they made meatballs for all of us—a Gargano family recipe. Mike drove me back and forth to their rented condo and took us to tour the construction site, now thankfully in full swing. We took them to dinner in Boulder, where chef Ethan was still working; John and Jimmy joined us so my investors could meet my partners and taste Ethan's delicious cooking.

They loved Bird & Jim's location and were excited for me, but they were my parents, so were understandably apprehensive about the challenges ahead. They lifted me up, told me I could do it, and filled me with the confidence I desperately needed.

Money was flying out of the bank account as the construction expanded. The old building was revealing surprising layers that demanded attention. While I knew that stress wasn't helpful to the healing process, I'd still lie awake at night, in quiet panic about investing so much in the restaurant, not knowing if it would be successful.

After my parents left, I plunged myself into Bird & Jim, bringing the vision and vibe together. There were countless decisions every day: paint colors, electric fixtures, granite for the chef's counter at the open kitchen window, benches, upholstery, furniture for the lounge and bar, exterior siding. I worked with our climbing friend and artist Daniel Yagmin Jr. to develop our logo. Ethan and the team came over to the house where Ethan cooked and we would sample the fare he was developing for our first menus. Jimmy made the cocktails that would be on our list, and John came in with some celebratory wine—2013 Opus One—yes please. The gang was assembled and we were moving forward.

Jimmy sanded countless wooden chairs and ran all the tables back and forth to a local artist, Dave Landers, a shining example of the love I got from the community. When the restaurant team visited me in the hospital, Jimmy had taken out a letter and read it aloud: "Dave uses electricity to make designs on his wood-turned bowls. He wants me to let you know he would be happy to volunteer to work on your decorative project at the future restaurant. I am praying for you at this difficult time." It was signed "A friend of a friend, Susan," who was Dave's wife.

"I cannot believe it," I'd said, choking up. "Estes Park is so amazing. I am so lucky. The funny thing is, I've been sitting here thinking about how to finish the table legs but assumed Adam would never let me touch that machine again."

Adam smiled, and being the practical person he is, said candidly, "Of course I would—you'd never make that mistake again."

"You're right," I agreed, even though I knew I could never bring myself to try the Lichtenberg technique again.

With my busy days and the slow but steady progress on the restaurant, I was starting to feel almost human again. It was early June, and we'd all accepted that we weren't going to open by the middle of the month. The restaurant was still a construction site, at the framing stage. I would see friends around town and give them updates—on my hands, and on Bird & Jim. Mike, Adam, and I had settled into a routine, and the days seemed more livable—bearable.

"We are going to the park tomorrow," Adam said one day. "Do you want to hike and hang out while we climb? Chaos Canyon—you love it up there," he said smiling.

My throat constricted. "I know, but no thanks," I said. "I'm not ready to face Chaos yet." Chaos Canyon was one of the spots where I'd learned to climb, a talus-filled gulch between the majestic peaks of Hallett and Otis. The canyon boasts world-class boulder problems above beautiful Lake Haiyaha. "I'll just stay here and get stuff done," I said.

I'll go back there someday, I thought, *but I need more time.*

Once again, I jammed climbing into its trunk, steering my mind to more immediate concerns. For instance, bathroom wallpaper for Bird & Jim. I was thinking peacocks in one bathroom and maps in the other. *That'll be a good project.*

"I think I'll be good on my own," I told them, then realized I hadn't been alone since I'd been home. "I guess my only concern is doorknobs, but it's not like I'm going anywhere," I said. In fact, I hadn't driven a car yet. With Mike leaving in mid-June, my next goal was to be able to grip the steering wheel.

As it turned out, I didn't spend that day alone. Sarah—a good friend and fellow climber who happened to be traveling through the area—reached out to see if we'd be around.

"The guys are going to Chaos if you want to join them," I told her. "I don't think I'm ready to hike up there yet."

"No, I'm good," she said. "I want to hang out with you. I can climb another day."

The next time Adam went climbing, I went for a hike with my friend Lindsey, who drove up from Denver. We hiked to the top of Crosier Mountain, a smallish mountain outside of the national park. "This is great," I said. "Getting out is just what I need. I am definitely not ready to go to a climbing area."

Back at the house later, I sat on the deck as Lindsey planted some flowers she'd brought with her.

"Thank you for the flowers, and the hike," I said. "I'm relieved that eight miles wasn't too challenging. My Peloton is bringing my fitness back." I shared with Lindsey that it was hard when Adam and our friends went off for a day of climbing. "I want them to go and have fun, but I feel sad and left behind."

Lindsey paused in her planting. "You should enjoy this downtime while you have it," she said, looking out at the Mummy Range.

At first, I was confused. How could I enjoy this "downtime"? It was a slow, torturous limbo. Turns out she was looking ahead. "Opening a restaurant in Estes Park, you won't have a second to spare in the summer," Lindsey added. She was right—summers are nonstop work.

"Funny, I hadn't thought about my time that way," I said. "I just want this to be over with—to be healed, and to have the restaurant open. But you're right," I said, drifting off in thought.

Of course I'd thought about how owning a restaurant would change my life and give me less free time. It was only later on that I'd realize there was practically *no* free time. At first, I'd naively believed that most of my time operating Bird & Jim would be spent on the floor, managing. Later, I'd realize that running a restaurant meant a thousand tasks, including handling payroll, invoicing, and paying the bills; making the schedule; refining procedures and solving problems; establishing core values, standards, and norms; being the HR department; navigating benefits and laws; taking care of advertising and marketing; and worrying over food cost and labor. It wasn't a full-time job; it was *several* full-time jobs.

The life of the old carefree Melissa, the climber with hands who ran off to climb in Rocky before work, was gone.

Chapter Thirty-Eight

Narwhal

Estes Park, June 2017

Even though a mid-June opening wasn't happening, we were going to have a champagne toast regardless, amid the saws, nail guns, and busy crew. We acquired our liquor license on June 13, 2017, in time for that target date, now a mockery. The crew was still installing windows and framing the walls and bar. "At least I can see the walls going up," I jested, "even though I can see right through them."

I had been able to drive myself. It's amazing what motivation did for my self-sufficiency. Mike had left after spending a month helping me adjust to daily life, and Adam was working, so I had to get to the restaurant on my own. Gripping the steering wheel for the first time in months was a bit intimidating, but also a breath of freedom and independence. I felt like a teenager who'd just gotten her license as I drove down Fish Creek Road. It took all my focus and, as with most things, multitasking was out. No drinking water while driving, for example.

I rolled down the window and bathed in the crisp air. I placed my elbow on the edge of the window and noticed my fingers no longer reached the top of the frame. A shorter reach now, it dawned on me. My thoughts drifted to climbing—my "ape index" (the distance from longest finger to longest finger) was shorter now. I wondered how it would affect my climbing, if I ever got the chance to try.

I met John (the wine director and managing partner) and Jimmy (our whiskey expert and bar manager) at the site and checked in with the climbing friends the contractor had hired: Kiel, Chris, and Jim. They brought me up to speed on the progress.

"The live-edge walnut bar will look great," I said. Our friends Josh and Kent were making the bar top and wine storage area, and I stopped to chat with them. As I was leaving, they realized their sander was unplugged from the extension cord. Instinctively I reached down to plug it in. I paused, propelled back in time to my near-fatal mistake. But I continued the motion and plugged the sander into the extension cord and looked up. Everyone—construction workers and partners—had gone silent, staring at me. I chuckled. "This should be safe enough."

We worked our way around the layout, marveling at how the dining room opened up with the low popcorn ceiling gone, revealing beams and old wood.

This could be great.

My passion for climbing was still in its trunk, but there was a glimmer of hope. Our friend Jackie Hueftle had started a company called Kilter Grips, which manufactures climbing holds. Years later, they also produced the Kilter Board, a modern take on a climbing wall. It's filled with hundreds of various holds, designed by Jackie and her partners, including Ian Powell. The holds light up around their edges. Using an app, you can concoct a nearly infinite number of problems, or try problems set by others. The holds light up with corresponding colors showing where you place your foot and the hold you should grab with your fingers.

Jackie invited Adam and me to their studio in Boulder to see what holds might work for my new hands. It was fun to see their company taking off. We checked out displays, walked through their warehouse, and met with Ian and their cross-brand partner, Peter Juhl. We sifted through different holds, seeing what my remaining fingers could grip. Incut edges seemed to offer some hope. Jackie and Ian gave me some, and back home, Adam drilled holes and bolted them to the side of our stairwell.

I stood under the holds, my hands in compression gloves with just a few scabby areas still healing, figuring out how to place my fingers on them, learning what my new grip might be able to do. Every day I gradually added more pressure to the holds while keeping my feet on the ground. It was a tiny step, but it fueled me with joy. *There is some hope,*

I whispered to myself. I was planting a tiny seed of climbing optimism. Maybe it would grow into a vine that I could weave into my net.

My sister Alison and her three children were coming to visit, and would stay in the apartment above our garage. It needed some sprucing up, so our friend Kiel generously helped me paint it on a weekend when he was off from the restaurant construction job. With gloves, I could use the paint roller with an extension pole. After forty-five minutes, however, I freaked out.

"I can't open my hands!" I cried out. After some time and considerable pain, I got the grip to release. Later, my occupational therapist in Boulder explained that this "contracture" happens as layers of scar tissue are continuously and rapidly produced.

When my sister and her family arrived later in June, it was an uplifting and delightful time. Other than her hospital visit, her last time in Colorado was for our wedding eleven years earlier, when her oldest child, Andrew, was four years old. Now Andrew was fifteen, and her twins Emelia and Mary were eleven. Somehow, they all crammed into the apartment.

We did it all: drove up Trail Ridge Road, hiked to Emerald Lake and showed them the boulders, played mini golf, took the kids to a ropes course, toured Bird & Jim's construction site, and spent a day in Boulder with Adam's sister Vicky and her daughter, Aspen. We hung out at night, playing games and watching movies. It was a fun visit that invigorated and distracted me.

One sunny day during their visit, Lisa met us at Performance Park at the edge of town, a spot for outdoor concerts with a short sport-climbing rock face where the kids could rope up. I gently touched the rock as Lisa helped my nieces and nephew climb, but I didn't dare attempt to pull on the coarse granite. With the Kilter holds at home, though, I saw a path. *This could happen*, I thought. Maybe I'll only advance enough to climb warm-ups, but at least I could see a path toward getting out and climbing again, even if it was just V0s. I knew I was far away from trying real rock, but this tiny bit of hope encouraged me to take the next step.

Two weeks after pulling down on the Kilter holds, my palms freshly free of scabs and my compression gloves on, I decided to try holds on our 60-degree climbing wall, starting with a couple of jugs—the biggest, easiest holds. I carefully bent my finger nubs around the edges of the jugs. Then, leaving my ridged thumbs pointed in the air, I placed one foot and then the other on equally large holes, gripping them with my stockinged feet. Pain shot through me, but I was on our climbing wall!

I eased my feet back to the mattresses below and let go of the holds. It took a few minutes to process the pain and breathe through it. Then I pulled back on the wall. This time, I bent my elbows, pulling my body into the wall. I held myself in for a few seconds and then straightened my arms. I repeated this motion and let go, once again hit with powerful pain.

After a few sets, my feeble arms grew tired and the pain became overwhelming. I couldn't shake off or push through this level of discomfort. It wouldn't subside, just intensify.

Don't push yourself. Baby steps.

Still, the climbing trunk was open. For the first time, I felt all right about lifting the lid.

You have miles to go, I reminded myself. It would be a grueling journey, and climbing would be totally different. Nevertheless, joy bubbled up in me. The sport I loved—that fueled me, distracted me, gave me so much joy—could be a part of my life again. It promised to be humbling, painful, and frustrating, but I would get to try. I cried with happiness.

When Adam came home from work that night, I greeted him with my good news: "I did pull-ins on the climbing wall today!" I described a pull-in: "I was simply holding onto the wall and straightening my arms, and bending them, pulling my body into the wall. But my feet were off the mattresses, and I was on the climbing wall." I was exuberant.

His joy matched mine and meant more than my movement on the wall. It gave us both a glimmer of hope for our future.

"Maybe no surfing for us," I kidded.

That night, I dreamed about climbing for the first time since the accident. In my typical climbing dreams, I'm in a beautiful setting with stunning boulders, climbing strong and proficiently. But that night was different. Friends surrounded me and spotted me while I climbed. I made moves and progressed up the rock face. "I'm doing it!" I shouted, thrilled.

I moved my right hand into a seam and advanced my left hand. Then I pulled my right hand out of the seam to reach for the next hold and screamed. *One of my fingers was gone—it was stuck in the crevice!*

I woke up, heart pounding, and looked at my hands. The fingers that I had left were still there. I flopped back on the pillow, vividly aware that I had a mental battle ahead in addition to physical challenges if I was ever going to climb on rock again.

A few days later, I texted Karla: "I'm heading to the site."

We'd kept missing each other, as she worked seven days a week at her restaurant, Ed's Cantina, and the busy summer season was hitting top gear, with the final weekend of June rapidly approaching.

She stopped by Bird & Jim with her dog, Lola, and was excited for updates.

"Hands first," she said.

"Well, the nail is growing as Ignatiuk hoped," I told her. "I call this the narwhal stage." My weirdly shaped, bulbous thumb with a nail growing out of the end reminded me of the whale with a tusk. I told her about my progress on the climbing wall and other daily accomplishments.

"And as far as Bird and Jim goes," I continued, "I think we're hoping to open in late July or early August. Even as I say that, I don't truly believe it, looking at the state of things."

As I gave her the tour, Lola would not leave my left thumb alone, sniffing persistently, trying to get closer.

I felt a faint memory trigger as I drove home.

"I've heard about dogs that can sniff out infections," I told Adam when I got home. "And this thing is getting bigger each day." I had no sensation in either thumb, so I held my left thumb up to my mouth to feel if it was hot. "Take a picture of my thumb so I can show Ignatiuk," I told Adam. (My level of dexterity wasn't up to the task.)

Dr. Ignatiuk texted back within minutes.

"He told me to squeeze it gently," I said as I put the phone down.

I gently squeezed the head of the narwhal and pus oozed from the flakey skin where it had been stitched. My heart sank. "Oh god," I said. "I think my thumb is infected." I told Dr. Ignatiuk, who texted back.

"He's calling in antibiotics," I reported to Adam. "He wants me on them for a few days, and then he wants to operate."

I had seen Dr. Ignatiuk at his office five times by now, but it had been almost a week since my last visit. I was also seeing the occupational therapist in Boulder, who was helping with splints for sleeping, scar tissue breakdown, and movement. At the doctor's visits, staff would X-ray my left thumb to check on the healing and nail growth, after which I'd visit with Ignatiuk for about ten minutes, reviewing the images.

He texted again, saying there was no need to come in for this week's office visit. The surgery would be June 30, just four days away.

"Sorry," I told Adam. "You'll have to take another day off."

During this surgery, Dr. Ignatiuk intended to tackle several problems with the left thumb. He'd clean up the infection, then repair the bone, which at some point had broken (it was fragile from extensive burns). He'd use pins that would remain in place for almost two months.

He also planned to advance the skin flap under the nail and increase the web of the left thumb by cutting and resurfacing the palm skin. For this, he'd be adding a new skin graft from my groin (yay—more pubic hair on my palm).

CHAPTER THIRTY-NINE

The Final Countdown

Estes Park and UCHealth, July and August, 2017

"The bones in your left thumb were like Swiss cheese," Dr. Ignatiuk said after the surgery on June 30, 2017. "But I was able to get two pins through to hold the compromised bones together. Those bones are very small. With this reinforcement, I hope they will heal."

It was eleven days later, and I was back in his office, where he was carefully removing the bandages. The bottom layer was a thick wad of cotton stapled to my palm covering the skin grafts that were resurfaced during the latest surgery. The staples were needed to get a tight, protective wrap that would help in the healing. As he removed the staples, I sweated with pain.

He paused. "Sorry—I didn't expect you'd have this much sensitivity."

I agreed. "It's surprising how much I can feel in my palms while my thumbs remain dead to sensation."

The narwhal stage was no longer. The skin flap from my arm was now extended under the nail, covering the bottom of the tusk. Stitches securing this new look traveled around the outside of the thumb, over the top, and down into the deepened web, with a new gusset of added skin. My thumb looked like an oddly stuffed, stitched-up doll that had seen better days. More frightful were the heads of the two pins that jutted out of the back of my hand, holding my thumb bones together.

Back home, I feared catching the pins on anything—a towel, my clothing, even the shower door. I moved slowly and deliberately and limited my excursions. No hiking for now; while the doctors hadn't said no to this, I was too afraid of tripping or snagging the pins. I could still pour myself into the Peloton, though, spinning out my angst and anxiety, temporarily alleviating some of my burdens.

The surgery was a step forward for my rebuilt left thumb, but a step back for my climbing. Instead of pulling on our climbing wall, I tried to train my right hand's new crimp grip—a basic in climbing, with three versions. The *open-hand crimp* is straight fingers using the end pads of your index, middle, and ring fingers, with your pinkie; the *half-crimp* uses all four with bent knuckles rolling up on the top digits of the fingers; and the *full-crimp* adds the thumb, wrapping it on top of the index fingers.

Well, I didn't have all those fingers anymore, or thumb-wrapping ability. The missing middle finger, once the longest, was now the smallest of all the amputated fingers, gone at the first knuckle. This was the knuckle that had always given me problems and was perpetually swollen; now it was gone. Next to that was my shortened, club-like ring finger, which added complications to this grip. In addition, this finger was crowned with a challenging skin graft that tended to callous and blister at the same time.

In my new crimp complex, the long index finger, with its original length and pad, had to bend high in the air. To enable the shortened ring finger to reach an edge, I had to force my wrist to turn out to the right, to compensate for the missing length. The nub in the middle was useless in this application. The ridged thumb pointed up and out to the left. What would that nub do when I pulled down and climbed on a crimp? Would I be able to keep it up in the air?

With my climbing comeback on hold, my focus turned to Bird & Jim. In July I met with Ethan and the food reps, including Kind Coffee, to craft a unique blend to serve at Bird & Jim. It was bold, and we called it "Isabella's," in honor of that bold lady of the nineteenth century, Isabella Bird. John, our sommelier partner, set up tastings with wine reps so we could build our wine list.

I was big on Burgundy, thanks to our 2002 trip, my first to Fontainebleau, France. On a rest day, we had headed south in our rental car, a map and a *Let's Go France* guidebook on my lap.

The Final Countdown

"It's November first, isn't it?" I asked. "This town, Beaune, is about a half-hour ahead, and it has this famous wine auction every year. It's called *Hospices de Beaune*, and it's a three-day festival. Let's go!" Walking around Beaune, drinking the world's best Burgundy, I fell in love with the wine. Although I'd become passionate about quality wine, I still had lots to learn. John, our reps, and the Court of Master Sommeliers could teach me.

A restaurant that's also a construction site was not the best place for wine tasting. "We can't taste in here," I'd declared. "It's too loud, and I don't want to get in the way." In early August, John had moved a few tables outside on the patio, which ran the length of the building, and we set up weekly meetings with different wine reps. Pouring just a little taste in the glass, I rejoiced that I could grip the stem and raise the glass to my lips, enjoying the splendid view of the Rocky Mountains—an ideal way to build our list.

Looking straight ahead, across the road, you could see the peaks called the Twin Sisters in the distance; to the right was the classic Front Range, all the way from McHenrys Peak to Flattop Mountain. We waved at friends who drove by.

"Why didn't Vic use this patio?" John asked.

I explained that Vic had thought the extra outdoor seating would have been too much for the staff to handle. "The drinks railing we're putting out here is Vic's idea," I told John. "He said that if he were doing the remodel, that'd be one thing he would add."

"Great idea. It's nice we can carry on with the things Vic wanted," John said, and nobody could argue.

Reality settled in as the first week of August ended. We were still many weeks away from opening and had to face the fact that an August opening was out. We decided to aim for the end of September.

"We can catch the tail end of the season," I said, making a stab at some optimism, reminding the team that Estes stayed busy until late October. "We will get a taste of volume and the busy season," I said. "Although it'll be rough on finances heading into the slow off-season, we'll make it through the winter," I said, trying to encourage the team, and myself.

On board with trying to make the best of a situation that was ultimately out of our control, Ethan agreed, adding, "This'll give us time to work out any kinks and be ready for next summer." John and Jimmy tossed out another idea: "There are the holidays, and we can do wine-and-whiskey dinners." I liked it. "I'd love to do a special menu for the twelve days of Christmas," I said. "And of course, a New Year's Eve four- or five-course menu with wine pairings."

Still trying to look at the bright side of another crushing delay, I shared some recent medical news. "For me, the delay is okay, I guess, since I have surgery on August 21." This surgery would mean five to seven days back in the hospital, I told them. "Funny, I was so afraid to leave the hospital, but now I am dreading going back." Still, I definitely wanted the surgery behind me before opening. "And I'll be rid of the pins in my thumb."

"What are they going to do?" they asked.

I paused to explain, as I was still getting used to the latest medical procedure that seemed like a science experiment to me. "They're going to take the skin, nerve, and an artery from the back of my index finger and move all of that over to my thumb. It'll create more length and give my left thumb some sensation." They listened, shaking their heads. (To this day, when I touch my left thumb tip, I feel it on the back of my index finger, since that's the way the nerve is programmed. Ignatiuk hoped my brain would rewire this connection, but it never occurred.)

I checked in on August 21, and Ignatiuk operated during a solar eclipse, whose path of totality crossed over Wyoming, a few hours north. All I remember was the mistake I made, telling the anesthesiologist I didn't need the pre-anesthesia cocktail before going into the ER. This meant I stayed conscious for the roll down the halls and seeing the operating chamber for the first time.

I was shocked at how cold it was in there. I heard nurses and doctors chitchatting about their weekend between work directives and pushing equipment into position; then someone reached for my arm and secured it on a table next to me. *This was a huge mistake*, I thought, verging on panic. Thankfully, they lowered the mask to my face and I breathed in deeply.

I woke up on the seventh floor of the UCHealth inpatient pavilion, once again in the care of charge nurse Grace and her team, with a left thumb boasting a surprising new length and shape. The patch of skin from the back of my index finger was stitched onto my thumb tip by four corners. The meaty mass of the inside of my thumb was visible in between the four corner stitches. This freshly laid skin patch was a dark, dusky purple.

Oh no, this again.

I thought about the lost thumb tip, grateful that I'd still retained the nail for this flap surgery. For the next few days, a resident or Ignatiuk would come in and poke the new graft, hoping for signs of "capillary refill," meaning those small blood vessels were working properly. The skin transplant was questionable initially, but eventually it thrived.

I went home on August 27 with more stitches and seams holding together patches of skin—and another half-inch of a left thumb. The pins were gone, too, and I was grateful all the way around. Work on the left hand was complete; the next step for that thumb was letting it heal.

During my stay, Dr. Ignatiuk shared some news with us: He and Jess were moving to New Jersey. They planned to start a family and wanted to relocate closer to Jess's family.

"I'm sad to leave the mountains, but happy at the prospect of starting our family," he said.

"I'm a little scared about you leaving," I confessed, "but happy for you and Jess."

He said he wouldn't leave until my hands were finished. There'd be one more surgery on my right hand in November.

"Sounds good," I said. "Permission to pull onto climbing holds?" I asked.

He smiled. "Yes, just take it slow."

I assured him I would, and that I'd leave my left thumb out of the mix. I told him I'd let him know when we held the soft opening at Bird & Jim, hoping they could make it up to Estes Park.

"We wouldn't miss it for the world," he said.

Chapter Forty

Bird & Jim
Estes Park, September 2017

September marked five months since the accident. I opened the mental box where I'd stashed away all those apprehensions about working in a restaurant again. *How would my new hands function? What could I pick up?*

My wine-tasting had disclosed I could manage the stem of a wineglass or a coupe, but I couldn't grip a pint glass. Could I carry plates and place them smoothly on a table? Would my skin grafts be able to handle the constant hand-washing of restaurant work? Beyond that, I returned to questions I'd had before the accident: *What kind of owner-operator would I be—what kind of boss?* Especially with my physical limitations.

I'd worked for two dramatically different owners over my eighteen years at the Dunraven. Dale had employed me for twelve years; Andy, for the subsequent six. Dale had purchased the historic restaurant from the founder years before I came to Estes. He could be challenging to work under. This was the family's livelihood, and as such, he took it seriously, and rightfully so. He was a hands-on owner and was there the majority of the week. If you did your job with just a few mistakes, no problem; but the chaotic nature of restaurant work made that unlikely.

The Dunraven's incredibly competent, dedicated staff was a small brood and included Dale's wife (also his business partner) and their three children. Most of my coworkers had been there for more than twenty years. Dale and I had our confrontations but managed to find mutual respect. The management style had dramatically shifted when Andy bought the place in 2011 and introduced a new vibe at work: Let's have fun and get the job done.

What would my style be? I had endured tremendous stress with the accident. A different version of me was evolving, but the stress of healing and enduring surgeries while trying to open a restaurant was oppressive. I was taxing my family with this investment and tying my success—or failure—to family finances. I didn't want to bring that anxiety to my staff. I could share that with my partners, who had signed into ownership with sweat equity (plus a salary) and no personal financial investment or risk. If something happened, they could walk away and find another job.

I did not have that escape. Also, I knew that my impairment added to the stress of the opening. I wondered: *Would my stress and sadness turn me into a detestable tyrant I didn't want to be?*

There was another consideration. I was a woman, which meant I'd already run into some disrespect during this endeavor. I'll never forget the equipment salesman who felt the need to condescendingly explain that an ice bin needed to be connected to a drain, and the loan officer who rudely dismissed me—all because I was a woman, or because they had lessons to learn. I wanted to be a boss bitch, but in a good way, not a bitchy boss. I'd seen that Karla could do it, despite her numerous stories of being mansplained to, demeaned, and underestimated.

I was barreling into my restaurant dreams, yet I was vulnerable. The accident had softened my edges in some ways, while simultaneously hardening them. I saw that my vulnerability could spin me either way and leave me weeping or filled with wrath. The gratitude I felt for surviving, and for the help of my doctors and care team, put me in a fairly positive healing state, as opposed to bitterness, which could've been an option. Sure, I was frustrated and angry that this had happened to me, but I'd found peace through thankfulness, which outshined those thoughts.

I acknowledged that I was changing. The Melissa of April 1, 2017, was vastly different from the woman now struggling to heal. I'd had the rug pulled out from under me, and uncertainty loomed everywhere. Of course this had altered me as a person. But I'd also been forced to learn how to ask for help and delegate the things I did not excel at before. In the restaurant of my dreams, I was always participating, not dictating. I wanted to be a competent leader who earned the respect of my staff—someone people could look up to, not pity or fear. I wanted to create a successful restaurant and pleasant environment for customers and employees, fostering a safe, happy, and lucrative workplace. I wanted to build a Bird & Jim crew that would rival the dream team I'd left behind at the Dunraven. Not having full use of my hands also humbled me, taking the almighty ego out of the scenario. Still, the stress of healing, functioning, and pursuing success was relentless.

After the opening, a friend told me, "Well, at least the accident made you a better person." I tilted my head, unsure whether to take this as an insult or a compliment.

"True," I conceded, shutting down my internal debate.

What did it matter? I am who I am today, thanks to the good and the wretched. What I'd endured had taught me perseverance, fortitude, and an appreciation for life that I had never believed I was capable of. There was no answer to these unknown worries, just deep conviction that I'd give it my all. I vowed to take the middle road as an owner-operator, placing these future unknowns back in their respective boxes in my mental closet. *You will confront these plaguing quandaries and resolve them, lightening your load. Be competent and kind*, I told myself. *You know how to do this.*

I backed out of the closet and closed the door, for now.

As a manager, however, I was lacking something crucial: a team. We had the supervisors for the kitchen and the bar and the business, Ethan and Jimmy and John. But the question was obvious in September, as the tourist season wound down and summer help returned to school: "How will you get a staff at this time of year?" My answer: "I am going to hire anyone with a pulse. We will figure out who works and who doesn't as we go along."

In that week following my last hospital stay, with open wounds, stitches, and a splinted hand, we interviewed applicants at the construction site and gradually assembled a team. Some crew members we hired are still a driving force at Bird & Jim today.

When the new hires would ask "When do we start?," we could only give them an educated guess. All I knew was that once we had passed inspection, we would open.

By mid-September, it was starting to look like an actual restaurant. Walls up, painting done, fixtures wired. At night, we turned the construction site into a practice restaurant, getting the flow and feeling, positioning tables, tweaking floor plans, and numbering tables. Ethan and his team brought the kitchen up to speed. We tasked any visiting family or friends with jobs, assembling lockers for the too-small office; setting up storage space, including shelves and drawers; arranging tables, chairs, barstools, sofas, and love seats for the lounge. A crucial part of our vision for the restaurant was this lounge area off the bar, by the picture windows, with comfortable sofas and love seats, and tables if people wanted to eat right there. The look was coming together.

It was exciting to unpack boxes of items I'd ordered and see how it all worked together. It started to look kind of fantastic, once everything was in place, including the old tables sanded and adorned with Lichtenburg designs on the legs; thanks, Dave. I loved the whole vibe we had created, but I had to wonder: Would Estes love it or hate it? Is this too much for our laid-back town? What about the 4.5 million visitors every year? I wanted to make a restaurant for everyone, from the guy getting off his construction job to a family coming to celebrate a special occasion. I whipsawed between excitement and dread, and slept very little in the nights before the opening.

At the end of September, I pulled stitches out of my hand before driving to Bird & Jim to help train the staff. We had some rehearsal customers lined up: Charlie, Cheryl, and Vicky and her children. Our new staff greeted them, walked them to their table, and let them settle in before handing them menus. There were lots of operational details unsettled (Where's the sugar go? The coffeemaker? The to-go boxes?), so we focused on hospitality. The place still felt like a construction site. We promised the team that as opening day got closer, we would create some SOPs (standard operating procedures) for all of us.

Jimmy worked with the bar team, stocking the shelves and practicing cocktail recipes. Ethan could only do so much, since some kitchen equipment wasn't yet installed. But with long nights and arduous work, the kitchen was clean, prepped, and ready for opening. John trained staff on how to open wine bottles. I onboarded staff, wrote the handbook, worked on floor charts, and built half-complete SOPs, including opening and closing duties, job roles, "how-to" diagrams of how to set a table and roll silverware in our handmade cloth napkins, and created menu buttons in the point-of-sale system.

Our invitation-only soft opening nights were set for October 2 and 3, 2017. Although I was able to perform my personal self-care, it was time-consuming. I arrived at the restaurant and asked a friend, who was also a new team member, to put my earrings and necklace on me, since Adam was still working when I left the house. The staff saw food for the first time (we couldn't cook until the fire marshal had approved the hood system, which happened on October 1).

We opened the doors, and invited in customers. Friends and acquaintances filed in as we simpered and beamed. It disheartened me that I could only hand out menus and pick up empty wineglasses, but I went through the motions with a smile.

People came in wide-eyed, wowed by the new look and feel. They scanned the large lounge and bar area from the entrance, yet their gaze typically fell on my hands. I kept smiling and assuring people I was doing just fine.

We survived the first night. It was fantastic and brutal all at the same time as we bumped into each other, trying to find our rhythm and flow. The food was delicious, but the timing of appetizers and entrees was a fiasco. The kitchen team struggled with courses and how the ticket items printed, and to what station, missing some items and making food for entire tables twice, slowing them down as they learned extemporaneously.

After closing, we read the comment cards people had filled out at our request: "Didn't like your choice of music," "The music was too loud," "Our meals came out too quickly," "Our meals came out too slow," "Everything was perfect," "We love the music and the vibe," "A wonderful experience from food and wine to service." In short, it was not horrible—just a few kinks to work out—and we did it all again on the second soft-open night.

October 3 was a blur. It was my forty-fourth birthday, and that afternoon I'd learned that my brother and father had rushed Mom to the hospital. She had developed sepsis following back surgery, and their updates added yet another mammoth worry—much more important than a forgotten drink order.

Lessons from the first night gave us more confidence for the second. This time, my list of invitees included close friends, the people who cared for me and visited me in the hospital countless times. That meant Karla, Bronson, Quinn, Jen, Marsha, Kathleen, Andrew, and Jackie, and all of the friends who'd helped with construction: Kiel, Chris, and Jim; Dave, who'd finished the table legs; and Mary Ellen and Walt. And of course, Dr. Ignatiuk and Jess.

Well into the evening, I gave myself a birthday present. I stopped flying around the room, checking on everything, and sat down with Adam, some close friends, and Dr. Ignatiuk and Jess. This was special; this was wonderful. I looked around at the exciting new space that we'd imagined and made a reality. I looked at my friends, my husband, and the surgeon who had restored my life. I was celebrating being alive, enduring, and working nonstop to reach this point. It was surreal; I was both giddy and stunned.

"Well, at least you're not all eating at 'Melissa's,' a restaurant named after its dead owner," I joked. Most people chuckled; some were speechless. "Too soon?" I laughed.

I could feel the fabric of my protective net surrounding me that night, in the restaurant I'd fought so hard to create. I had literally invested my blood, sweat, pain, and tears. I was dazed, as if living in a dream, which, in a way, I was. I had dreamt and thought about this moment for years, from the old me before the accident to the new me, who I was still trying to let in and understand.

As I crawled into bed later that night, Adam looked at me. "Well," he said, "are you happy your dreams came true tonight?"

"Yes, I am," I said. "But in my dreams, I always had my hands."

It was a constant struggle to adjust and accept the new me. I was continuing to move through life because it was my only option—pushing forward to reach this juncture. After the opening nights, I understood this moment as the beginning of years of refinement, providing me with more to focus on, meaning Bird & Jim and my personal healing evolution.

The carefree, climbing-obsessed old Melissa became a new person who had sustained intense trauma, dug deep to find a way through, and opened a restaurant. Now, the new me had to pour all I had into Bird & Jim, an endeavor filled with positivity but also uncertainty and fear. Devoting all of me to the restaurant had become an inherent part of my life's path. And since climbing was no longer an accessible, carefree, fun activity, I filled that hole with the restaurant. I had never intended to diverge completely from the old me, so I hoped the two would become one someday.

I tried to explain my emotions to Adam, the happiness alongside the melancholy. I told him it sometimes felt like I was wearing a cloak of sadness. "In the beginning," I said, "it was made of this heavy, thick rubber material. Now, after all this time and all of my surgeries, and learning how to function, it's more like a thick, wool suit on a warm day that I can't shed." I smiled. "Maybe one day it'll be cotton, then linen. Maybe I can get to a fine gauze."

I wanted to feel the happiness and joy of accomplishing what we'd worked so resolutely toward, but there was a barrier. Some of it was mental, and some just reality. We had many days to go before the restaurant would operate smoothly. There'd be a myriad of hardships and challenges. I tried to let the light in and feel the accomplishment and satisfaction. I struggled to allow myself to feel the true highs of this week, not just because of the work ahead, but because of the trauma and of what my soul and psyche had endured. I found the strength to save myself from living in the severe lows, but due to the mental scar tissue associated with my suffering, the extreme highs eluded me. I hoped my healing would continue, enabling me to feel authentic, unencumbered joy.

I also began to understand that no single moment would define a point of complete healing, of being 100 percent back in any game, whether it was the restaurant, climbing, or life. The road toward healing would be a journey based on the effort and spirit I contributed.

I fell asleep the night of my birthday reminding myself that I'd faced the fears of working in my new restaurant with my new hands. I decided to grab that box in my mental closet and throw it away. This was just the beginning of recovery. I knew more healing was ahead of me, but I realized I could do it. I needed to open and eventually discard more boxes in my closet, but it felt good to confront and remove even one.

"I will get better about being happy," I told Adam as we lay in bed. I knew this and believed it. It wasn't like flipping a light switch; it would only come with time, patience, and hard work.

In the coming days and weeks, Bird & Jim was a hit, and I was delighted. The community welcomed us, and we got our name out to the fall visitors coming to Estes Park to enjoy the season. The Autumn Gold Festival and the Elk Fest brought in a steady stream of customers to celebrate the beauty of autumn in Estes Park. There were still some kinks to smooth out, but we started off with a bang.

For me, there was more functionality to gain and deeper satisfaction to attain. I told myself, *Welcome in the good, and be open to the happiness I'm struggling to feel.* My net was reinforced, almost buoyant with this success and the love I felt from the community, and the opening of what I had worked so hard for—Bird & Jim.

CHAPTER FORTY-ONE

Opening the Climbing Trunk
Estes Park, October 2017

I WAS PEDALING AWAY ON MY PELOTON WITH A MILLION THINGS ON MY mind when my phone buzzed. It was nine days after our official opening, on October 12. I'd been debating whether to try my first climb on our garage wall and (as always) thinking about the restaurant. That's why my phone was in a holder opposite my water bottle—I had learned quickly that owning a restaurant meant never disconnecting. Though we were only open for dinner at this time, there was always something.

Climbing took up much of my brain space, too. In September, once I was out of the splint from the August surgery, I got back on the climbing wall and returned to where I'd left off with pull-ins. When I thought about making moves on the wall, though, I was reluctant, afraid I'd hurt myself or undo any of the good the doctors had done, even though they'd given me permission to climb lightly.

I also dreaded the pain and my lack of strength. *Will you even be able to do this?* I wondered. As a climber naturally would, when I did pull-ins, I eyed the next hold and thought about the movement. But I couldn't fathom reaching out and making contact. I also thought I could choose to give myself a break, just as my Peloton instructor called out to add resistance and sprint.

That's when the phone buzzed with an incoming text. It wasn't the restaurant. It was from a friend, and the message was grim. It was about a friend and climbing partner, Quinn Brett, a skilled climbing ranger who had been at the Bird & Jim opening, heading out directly afterward to climb at Yosemite.

The message was horrifying: Quinn had taken a bad fall from more than 100 feet while attempting a speed ascent of the Nose, one of the routes up El Capitan. She was alive, but in the hospital with head trauma and a fractured spine. They were operating, but surgeons were already saying she would never walk again.

I slowly stopped pedaling and sat there, numb.

Just like that, another devastating tragedy. Nine days ago, Quinn had been full of life, finishing her season as a climbing ranger and excited to start her off-season adventuring.

I texted back naive words of encouragement. "You never know—my doctors said I'd only have four fingers—maybe Quinn can defy the prognosis and walk again." (Woefully, time would prove that Quinn's doctors were correct.)

Quinn was a dear friend, one I had dreamed of someday climbing with again, when I allowed myself to dream. Now this. Somehow this hardened my resolve, and I decided that today would be my first attempt to link moves on our wall. *Someday had to come sooner or later. Might as well be today. I'd do it for Quinn and me.*

After a cool-down ride and some breakfast, I went into the garage and put on my climbing shoes. A friend from Kentucky was visiting, Cletus, and he was ready to climb with me and cheer me on.

I approached the wall and wrapped my palms around the plastic holds, placing my feet on equally large holds. When I shifted my weight off the mattress and onto the wall, pain shot through my hands and reverberated through my body. A stomach-churning, sloshy feeling accompanied by pain from my grafts was almost enough to make me quit before I started. I looked up to the right at the next jug, 3 feet away. I wanted to reach out and grab the hold, but my brain told me, *No—you don't have fingers. It'll hurt worse—you can't.*

I overruled myself, moved my hand, and latched the hold. The internal battle between my brain and my will continued, distracting me as I moved my foot, gracelessly, carelessly, to make the next hand movement. My foot slipped, I released the holds, and I stepped off and away from the wall. Quickly I examined my hands to make sure all of the skin was still in place. Pain screeched through me. I paused and breathed through it. If I could keep my foot on, maybe I could pull through a few more moves, I thought. Annoyed at myself for sloppy climbing, I tried to calm my nerves. *You know how to climb. You can do this.*

I pulled back onto the wall, repeated the first move, shutting down the chatter of my brain's warning signals again. I placed my foot with intention and dynamically reached out for the next hold, snagging it. My nubs and skin grafts were smashed onto the hold, causing ghastly pain. Yet I kept going, moving my feet and advancing my right hand one more time. I set up for another move, but the pain made me decide to step off.

I turned and realized that Cletus was videoing these attempts. He lowered the phone and smiled. "Don't call it a comeback," he said with a sly smile.

I shook my head. "That's enough for now."

I walked outside, unconsciously standing where the accident had occurred, bent over and nauseous with pain.

"I cannot believe I just did that," I choked out. It took about ten minutes to work through the throbbing agony, and then I went back for more.

This time, I made five moves in a row, starting close to the bottom of the board and linking to the top. Grabbing a large hold at the top of the board, I felt another gross sensation as my palm skin smooshed with the pressure, feeling connected but oddly loose.

"That's good for today," I told Cletus.

This was a new situation for me, tough to absorb: I wanted to keep going but knew I physically could not. My arms were so weak, and the pain became intolerable.

I started calculating a different approach for next time.

"I'm not ready to wrap both palms around that huge jug yet, after that sloshy feeling," I said. I told Cletus that between the first two tries, the pain had subsided a bit, "But now it's not going away." I thanked him for being my witness and encouraging me. "It wasn't much, but at least it was something."

He scoffed. "Are you kidding me? That was incredible, Mel!"

When Adam came home from work that night, we talked somberly about the news from Yosemite. But then I excitedly showed him the videos of me linking moves on our wall. This showed me there was something else in my climbing trunk besides sadness—there really was hope. I had lived through six months of trauma, fears, and distress, with a central thought: I would never be able to climb again. It was the refrain I'd first screamed on the ride to the hospital, staring at burnt bones.

While this day's efforts opened the door to the old Melissa, the session also undoubtedly demonstrated how challenging the journey back into climbing would be. If not for my love of the sport, I wouldn't have tried it with missing fingers, fused and oddly shaped thumbs, and skin grafts. Climbing was part of my inner fabric.

"It was so painful, but all of my skin is still on my hands, so that's a good start," I told Adam.

"I can only imagine how much that hurt," he said. "I am super proud of you."

I knew I had a long way to go. Instead of rhythmic, instinctive moves, I had to convince my brain that this was what we were doing. I had to force the motion.

"There was no style or grace, just desperate grabbing," I said as I rewatched the videos.

"It'll come together," Adam said.

That night, I settled into bed feeling satisfied that I had faced two enormous challenges: functioning in the restaurant and climbing. I was flabbergasted that I could see a path back to climbing with fewer fingers, ridged thumbs, and marred hands that were 70 percent covered in grafts. In my deepest despair, I'd never believed I would have the opportunity to try again at the sport I loved so much. My effort that day was maximal; the results, feeble. I still couldn't imagine latching holds dynamically and pulling down hard onto real rock; not yet, anyway. This comeback would take years of dedication and arduous training, but I was determined, and somehow, ecstatic.

It had been an emotional day. Lying there in bed, I couldn't stop thinking about Quinn and her anguish. Never walking again, for someone so active—for anyone? It reminded me how lucky I was. I got to try.

Quinn was granted the gift of survival, to be among the living, but her road would be exponentially more challenging than mine.

I stopped thinking of anything else and started to pray for Quinn.

CHAPTER FORTY-TWO

Every Girl's Dream

Estes Park, October–December, 2017

THE STORY OF MY ACCIDENT AND RECOVERY—AND THE RESTAURANT—had reached a Denver TV station. A reporter from the NBC affiliate, Channel 9, did an inspirational story about me that fall. I was at the point where my left hand had healed enough to begin laser hair removal on my palms.

Some grafts had come from my groin area, so my palms had pubic hair—strange, but true. Skin grafts have DNA and continue to do what they are programmed for, no matter where they're moved to. They'll grow hair, for instance, or they won't toughen up. I wanted the hairs zapped before my final surgery, scheduled for November.

The TV station interviewed me and Dr. Ignatiuk and aired their feel-good segment on the five o'clock news. After it aired, Dr. Ignatiuk messaged me: "Of course, the story focused on the pubic hair." I texted back a quote from the story: "Strong will need more laser hair removal, but hairy palms seem a small price to pay for hands that work." I added: "Every girl's dream."

Dr. Ignatiuk said he was writing a paper about the bilateral flaps. "I suspect it will get published, since it has never been done before, and because of your success."

I found it comforting that my case and what I'd gone through might help others.

My restaurant skills were another work in progress. I was healed enough that I could now awkwardly carry plates to tables. My fingers gripped with everything they had, but my thumbs awkwardly jutted out. A full water pitcher was demanding on my wrists and would make my arms shake. I'd also started to clear plates and clean tables, which meant frequent hand-washing, dipping my hands into buckets of sanitizer, and wringing out rags to wipe tables. These chemicals are nasty on regular hand skin. My hand grafts—harvested from my thighs, arms, and groin—dried out and hurt more with this abuse. At night, I would coat my hands in a heavy lotion, put argan oil in silicone-lined gloves, and sleep with my hands nestled and soothed. Then I'd repeat the torture the following day.

I frequently dropped things and was picky about what I touched and how I carried glasses and plates. Unless the glassware had a stem or a narrow grip, I had to hold it with two hands. I adapted, learned, and progressed. I was self-conscious at first, but moved on. *You've come this far—if anyone wants to judge, well, screw them*, I coached myself.

Some things were just off the list: buttons (eventually doable, thanks to a button-fastener hook a friend sent—thank you, Nora), earrings with backs, necklace clasps, lids, and doorknobs. With time, some of these maneuvers became part of my compromised movement repertoire, while others still required two hands or assistance. But I was gradually becoming more capable.

I also progressed in climbing, performing two climbs to eventually five climbs on our wall, in a session. I started doing pull-ups on our hangboard to build strength and training before the inevitable downtime that would come after the next surgery. I was a shell of my former self, but hope grew with my progress.

Knowing that the November surgery would be my last helped me find strength to face another round under the knife. Happily, it wouldn't require a hospital stay. The skin under my right middle-finger nub was contracting, pulling the nub down. This motion was awkward, and the nub ground painfully into anything I grasped, especially climbing holds. The plan was to release scar tissue at the nub with debriding and resurfacing, Dr. Ignatiuk had explained. "Depending on the debridement, we might need to add a graft to the right finger and base."

As for my right thumb, Ignatiuk planned to "advance the existing skin flap graft to realign the tip, adding some skin next to the outside edge of the nail. When we advance the graft, we will add skin to the base of the right thumb."

The November surgery went well, and soon I was back on my Peloton, my right hand in a cast. I couldn't climb for a while, but again, at least I could get some sweat and energy out, and this time, I knew I had something I could return to—climbing.

My new worry revolved around Adam leaving for Hueco Tanks and my having to face life on my own for a while. By Thanksgiving, his tree service had finished putting the Christmas lights up for Estes Park. We typically exited for El Paso as soon as the lights were up and celebrated many "Tanks-givings" in Hueco. This year, Adam stayed until November 29 before leaving. It was a one-two punch: being alone and not going climbing with Adam in the place we both loved.

"Who knows if I could even climb there?" I told Adam one night before he left. The holds are notoriously sharp and the climbing is steep. Maybe some of the roof jugs would be doable, I mused, rather than the incut thin crimps. "I can't imagine putting my body weight on my palm grafts on real rock," I told him. Besides, I had stitches in my thumb and a raw graft on my nub. And I couldn't leave the restaurant anyway, so it was a moot point.

I must have said this a hundred times, talking myself into accepting the inevitable. "I want you to go," I half-lied. I was stressed about doing stuff for myself, but thankfully, our friend Andrew was able to step in to help me with anything I might need, while also running the tree crew so Adam could get away.

Andrew had been living in the apartment above the garage with Ben, another climber friend and tree crew member. They had both helped tremendously with the pets and the tree service when we were in the hospital. "God knows Adam deserves to get away after making so many sacrifices, and catering to me," I'd told them.

"My love," Adam broke in, "I'll be back to see you for Christmas." He reminded me that we'd also meet in the Caymans to visit my parents at the end of January, and he'd be home in early March.

I knew this was how it had to be. I wondered about the flight to meet him in Houston en route to the Caymans, fumbling with my bags and going through airport security without assistance. But that was two months away. There were plenty of other things to worry about in between. I sulked as he drove away.

When Adam was home for Christmas, he saw me with grocery bags in each hand. "Wow, look at you, carrying bags!"

What was he talking about?

Oh yeah. I suddenly realized that with him gone, I had grown more capable. We were planning a Christmas dinner with Quinn, her parents, and some others. Quinn was recently out of Craig Hospital in Denver and was learning to adapt to life without the use of her legs.

I shrugged off Adam's compliment, not wanting to celebrate a return to mundane tasks like lugging groceries. I wanted to be living the life of the old Melissa, climbing in Hueco, but I knew I had plenty to focus on at Bird & Jim. We had a series of wine-and-whiskey pairing dinners planned for the winter, trying to keep a revenue stream and excitement high in our first slow season. Karla and I took a level-one sommelier class in Boulder, and I was spending time with Quinn and friends, visiting museum exhibits, taking strolls, and enjoying happy hours.

A frequent occurrence was reconnecting with friends I hadn't seen in a while.

"I'm sorry I didn't reach out when you were in the hospital," one friend told me. "I was going through a hard time and felt ridiculous, knowing what you were going through."

I paused, feeling empathy. "You don't have to burn your hands off to be going through a tough time," I said. "There are people all around us who are navigating difficulties. People are losing loved ones, dealing with a diagnosis, suffering from depression or addiction, enduring chronic pain, hurt from dysfunctional relationships. Lots of people are feeling discontented and lost. Life is full of trials and hardships. One trial doesn't have to outweigh the other to be valid or significant." I told her how navigating any tumultuous period can give us tools to help us face the next tough stretch. "And the way life is going, I am sure there will be other challenges," I said. "We are stronger than we give ourselves credit for."

I continued to share more stories of the support I'd received, hoping I could be a thread in her net, providing encouragement the next time hardship came her way.

CHAPTER FORTY-THREE

Hello, Old Friend

Estes Park, December 2017–March 2018

A LITTLE MORE THAN A MONTH AFTER THE NOVEMBER SURGERY, I started pulling on the Kilter holds on our stairs. These holds were my training wheels after surgeries, and I was now on take three of my dogged return to climbing.

The middle right nub was still delicate and sensitive, so I wore rubber kitchen gloves for protection. On smaller crimps, when my right index finger (regular-length) and ring finger (partial-length, club-like) gripped an edge, the middle nub sank past the hold, unable to join the party. If the hold was large enough and the nub could reach, it hurt as it ground into the plastic. Eventually, I experimented with buddy taping—taping the nub to an adjacent finger—but that didn't help. I was recently out of a cast, and found that I could strengthen what I had left by holding onto a wooden training edge—weight training for your fingers. I added a 5-pound dumbbell attached by webbing to an eyebolt at the bottom of the wood block. Ultimately, I learned that dropping the nub produced the strongest grip power I could attain.

By January of 2018, I was back on the climbing wall, and the gloves were off.

During one of my first sessions back, I had my first "real" fall (meaning, something other than a foot slip or intentionally stepping off). I ripped off a jug, dry-firing out of nowhere, to use climbers' jargon. I was fully engaged, weighing a hold and pulling hard, and my hand violently slipped off the hold without warning, resulting in an explosive fall.

I thumped onto the mattresses and immediately checked my hand, seeing that the right nub had forfeited a chunk of skin. I panicked and texted Dr. Ignatiuk a photo, saying "You worked so hard to put this skin on, and I just ripped it off climbing! Will it grow back?"

He assured me it would.

I learned that dry-firing was to be a common occurrence with my new fingers. Without distal phalanges (the bones at the tips) or active thumbs, either hand tended to rip off holds unexpectedly. This was tough for my spotters, and I warn people of this tendency to the present day.

Salve and climbing tape would be part of my climbing future. Initially, applying tape directly to the skin grafts was a stomach-churning thought.

"I cannot imagine taping this hole or the grafts," I told Adam in one of our nightly calls, while he was at Hueco. "Taking it off would yank layers of skin with it, causing more damage than protection."

He suggested I buy pre-tape.

"What's that?" I asked.

He explained that it's a foam-like tape that protects skin from the adhesive. "Something climbers would never think to use because we want the least bulk and most friction," he said. "But in your case, it sounds like a good idea."

While I waited for Amazon to deliver the pre-tape, I was comforted to see the graft happily re-growing. Adam was correct: The pre-tape under the climbing tape resulted in less-quality contact with the holds, but nothing was ideal about my new grips anyway. At least it would keep me going. I sensed that the harder I tried, the more skin I'd lose—that this would be part of the routine.

And this was just on plastic; I couldn't imagine what real rock would be like.

Climbing outside dominated my thoughts, especially with Adam in Hueco. I was terrified to try a boulder problem on natural stone, but I knew I didn't want to climb on plastic holds indoors for the rest of my life. So much of the joy of climbing is being outside in beautiful surroundings, gripping gneiss, granite, sandstone, or the syenite porphyry of Hueco. The distinctive smells of the forest and the desert, the wind rippling through aspens, or the rush of a river—all of that was part of the visceral adventure.

I hoped to try my first outdoor climb as soon as the weather allowed. I thought about boulder problems and moves that might be a good reintroduction. I wanted it to be a familiar climb so my body could rely on muscle memory while I focused on how to grip the holds with my new hands. These thoughts distracted me when awake and filled my dreams at night with a combination of hopes and fears. I knew this goal would be more emotionally and physically taxing than my first wall climb. I would need a strong, reinforced net to face it.

Adam returned in mid-March. I kept my plans quiet and watched the weather. I had settled on the Boxcar Boulder in RMNP's Wild Basin area for my first outdoor climb. I had climbed on this boulder for years before I met Adam, and for years after. I had in mind a traverse that was my project in 2000 as a rookie climber. I'd spent countless hours at this boulder, teaching myself how to climb, and eventually this traverse became a warm-up. It was close to the ground, so I wouldn't have to worry about falling, just moving and grabbing. The sequence was burned into my memory; I could see each handhold and foot jib without looking.

When the forecast looked good, I said to Adam, "If it's not too cold, I want to go to the Boxcar and try the V2 traverse this weekend."

"Really?" he said, a little surprised. He agreed it was a good place to start. "You say the word, and I'll be ready," Adam said.

On March 25, 2018, a week before the one-year anniversary of the accident, I decided that today was the day. I cried silently as I packed my climbing bag and crash pad—a ritual I had not performed in more than a year. Who knew that putting chalk and climbing shoes into a bag could be so emotional? I had done it for seventeen years without even thinking about how special it was.

"I am afraid it will be too cold," I said on the ride to Wild Basin. "But I have to try. I have to touch a real rock problem."

Adam tried to calm me: "We'll just go and see—no pressure."

True, technically there was no pressure; I could try this problem any day. But somehow, just going through the motions, packing and driving to the rock, felt like a lot. I had pointedly avoided climbing areas during my recovery, only going when my sister, nephew, and nieces visited. Even then, they were brief visits, showing them boulders I used to climb on. Bringing my climbing gear out to a rock was different, and this was intense.

We unpacked at the boulder. It was in the low 50s and overcast, normally pleasant weather for climbing. But I feared the chill would make it unbearable for my hands to function and endure the pain of grabbing real rock.

"If it's too cold, you don't have to do this," Adam reminded me.

"I know," I replied, lying. *I have to do this today.*

I slowly walked around the boulder, passing the front-side problems, feeling drawn to the steep side, the opposite side of the wall I intended to climb. With my left hand, I touched a pinch hold on a V9 I used to have wired and could repeat several times in a session. My new nubs nestled on the small edge, and my tiny left thumb tip rested on the top part of the hold that was curved, as if it was made to cradle a thumb. Seeing my deformed digits on a pinch that I'd once dominated, I couldn't hold back the tears.

Enough of this, I told myself. First things first—and that is the traverse.

I tore off small squares of pre-tape, placing them on different skin grafts and nerve bundles, then taped over the protective foam. Trying to yank my climbing shoes on, I joked, "This might be as hard on my fingers as climbing." I put my big down mittens on to keep my hands warm as we arranged our lineup of Organic crash pads. We'd brought enough pads to make a runway following the traverse, so Adam could spot me and not have to shuffle pads.

Removing my mittens, I wiped the tears from my eyes and walked over to the start. I chalked up and took a deep breath. *You know this climb; feel the holds, adjust when needed, and let your body guide you.*

I dropped the chalk bucket, clapped the excess off my hands, and placed each hand on the starting holds, taking one foot and then the other off the ground. Shifting my weight, I matched hands and then reached to my left, touching the first hold, a sloper, making full contact with my palm and fingers. My thumb did not know what to do, and my brain started with its warning signals. I overrode them. *Trust it and move; Adam is right there*, I told myself, drowning out the negative but real mental chatter.

I matched hands, and the grip felt equally awkward and wrong, with my right hand having to twist uncomfortably to get the short right ring finger to make contact. The taped nub smashed into the rock.

Just keep moving, I commanded, and I did. I carefully grabbed each granite edge, positioning my fingers into the seam of the rock, wondering with each movement if I would rip off the rock. I grabbed one hold after the other, moving my feet as I progressed. I doubted each grip and readjusted repeatedly. My brain fired off warnings despite my efforts to quell them: *You don't have fingers. Your skin is coming off!* My muscles and my will battled my brain. And muscle memory won, defeating fear, terror, and alarm. *I did it.*

The familiar movement had felt awkward, unlike the fluid dance I once commanded across the rock. I dismounted and bent over with pain.

Adam patted my back. "It looks like it hurt a little at the end," he said.

He was right, but also wrong—it hurt the whole time—but I didn't correct him. What he saw as pain at the end was me fumbling the holds, wanting to keep my fragile thumbs away from seams and keep them from absorbing too much pressure. Maybe the brittle bones could withstand the strain, but I didn't want to push them.

I put my mittens back on as Adam went over to shut his camera off. I hadn't realized he was recording, wholly lost in my tunnel, facing this boulder problem. I wiped more tears away with my sweatshirt sleeves.

"That's it—I'm done. My fingers can't take anymore," I said. "I did what I came to do. Let's go home."

Epilogue

"You're getting well," Samuel said. "Some people think it's an insult to the glory of their sickness to get well. But the time poultice is no respecter of glories. Everyone gets well if he waits around."
—John Steinbeck, *East of Eden*

I lived into the forty-fourth year of my life with my original hands. The loss and trauma I suffered on April 2, 2017, will never go away. I will forever wear a thin cloak of sadness and forever miss my hands. But I feel privileged to use these beautiful scientific works of art that Dr. Ignatiuk and his team created, and I hope I can use them for another forty-four years. I did everything I could to not let scar tissue build up—both real and metaphorical—that would hinder my physical hands, and my spirit.

I learned not to live in the extreme lows that life presented, thanks to the webbing in my net. I learned that time and effort would allow me to reprogram, permitting myself to feel life's high moments along with the low. I was patient with myself.

Initially, I was guarded, always bracing for the next tragedy. Indeed, they came. The breakup of Bird & Jim's original partnership; the COVID-19 pandemic; the deaths of Cheryl in 2018, my brother in 2020, my father and Charlie in 2021, and my sister's husband in 2024. The stress began to manifest in migraines. I unrolled my safety net and helped myself remember acceptance, forgiveness, and how to ask for help.

Ironically, as the dust of life settled, I had to save the new Melissa, who was strong and determined but needed a break after pushing through the trauma, stress, and grief. We hired a general manager, teamed up with a new chef, and opened our second establishment, Bird's Nest, with a café and pizzeria downstairs and private event space upstairs.

With the help of the Bird & Jim and Bird's Nest teams, I found the support I needed to welcome back the previous version of me—the carefree young woman with a passion for climbing, and life. The two versions of me, from before and after the accident, began to merge.

Lifting this tremendous weight has empowered me to return to my healing journey, stuffed in various boxes. My brain has successfully reprogrammed to my new hands' altered shape and length. I also freed myself from the stress response my brain had become accustomed to. The headaches mostly faded. Joy returned as a frequent companion, flooding in with life's high points.

Today, writing my story, I find myself uniting with another rendition of myself: the young girl who ventured far away from the family nest to attend university. An insecure young woman, yet headstrong, opening and closing doors, trying to discern what life was all about, seeking a path, friendships, and love. This young woman's passion for writing never dissipated.

As much as my aging body permits, I pursue my quest of recapturing the strength I possessed before the accident. I have to be much stronger than I was before to climb any problems. My training focuses on strengthening my weaknesses, ranging from my right arm, to grip strength overall. Keeping overall fitness up is also important, so my body can assist my fingers. Thanks to my continued dedication to my Peloton bike, my new treadmill, and the great instructors' core and strength classes, I stay fit. To this day, I look forward to working up a sweat on my Peloton. My first ride was May 28, 2017—3,365 rides ago.

We invested in an Original Kilter Board home wall and remain grateful to our friends at Kilter for continuing to produce stellar climbing products. Thanks to our friends at Organic Climbing, I now have a crash pad adorned with my chalk hand prints to cushion my falls. Adam and I continue to spend time in Hueco, where we built a permanent home on our land in 2019, purchasing the adjacent 5 acres in 2022. We also continue to volunteer with the climbing rangers in RMNP as bouldering stewards.

Epilogue

When I first got back onto the rocks on a regular basis, I was humbled, embarrassed, and frustrated. I'm so thankful for Adam and our friends who climb with me, well under their own abilities, encouraging me and cheering me on. Each season I find increased strength on the rocks, surprising Adam, and myself. The hard work is paying off; I've gained additional power, and am now able to grab, hold, and move off of holds I never thought I'd be able to touch again.

After a few years, I began to just climb—reaching out and grabbing without trepidation and mental alarms. I still cannot walk up to just any problem and give it a try. My hands will never be able to grip certain holds. The ends of the nubs are not tapered like normal fingertips and sometimes just do not fit on the holds. There are many problems left undone that I will never get to try again. The skin grafts do not hold up to rock surfaces, tearing and cutting and adding to the difficulty.

No matter how frustrated I get when climbing, I steer myself to come full circle. I am grateful that I survived and get to participate in the game of life and try this silly sport that means the world to me. Despite the lingering limitations and pain, I am thankful for my hands, and each night I put them to rest in compression gloves to heal as much as they can for the next day's encounters. The journey back toward climbing and restaurant ownership has taught me to continuously rely on and reinforce my support network.

Healing and learning will never end. Joy and hardship continuously flow into our lives. We all have scar tissue from going through something difficult, and we will again. Whether it's health-related, coping with grief, an injury, or struggling with self-love and self-doubt, we all have trials and pain. As we navigate one of life's challenges or provide support to others, we're weaving fibers for our net.

Every day, we can add to our safety net, providing the light, and lightness, to live in our strength. I hope my story can become part of your net. I lay my pain, heartache, tragedy, and triumph at your feet, hoping you will also find the strength you need in dark hours to pull yourself out of despair, shining a light on your path.

Aedh Wishes for the Cloths of Heaven

Had I the heavens' embroidered cloths,
Enwrought with golden and silver light,
The blue and the dim and the dark cloths
Of night and light and the half-light,
I would spread the cloths under your feet:
But I, being poor, have only my dreams;
I have spread my dreams under your feet;
Tread softly because you tread on my dreams.

—W. B. Yeats

Appendix: Surgery Notes

April 4, 2017

Author: TeBockhorst, Seth, MD
Filed: 4/4/2017, 7: 17 p.m.
Service: Plastic Surgery
Date of Service: 4/4/2017, 7:12 p.m.
Editor: TeBockhorst Seth, MD (Resident DEA)
Brief Post-Op Note:
Post-Procedure Diagnosis: Electrical burn bilateral hands, left shoulder, lower chest
Operation/Procedure performed: R hand FPL debridement skin and soft tissue debridement (5×5 cm); long finger revision amputation

L hand: FPL debridement: skin and soft tissue debridement (10×5 cm) thumb IP joint decortication and immobilization; long and ring finger distal phalanx bony debridement
Proceduralist: Ignatiuk
Assistants: TeBockhorst
Description: See dictation
Complications: None
Findings: See dictation
Estimated Blood Loss: None
Was hemorrhage/hematoma a procedural complication? No
Post-operative Check Note
Sip Procedure(s): Irrigation and debridement bilateral hands
BURN, ELECTRICAL
Electrical burn
S/p Procedure(s): Irrigation and debridement bilateral hands

R hand: FPL debridement; skin and soft tissue debridement (5×5 cm); long finger revision amputation

L hand: FPL debridement; skin and soft tissue debridement (10×5 cm); thumb IP joint decortication and immobilization; long and ring finger distal phalanx bony debridement

(4/3/2017–4/4/2017)

Keep post-op care

Chen-Han Wilfred Wu, MD, PhD

General Surgery PGY1

Email: Chen-Han.Wu@ucdenver.edu

April 6, 2017

Right hand debridement of FPL tendon, skin, and soft tissue with a total area of approximately 5×5 cm and amputation of long finger at the level of the DIP.

Left hand FPL debridement, skin and soft tissue debridement, 10×5 cm, thumb IP joint decortication of articular cartilage and suture immobilization with plans of arthrodesis after soft tissue coverage obtained, long and ring finger distal phalanx bony debridement.

SPY angiography.

DATE OF SERVICE: 4/6/2017

RESPONSIBLE STAFF SURGEON: Ashley Ignatiuk, MD FELLOW OR CONSULTANT

HOUSE STAFF SURGEON: Seth TeBockhorst, MD ASSISTANT

PREOPERATIVE DIAGNOSIS: Bilateral hand electrical burns.

POSTOPERATIVE DIAGNOSIS: Bilateral hand electrical burns.

OPERATIVE PROCEDURES: Right hand debridement of FPL tendon, skin, and soft tissue with a total area of approximately 5×5 cm and amputation of long finger at the level of the DIP.

Left hand FPL debridement, skin and soft tissue debridement, 10×5 cm, thumb IP joint decortication of articular cartilage and suture immobilization with plans of arthrodesis after soft tissue coverage obtained, long and ring finger distal phalanx bony debridement.

SPY angiography.

ANESTHESIA: General.

APPENDIX: SURGERY NOTES

COMPLICATIONS: None.
ESTIMATED BLOOD LOSS: 20 mL
CLINICAL HISTORY: The patient is a pleasant 43-year-old lady who presented to OSH after sustaining high-voltage electrical injury while renovating a building and picking up a live electrical cable. She sustained a total of 2% total body surface area full-thickness burns to her bilateral hands with subsequent exposed tendon and bone. She was transferred to the hand service for definitive management after she was deemed medically stable from a cardiovascular and renal standpoint. I discussed debridement of her wounds using SPY angiography in order to obtain a conservative debridement and to assess the demarcation of vascular injury. The risks and benefits were reviewed, and informed consent was obtained.

DESCRIPTION OF PROCEDURE: She was identified in the holding area, and the operative sites were marked. She was brought to the operating theatre in stable condition, placed onto a regular OR table with both arms on an arm board without tourniquets.

Preoperative timeout was taken to ensure the patient's identity, the operative procedure, as well as the operative location. General anesthesia was administered. The hands were then sterilely prepped and draped.

We began the procedure by removing all of the blisters and easily debrided tissue from bilateral hands. We then performed SPY angiography using 3 mL of indocyanine green. The level of decreased vascularity was marked on her bilateral hands. We then proceeded with a more thorough debridement according to the levels revealed by the SPY angiography. On her right hand, the FPL tendon was completely debrided and was found to be in discontinuity. The skin and soft tissue were debrided from the thumb as well as the thenar eminence, measuring a total of 5×5 cm. Her long finger had significant exposure of the distal phalanx with no soft tissue coverage, and we, therefore, proceeded with revision amputation with disarticulation through the DIP joint. The hand was irrigated and the amputation closed with a single 3-0 Monocryl suture. Traction neurectomies were not performed at this time.

For the left hand, the FPL tendon was also in discontinuity and debrided. Skin and soft tissue injury was much more significant, and a total of 10×5 cm was debrided. The thumb IP joint was exposed, and we, therefore, proceeded to remove the articular cartilage and perform a provisional arthrodesis with a 2-0 Monocryl suture placed through the head of the proximal phalanx and sutured to the soft tissue of the distal phalanx. The long and ring fingers had exposed distal phalanx, however, deemed possibly salvageable. Therefore, the nonvascular bone was debrided with plans of soft tissue coverage at a later date once the hand has demarcated.

The wounds were again thoroughly irrigated, and repeat SPY angiography showed good vascularity to all the remaining tissue; however, we do expect this to evolve within the next weeks and possibly into the next months. The hands were then dressed with Xeroform and gauze and immobilized with a volar splint.

She tolerated the procedure well. There were no complications. Final instrument count was correct. She left the operating room in stable condition.

OT Assessment: Pt is a 43 y.o. who sustained electrical injury to bilat hands, pt s/p R FPL debridement, long finger revision amputation, L thumb IP joint decortication and immobilization, long and ring finger distal phalanx bony revision. Pt s/p casted from Plastics in OR. Pt was educated on not bearing weight through bilat hands when completing bed mob. Ace wrap was applied to the outside of her cast on her RUE in order to place stylist and utensils in Ace wrap to increase indep with ADLs and IADLs while hands are casted. Pt will cont to benefit from skilled OT.

April 9, 2017

Bilateral completion amputation of the long and ring fingers at the level of the DIP joints.

Bilateral revision thumb IP arthrodesis.

Bilateral creation of pedicled skin flaps from bilateral forearms, measuring 10×4 cm.

Use of SPY angiogram.
DATE OF SERVICE: 4/9/2017
RESPONSIBLE STAFF SURGEON: Ashley Ignatiuk, MD

Appendix: Surgery Notes

FELLOW OR CONSULTANT: Laura Boschini, MD
PREOPERATIVE DIAGNOSIS: Bilateral hand electrical burn.
POSTOPERATIVE DIAGNOSIS: Bilateral hand electrical burn.
OPERATIVE PROCEDURES: Bilateral completion amputation of the long and ring fingers at the level of the DIP joints. Bilateral revision thumb IP arthrodesis. Bilateral creation of pedicled skin flaps from bilateral forearms, measuring 10×4 cm.
Use of SPY angiogram.
COMPLICATIONS: None.
ESTIMATED BLOOD LOSS: 50 mL
CLINICAL HISTORY: This is a pleasant 43-year-old lady who is known to me for bilateral hand electrical burns. She was first taken to the operating room on April 6, 2017, for debridement and use of SPY angiogram to determine the level of viable tissue. She returns to the OR today for repeat debridement, SPY angiogram, as well as amputations and flap coverage of her bilateral thumbs using forearm flaps. Risks and benefits were reviewed in detail and informed consent was obtained.
DESCRIPTION OF PROCEDURE: She was identified in the holding area and the operative site was marked. She was brought into the operating theatre in stable condition, placed onto a regular OR table in the supine position with both arms on an arm board. Preoperative time-out was taken to ensure the patient's identity, the operative procedure, as well as the operative location.
We began the procedure by using SPY angiogram in order to determine the level of viable tissue, which was marked. The hands were then bilaterally sterilely prepped and draped. We began the procedure by removing all of the nonviable skin, and performing revision amputations of her bilateral long and ring fingers at the level of the DIP. Traction neurectomy was not performed in order to preserve vascularity.
Next, we turned our attention to her bilateral thumb IP joints. Previous suture mobilization was performed on her left thumb. Her right thumb was decorticated of all articular cartilage. On both thumbs, we used a 26-gauge tension band wire in order to immobilize the joint.
The wounds were then thoroughly irrigated, and her arms were crossed, and we determined the best position for creation of forearm

flaps. These flaps measured approximately 10×4 cm. The forearm skin was incised down to the fascia and the subcutaneous tissue was elevated off of the brachial fascia.

Good vascularity of the flaps was maintained at all times. We then proceeded to inset the flaps onto her bilateral thumbs using 2-0 Monocryl for the base and 4-0 Monocryl for the tips. The flaps were tailored to the contour of the defects. At the end of the procedure, the flaps remained viable. All of her open wounds were dressed with Xeroform, and her arms were immobilized together using Coban.

She tolerated the procedure well. There were no complications. Final instrument count was correct. She left the operating room in stable condition after general anesthesia was reversed.

POSTOPERATIVE PLAN: She will remain admitted to the Burn ICU. She will be followed closely by plastic surgery. We will leave the pedicle flaps inset for approximately 2½ weeks before division of the pedicles. She may require further skin grafting at a time.

May 1, 2017

Bilateral arm flap division and inset into bilateral thumbs with primary closure of both donor sites.

Left thumb distal phalanx amputation at the level of the middle of the distal phalanx.

Removal of hardware from left thumb.

Debridement of chest full-thickness burns, 7×4 cm total area of sharp debridement, including full-thickness skin.

Split-thickness skin grafting to chest. Total area is 7×4 cm.

Debridement full-thickness burn, left hand. Total area of 11×5 cm. Split-thickness skin grafting to left hand, 4×4 cm. Full-thickness skin grafting to left hand, 7×5 cm.

Debridement of right hand full-thickness skin burn, 11×5 cm. Split-thickness skin grafting, 3×4 cm. Full-thickness skin grafting, 8×5 cm.

Application of disposable wound VAC, 7×4 cm total area.

DATE OF SERVICE: May 1, 2017

RESPONSIBLE STAFF SURGEON: Ashley Ignatiuk, MD

HOUSE STAFF SURGEON: Seth TeBockhorst, MD

Appendix: Surgery Notes

PREOPERATIVE DIAGNOSIS: Bilateral hand electrical burn.

POSTOPERATIVE DIAGNOSIS: Bilateral hand electrical burn.

OPERATIVE PROCEDURES: Bilateral arm flap division and inset into bilateral thumbs with primary closure of both donor sites.

Left thumb distal phalanx amputation at the level of the middle of the distal phalanx.

Removal of hardware from left thumb.

Debridement of chest full-thickness burns, 7×4 cm total area of sharp debridement, including full-thickness skin.

Split-thickness skin grafting to chest. Total area is 7×4 cm.

Debridement full-thickness burn, left hand. Total area of 11×5 cm.

Split-thickness skin grafting to left hand, 4×4 cm. Full-thickness skin grafting to left hand, 7×5 cm.

Debridement of right hand full-thickness skin burn, 11×5 cm. Split-thickness skin grafting, 3×4 cm. Full-thickness skin grafting, 8×5 cm.

Application of disposable wound VAC, 7×4 cm total area.

ANESTHESIA: General.

COMPLICATIONS: None.

ESTIMATED BLOOD LOSS: 50 mL

CLINICAL HISTORY: The patient is a pleasant 43-year-old lady well known to myself for bilateral hand electrical burns. She had bilateral forearm flaps, which were performed 3 weeks ago. She comes to the operating room today for division and inset of her flaps as well as skin grafting to any open areas. We will also debride any nonvitalized tissue. The risks and benefits were reviewed in detail. Informed consent was obtained.

DESCRIPTION OF PROCEDURE: The patient was identified in the holding area, and the operative site was marked. She was brought to the operating theatre in stable condition, placed onto a regular OR table. Preoperative timeout was taken to ensure the patient's identity, the operative procedure, as well as the operative location. General anesthesia as well as bilateral supraclavicular blocks were placed.

We began the procedure by sterilely prepping and draping the tube flaps from bilateral forearms to her bilateral thumbs. We then divided the flaps in order to allow both of her arms to be placed onto an arm board.

The arms were then sterilely prepped and draped, as well as her chest, bilateral groins, and her left anterior thigh.

We began the procedure by debriding all devitalized tissue for a total area of 7×4 cm on her chest, 11×5 cm on her left hand, and 11×5 cm on her right hand.

The debridement was sharp, including full-thickness skin.

The left thumb tip showed poor vascularity and necrotic tissue, which was debrided, resulting in exposed distal phalanx. We, therefore, proceeded with revision amputation of the left thumb distal phalanx. The previous arthrodesis showed exposed hardware; therefore, the dental wire was removed and the wound was thoroughly irrigated.

Next, we proceeded to inset the bilateral flaps. The left flap was gently thinned out of excess granulation tissue in order to allow the flap to cover part of the thenar eminence. Inset was performed using 3-0 Monocryl suture bilaterally. The flaps showed good vascularity at all times.

Next, we proceeded to harvest a split-thickness skin graft from her left anterior thigh using a Zimmer dermatome set to 0.012 inches. The donor site was dressed with fiber. The skin grafts were placed onto the chest wall as well as onto the left hand and right hand after being meshed 1:1.5. Skin grafts were secured using Dermabond glue. A Prevena wound VAC was placed to bolster the 2 sites of split-thickness skin grafting on her chest. The total area of split-thickness skin grafting on her left hand was 4×4 cm and on the right hand was 3×4 cm.

We then proceeded to harvest a full-thickness skin graft from her right groin measuring 15×5 cm. The donor site was closed primarily using 3-0 Monocryl and 3-0 V-Loc suture reinforced with Steri-Strips. The skin graft was then placed onto the left hand for a total area of 7×5 cm and on the right hand for 8×5 cm. The skin graft was inset using 4-0 Monocryl suture. The bilateral hands were then dressed with Xeroform and wet-to-dry gauze, followed by Webril and plaster.

She tolerated the procedure well. There were no complications. Final instrument count was correct. She left the operating room in stable condition.

POSTOPERATIVE PLAN: She will remain in hospital admitted under the plastic surgery service and we will assess the skin graft take in 5 to 7 days. If she wishes to go home before this, we will allow it; however, we will keep her in the hospital until we are happy with her pain control and mobilization.

If she is discharged from the hospital, she will follow up in the hand surgery clinic, where her bilateral hands and donor sites will be checked to assess the skin graft take as well as healing of her donor sites. We will wait until the skin grafts are stable to start initiating hand therapy for return of range of motion. She may require additional procedures for her thumb IP joints until they show good fusion.

ASHLEY IGNATIUK MD

June 30, 2017

Sharp debridement of left thumb including subcutaneous tissue and bone, 3×2 cm

Revision left thumb IP joint arthrodesis

Advancement left thumb fasciocutaneous flap from previous cross arm flap

Left thumb first web space deepening with and resurfacing with FTSG [full-thickness skin graft] from right groin donor site, 5×7 cm

RESPONSIBLE STAFF SURGEON: Ashley Ignatiuk, MD
PREOPERATIVE DIAGNOSIS: Bilateral hand electrical burns
POSTOPERATIVE DIAGNOSIS: Bilateral hand electrical burns
OPERATION PERFORMED:

Sharp debridement of left thumb including subcutaneous tissue and bone, 3×2 cm

Revision left thumb IP joint arthrodesis

Advancement left thumb fasciocutaneous flap from previous cross arm flap.

Left thumb first web space deepening with and resurfacing with FTSG from right groin donor site, 5×7 cm.

ANESTHESIA: General anesthesia
ESTIMATED BLOOD LOSS: Less than 5 cc.
COMPLICATIONS: None
CLINICAL HISTORY: Melissa Strong is a 43 y.o. female who has had multiple previous surgeries for bilateral hand electrical burns.

Her left thumb IP joint has dislocated dorsally and the volar pulp has necrosed, leaving her with exposed distal phalanx and minimal support for her nail bed. She also has a significant contracture of the thumb/index web space. We discussed revising her thumb IP joint fusion, advancing her previous flap and releasing her thumb/index web space with possible FTSG, including the risks as well as the benefits, and she was agreeable to proceed. Informed consent was obtained.

DESCRIPTION OF OPERATION: Melissa was identified in the holding area and the operative site was marked. She was brought to the operating theatre in stable condition, placed onto a regular OR table in the supine position with the operative extremity on an arm board. A preoperative time-out was taken to ensure the patient's identity, the operative procedure, as well as the operative location.

General anesthesia was induced and the hand and right groin were then sterilely prepped and draped. We did not use a tourniquet.

We began by opening the distal flap of her left thumb; a small amount of pus was encountered and sent for culture. We then debrided the wound, including about 7 mm of the middle phalanx, the proximal portion of the distal phalanx, as well as subcutaneous tissue. The thumb IP was then reduced and stabilized with 0.035 K-wires × 2 under fluoroscopic imaging. The position of the fusion was satisfactory. The wires were bent and cut.

We then elevated the distal aspect of the flap and advanced it about 5 mm to allow coverage of the volar thumb defect. Release was carried back into the thumb/index web space. A significant amount of scar tissue was excised, resulting in a defect of approximately 5×7 cm. The advanced flap was sutured to the nail plate using 4-0 Monocryl.

We then harvested an FTSG from her right thigh. The donor site was closed primarily with 4-0 Monocryl and dressed with Telfa and a Tegaderm. The skin was defatted and fenestrated using a 15 blade scalpel. The skin graft was sutured in place on the left thumb/index web space using 4-0 Monocryl and bolstered using Xeroform and sponges. A thumb spica splint was applied.

She tolerated the procedure well, no complications. Final instrument count was correct. She left the operating room in stable condition.

APPENDIX: SURGERY NOTES

POSTOPERATIVE PLAN: Melissa will go home from the hospital today. Arrangements made to follow up with me in clinic in two weeks for suture removal and to assess FTSG take. She should keep the dressing intact, keep the hand elevated, and begin moving her fingers as much as possible to prevent stiffness. If she has any difficulty between now and follow-up, she has been told to contact me, and I would be happy to see them sooner.

August 21, 2017

DATE OF SERVICE: August 21, 2017
RESPONSIBLE STAFF SURGEON: Ashley Ignatiuk, MD
HOUSE STAFF SURGEON: Salih Colakoglu, MD, Resident DEA
PREOPERATIVE DIAGNOSIS: Bilateral hand electrical burn.
POSTOPERATIVE DIAGNOSIS: Bilateral hand electrical burn.
OPERATIVE PROCEDURE: First dorsal metacarpal artery innervated fasciocutaneous flap to left thumb tip.
Removal of superficial hardware, including 2 K-wires.
Full-thickness skin graft to left index finger, measuring 4×2 cm, right groin donor site, with scar revision of right groin.
Flap debulking, left thumb.
ANESTHESIA: General.
COMPLICATIONS: None.
ESTIMATED BLOOD LOSS: 10 mL
CLINICAL HISTORY: The patient is a 43-year-old lady who is very well known to me for bilateral hand electrical burns requiring complex reconstruction. We are focusing on her left thumb today, which had K-wires placed in order to promote fusion of the DIP. She also requires a sensate pad for her thumb, as well as reconstruction of the lateral and distal nail folds. This could all be accomplished with an FDMA flap from her index finger. We discussed the details of this surgery and debulking of the previous flap to her left thumb at the same time, including the risks, as well as the benefits, and she was agreeable to proceed. Informed consent was obtained.

DESCRIPTION OF PROCEDURE: She was identified in the holding area, and the operative site was marked. She was then brought to the operating theatre in stable condition, and her left arm was placed onto an arm board. A preoperative time-out was taken to ensure the patient identity, the operative procedures, as well as the operative location. General anesthesia was administered. Her left hand and right groin were then sterilely prepped and draped.

We began the procedure by examining her thumb IP arthrodesis under fluoroscopic imaging. The fusion appeared to be complete. We, therefore, removed the K-wires, and there was no movement with stressing under fluoroscopic imaging. We, therefore, proceeded to harvest the left index finger 1st dorsal metacarpal artery flap. A skin paddle was designed to include the dorsal skin over the proximal phalanx of the index finger, extending from the midaxial lines on the radial and ulnar sides of the digit. The distal aspect was at the PIP, and the proximal aspect was at the MCP. The subcutaneous tissue was then elevated off of the extensor tendon, preserving the paratenon for subsequent full-thickness skin grafting.

A curvilinear incision was then made to the base of the index metacarpal and thumb metacarpal junction. Skin flaps were elevated, leaving the subcutaneous tissue intact. We then elevated the subcutaneous tissues, including the 1st index metacarpal periosteum, as well as the 1st dorsal interossei fascia in order to preserve the 1st dorsal metacarpal artery. Care was taken to preserve the subcutaneous veins, as well as the branches of the radial nerve in order to provide a sensate flap. The flap was then isolated on its pedicle, and the tourniquet was deflated. The flap showed good vascularity.

Next, we opened up her previous thumb/index web space incisions in order to make a tunnel for the flap. The thumb tip was de-epithelialized to receive the flap. We also debulked the previous flap by elevating the radial border and removing subcutaneous tissue, as well as a small portion of the skin in order to provide a better contour. We then inset the flap using 4-0 Monocryl suture, ensuring there was no tension.

The donor site was then closed by harvesting a full-thickness skin graft from her right groin, measuring 4×2 cm. We performed a scar revision of her right groin at the same time. The donor site was closed with 3-0 Monocryl suture. The full-thickness skin graft was fenestrated and inset using 4-0 Monocryl suture, and a bolster dressing was applied. We then put her thumb into a thumb spica splint.

She tolerated the procedure well. There were no complications. Sponge and instrument counts were correct. She left the operating room in stable condition.

POSTOPERATIVE PLAN: She will remain in hospital for postoperative flap monitoring. If there are any concerns for the flap, we will remove some of the sutures in order to decrease the tension on the pedicle. She will remain in the splint for an additional 2 weeks. The skin graft will be assessed on postoperative day #5. She will be discharged from the hospital once we have assessed a full-thickness skin graft take and can begin mobilizing her hand to prevent stiffness. She will follow up with me in clinic and contact me if she has any questions or concerns.

ASHLEY IGNATIUK MD

November 10, 2017

RESPONSIBLE STAFF SURGEON: Ashley Ignatiuk, MD

ASSISTANT: Kathryn E. Miller, PA-C

PREOPERATIVE DIAGNOSES: Right long finger volar scar contracture. Right thumb eponychial deformity.

POSTOPERATIVE DIAGNOSES: Right long finger volar scar contracture. Right thumb eponychial deformity.

OPERATIVE PROCEDURES: Full-thickness skin grafting to right long finger and right thumb. Total area is 7×4 cm, left groin donor site.

Excision scar contracture of right long finger, 3×5 cm.

Reconstruction right thumb eponychial fold using local tissue rearrangement, 7×3 cm.

ANESTHESIA: General.

COMPLICATIONS: None.

ESTIMATED BLOOD LOSS: 10 mL

CLINICAL HISTORY: The patient is a pleasant 44-year-old lady well known to myself for bilateral hand electrical injury. She has had multiple previous procedures. Her main complaint now is her tethering scar band on her right long finger volar surface, right thumb eponychial fold deformity, as well as a prominent scar on the right thumb base. We discussed management of these deformities including excision of the scar contractures and reconstruction of her thumb eponychial fold using local tissue rearrangement. The risks and benefits were reviewed, and informed consent was obtained.

DESCRIPTION OF PROCEDURE: She was identified in the holding area and the operative site was marked. She was brought to the operating theatre in stable condition, placed onto the operative table in the supine position with her right arm on an arm board. Preoperative time-out was taken to ensure the patient identity, the procedure, as well as the operative location. General anesthesia was administered. She did not require a tourniquet. The right arm was sterilely prepped and draped. She received perioperative antibiotics.

We began the procedure by excising the scar tissue from right long finger volar surface. We identified the neurovascular bundles, which were protected at all times. After release of the scar tissue, which was completely excised and discarded, she had a defect measuring approximately 6×4 cm with a tissue bed, which was amenable to full-thickness skin grafting.

Next, we turned our attention to her right thumb. A Freer elevator was used to elevate the scarred eponychial fold. We then incised the previously placed flap as well as her native eponychial folds. The eponychial folds were then advanced distally. The thumb flap was elevated from the thumb tip all the way to the thumb base and advanced forward approximately 1 cm. We then proceeded to inset the tissue using 4-0 chromic gut sutures and multiple Z-plasties in order to allow for advancement of the tissue and prevent further scar contracture.

Lastly, we harvested a full-thickness skin graft from her left groin measuring 8×5 cm. The skin graft was defatted and thinned, as well as fenestrated. Donor site was closed using 3-0 V-Loc suture, dressed with Telfa and Tegaderm.

We then proceeded to inset the skin grafting into her right volar long finger as well as the defect created by advancement of her thumb flap. A bolster dressing was applied.

She tolerated the procedure well. No complications. Final instrument count was correct. She left the operating room in stable condition.

POSTOPERATIVE PLAN: She will leave the hospital today, arrangement to follow up with me in clinic in approximately 11 days for removal of her bolster as well as her splint. If she has any difficulty between now and follow-up, she has been told to contact me and I would be happy to see her sooner.

ASHLEY IGNATIUK MD

About the Author

Melissa Strong, a sponsored rock climber, pushed her boundaries worldwide, excelling in her passion. Not one to settle, she aspired to open an exceptional restaurant in her small mountain town. A near-fatal electrical injury during renovations left her with partial hand loss, prompting a determined medical journey. (Follow the story with pictures on melissaistrong.com—warning, graphic content.) Melissa's memoir *Climbing Through* chronicles her journey from athlete to survivor. Based in Estes Park, Colorado, she manages the acclaimed restaurants Bird & Jim and the Bird's Nest when not inspiring others through speaking engagements or writing about rock climbing.

www.ingramcontent.com/pod-product-compliance
Lightning Source LLC
LaVergne TN
LVHW041554060526
838200LV00037B/1284